WHITEHALL AND THE S

British Foreign and Colonial Policy

ISSN 1467-5013

General Editor: Peter Catterall
Institute of Contemporary British History, London

This new series provides insights both into the background influences on and the course of policymaking towards Britain's extensive overseas interests during the past 200 years.

Whitehall and the Suez Crisis is the first in this new series.

Whitehall
and
the Suez Crisis

Editors

SAUL KELLY

ANTHONY GORST

University of Westminster, London

FRANK CASS

LONDON • PORTLAND, OR

First published in 2000 in Great Britain by
FRANK CASS PUBLISHERS
Newbury House, 900 Eastern Avenue, London IG2 7HH

and in the United States of America by
FRANK CASS PUBLISHERS
c/o ISBS, 5804 N.E. Hassalo Street
Portland, OR 97213-3644

Website www.frankcass.com

British Library Cataloguing in Publication Data

Whitehall and the Suez crisis. – (British foreign and
colonial policy; no.1)
1. Great Britain – Officials and employees 2. Egypt – History
– Intervention, 1956 3. Egypt – Foreign relations – Great
Britain 4. Great Britain – Foreign relations – Egypt
I. Kelly, Saul II. Gorst, Anthony III. Contemporary British
history
956'.044

ISBN 0 7146 5018 8 (cloth)
ISBN 0 7146 8077 X (paper)
ISSN 1467-5013

Library of Congress Cataloging-in-Publication Data:

Whitehall and the Suez crisis / editors Saul Kelly, Anthony Gorst.
        p.   cm. – (British foreign and colonial policy, ISSN 1467-5013)
Includes bibliographical references and index.
ISBN 0-7146-5018-8 (cloth) – ISBN 0-7146-8077-X (pbk.)
1. Great Britain – Politics and government – 1945–1964. 2. Great Britain
– foreign relations – 1945– 3. Egypt – History – Intervention, 1956. 4. Suez
Canal (Egypt) – History.
I. Kelly, Saul, 1957– II. Gorst, Anthony. III. Series.

DA592.467 1999
962.05'3 – dc21   99-045859

This group of studies first appeared in a special issue of
Contemporary British History [ISSN 1361-9462] Vol.13, No.2 (Summer, 1999)
published by Frank Cass and Co. Ltd.

Printed in Great Britain by
Antony Rowe Ltd., Chippenham, Wiltshire.

Contents

Introduction   **Saul Kelly** and **Anthony Gorst**   1

Alternatives to Nasser: Humphrey Trevelyan,
Ambassador to Egypt   **Michael T. Thornhill**   11

'A Modern Major General': General Sir Gerald Templer,
Chief of the Imperial General Staff   **Anthony Gorst**   29

Playing the Role of a Cassandra:
Sir Gerald Fitzmaurice, Senior Legal Advisor
to the Foreign Office   **Lewis Johnman**   46

The Mandarins' Mandarin: Sir Norman Brook,
Secretary of the Cabinet   **Keith Kyle**   64

In the Know? Sir Gladwyn Jebb,
Ambassador to France   **Christopher Goldsmith**   79

The Limits of Opposition:
Admiral Earl Mountbatten of Burma,   **Eric Grove** and
First Sea Lord and Chief of Naval Staff   **Sally Rohan**   98

The Missing Link? Patrick Dean, Chairman of
the Joint Intelligence Committee   **W. Scott Lucas**   117

Cadogan's Last Fling: Sir Alexander Cadogan,
Chairman of the Board of Governors of the BBC   **Tony Shaw**   126

In the Company of Policy Makers: Sir Donald Logan,
Assistant Private Secretary to the Secretary of State
for Foreign Affairs   **Chris Brady** 146

Transatlantic Diplomat: Sir Roger Makins,
Ambassador to Washington and Joint Permanent
Secretary to the Treasury   **Saul Kelly** 157

The Diplomats' Diplomat: Sir Pierson Dixon,
Ambassador to the United Nations   **Edward Johnson** 178

The Past as Matrix: Sir Ivone Kirkpatrick, Permanent
Under-Secretary for Foreign Affairs   **Ann Lane** 199

Conclusion   **John W. Young** 221

Bibliographic Essay   **Saul Kelly** 232

Abstracts   238

Notes on Contributors   243

Index   245

Introduction

It is easy to see why the Suez Crisis remains of such lasting interest to historians both British and international: it split the British nation and brought down the prime minister; it revealed with startling clarity that Britain could no longer continue the pretence of being a great power; it was brought to a head by a conspiracy, or collusion, between France, Israel, and Britain to overthrow the most charismatic leader in the Middle East, Colonel Gamal Abdel Nasser of Egypt; it complicated the intractable Arab–Israeli dispute and weakened the Western position in the Middle East; it was a test case for the United Nations; and it exacerbated Cold War tensions and raised the spectre of nuclear war.

Some 40 years after the Suez Crisis, it is possible with some confidence to outline the course of British and US – and to a degree, Israeli – policies (French and Egyptian policies remain largely obscure because of the continued closure of much of their government records on Suez). In the case of British policy, we have a much better understanding than before of the respective roles played by Eden, Macmillan and Lloyd and, for example, the splits in the Cabinet over the use of force against Egypt.[1] But concentration by historians on the activities of the political decision-makers has meant that only sporadic attention has been given by historians to the question of the role played, and influence exerted, by their advisers in the formulation and execution of policy.

The Suez Crisis has been described as '*the* greatest political crisis of the 1950s' which stretched the fabric of the British Civil Service 'to the point where it began to tear in private if not in public in an uncanny pre-echo of the dilemma faced by Clive Ponting about thirty years later'.[2] Yet there has been no proper study of the role of Whitehall in the Suez Crisis. We know that the Chiefs of Staff (and, in particular, Templer and Mountbatten) were divided in their views over the threat posed by Nasser and how to respond to it.[3] But no attempt has been made to define the precise roles of Templer and Mountbatten in the policy-making process. We know that the Eden government's legal advisers disagreed over the legality of the use of force against Nasser to make him disgorge the Canal, but we are unfamiliar with the twists and turns of the legal debates between the Foreign Office Legal Adviser, Sir Gerald Fitzmaurice, and the Lord Chancellor, the Earl of Kilmuir.[4] We know about the opposition of the Eisenhower administration and the United Nations to the use of force, which was reflected in the respective warnings of the British Ambassador in Washington, Sir Roger Makins, and the Permanent British Representative to the UN, Sir Pierson Dixon.[5] What we do not know about is how Makins and Dixon presented British policy and sought to reconcile it with the opposing position of the US and the UN. We know about the feeling of betrayal and outrage among Foreign Office officials (expressed not only in the resignations of Nutting and several junior officials but Paul Gore-Booth's 'round-robin' protest) at being 'kept in the dark' about the Sèvres Protocol by their Permanent Under-Secretary, Sir Ivone Kirkpatrick.[6] But we have no real idea of the roles played by Kirkpatrick and the other Foreign Office officials who facilitated the policy of collusion.

We know that the Chancellor of the Exchequer, Harold Macmillan, did not act on the briefings, advice and warnings about the need to protect sterling supplied by the Permanent Secretary to the Treasury, Sir Edward Bridges, and how the latter was excluded by Eden from the Suez inner circle and from seeing the most sensitive documents. We know about the resignation of the Economic Secretary to the Treasury, Sir Edward Boyle, in protest at the invasion of Egypt and the revulsion of junior Treasury officials at this action.[7] But we have a less clear idea of the influence the new Joint Permanent Secretary at the Treasury, Sir Roger Makins, had in fashioning and executing the strategy of the Treasury and the British government for obtaining much needed US financial and economic assistance following the rift in Anglo-American relations over Suez in November 1956.

We know that the Cabinet Secretary and head of the Home Civil Service (as the other Joint Permanent Secretary of the Treasury), Sir

Norman Brook, thought the Anglo-French intervention in Egypt to be 'folly', that he had serious doubts about Eden and that he found himself in a difficult position of having 'to be loyal to his Cabinet *and* the repository of people's worries in Whitehall'.[8] But we do not know how Brook actually managed to resolve this dilemma, perform his duties and manage the crisis. We know that the Prime Minister, Anthony Eden, lied to Parliament about Suez, and that this was known by Sir Donald Logan, assistant private secretary to the Foreign Secretary, Selwyn Lloyd, and the only man to have attended both secret meetings in Paris which led to the Sèvres Protocol. We know that neither Logan, nor any other official at the time, regarded it as part of their remit as civil servants to blow the whistle on Eden (in contrast to Clive Ponting, who broke the story about Mrs Thatcher and the sinking of the Argentinian cruiser, the *General Belgrano*, during the Falklands War). But we do not know what Logan thought about those secret meetings in Paris which led to the collusion about which Eden felt the need to lie.

Suez may have been '*the* greatest professional trauma experienced by the British Civil Service before or since 1957. Yet discipline held. Nobody flouted the rules or spilled the beans.'[9] Concentration on the moral dilemma faced by the British Civil Service over Suez obscures the more important, if more mundane, question of how the vast Whitehall machine actually functioned during Suez.

This volume seeks to answer this question by taking a cross-section of Whitehall during the crisis. It focuses on the roles played by key individuals in vital posts at significant times in order to show how the policy process worked during the crisis. Each essay deals with a key 'Whitehall warrior', and seeks to define their private and public attitudes to events in order to determine what influence, if any, they had on policy making and to highlight any dilemmas they may have faced. The sequence of essays is explained by the fact that each adviser has been allotted to the main phase of the Suez Crisis in which they played their most prominent role, although there are of course overlaps. Thus, Trevelyan, Templer, Fitzmaurice and Brook are in the first phase covering July to mid-September 1956; Jebb, Mountbatten, Dean and Cadogan are in the second phase from mid-September to late October, and Logan, Makins, Dixon and Kirkpatrick are in the third and last phase from late October to December. This selection is not random but neither is it exhaustive, if only for reasons of space.

Some obvious figures, like the British Ambassador in Moscow, Sir William Hayter, and the Chairman of the Chiefs of Staff, Sir William Dickson (who was on sick leave) have been omitted because they played only peripheral roles in the crisis. We have not included the civil servants in the service ministries or the Ministry of Defence in order to focus on the cleavage of views within the Chiefs of Staff between the two major figures in defence policy making, Templer and Mountbatten, about how to deal with Nasser. Partly for reasons of space and partly because it has also been covered (in William Clark's memoirs) we have not discussed the contribution of the staff in the Prime Minister's office. This selection represents a good spread of roles and opinion in Whitehall during the Suez Crisis. The essays in this book are based on new research in the relevant British archives by historians who, in some cases, have been able to interview their subjects or who have benefited from recorded oral testimony.

A further word needs to be said about the scope and organisation of the book and each of the essays. One of the questions which still remains unanswered after the opening of the records in 1987 was what regime did the British government think should replace that of Nasser if military action was successful. Michael Thornhill helps answer this question in his essay on the British Ambassador to Egypt, Sir Humphrey Trevelyan. This essay assesses the often divergent reports of Trevelyan and his embassy officials on possible alternatives to the Nasser regime. He also attempts to establish the extent of the Cairo embassy's collaboration with MI6 in this area. Thornhill also details Trevelyan's political input in the military planning (especially on the use of oil sanctions and psychological measures) which aimed at seizing the Suez Canal and overthrowing Nasser. Thornhill's analysis demonstrates how the Cairo embassy's attitudes on these issues shaped the advice being received in London during the diplomatic phase of the crisis.

There is no doubt that the Chief of the Imperial General Staff (CIGS), the professional head of the British Army, General (later Field Marshal) Sir Gerald Templer, was, in contrast to Trevelyan, an enthusiastic supporter of Eden's desire to use military force to solve the Suez Crisis and remained so throughout. It can be argued, as Anthony Gorst points out, that this enthusiasm resulted in Templer, who was the dominant figure on the Chiefs of Staff Committee, and to a lesser extent the other chiefs (the Chief of the Air Staff, Sir Dermot Boyle,

4

and the First Sea Lord, Lord Louis Mountbatten) accepting a political war aim – the toppling of Nasser – that was militarily unachievable and which contributed to the constant changes in the military plan in August and September 1956. Anthony Gorst has disentangled the role of Templer in policy-making during the crisis and highlighted the lesson that the CIGS drew from MUSKETEER, that future military interventions needed to be taken quickly and decisively in pursuit of a realistic war aim.

Lewis Johnman's examination of the role of the Legal Adviser to the Foreign Office, Sir Gerald Fitzmaurice, and the general legal debate within the British government over the use of force, reveals the determination of Eden to topple Nasser without declaring this as an aim of policy. Thus, the extreme narrowing of the advisory and policy channels threw much of Whitehall into confusion. The Suez 'insiders' (Eden, the Egypt Committee and a small number of senior officials) blocked or ignored any advice which did not suit their purposes and utilised entirely inappropriate means to justify their actions. Lewis Johnman shows that, as with so much of the advice given during the Suez Crisis, 'what was ignored proved to be correct and what was accepted proved to be wrong'.

It is one of the myths of Suez that the civil service was excluded throughout from the secret planning of the expedition against Egypt. But the crisis as a whole should not be confused with the desperate last phase of it. For most of the time, those admittedly limited number of civil servants who had clearance to receive documents (codenamed TERRAPIN) were kept fully informed and controlled the plans for the use of force. This was especially true, as Keith Kyle shows, of Sir Norman Brook, with his two committees – Defence (Transition), which met throughout the crisis and co-ordinated the reports of the specialist groups, and the Egypt (Official) – and his role as Secretary of the Cabinet and of the Egypt (Ministerial) Committee. It was only during the last phase that most civil servants were excluded, with the exception of Brook. As Secretary to the Cabinet he kept the minutes which chronicled the Cabinet's deliberations on the use of force against Egypt. It fell to Brook to undertake the unpleasant task of destroying any incriminating documentary evidence of collusion. Following Eden's departure for Jamaica to convalesce, Brook's calm was a great boon as he worked closely with Makins to restore order to Whitehall and to keep the machine running.

5

Most accounts of the Suez Crisis have tended to concentrate on the exclusion of the British Ambassador to Paris, Sir Gladwyn Jebb, from the bilateral Franco-British meeting on 16 October 1956 when Eden and Lloyd agreed to the Challe plan for collusion with Israel. But, as Chris Goldsmith points out, it is also important to recognise that the Ambassador had earlier played a part in shaping the British response to the nationalisation of the Suez Canal Company, especially the development of a common Franco-British approach. Chris Goldsmith shows that, as the crisis developed, Jebb became increasingly concerned about the implications of a continued commitment to a policy of force. However, there were limited opportunities to express such opinions by September 1956. By the start of October, Jebb was becoming increasingly concerned about the implications for Franco-British collaboration of the closeness of French relations with Israel, a worry which was reflected in his warning to Eden about the supply of French Mystère fighters to Israel. The Prime Minister chose to adopt another approach and took the first steps along the path to collusion and disaster.

Mountbatten's position as First Sea Lord during the crisis gave him a particularly central role. However, he was hardly a normal 'official'. As a member of the British Royal Family and with close connections with the British governing class he had been the Supreme Allied Commander, South East Asia and the last Viceroy of India. He was also a personal friend of Eden, which enabled him as First Sea Lord to influence policy but posed constitutional problems. Mountbatten's opposition to British policy over Suez, which Eric Grove and Sally Rohan show to have been consistent throughout the crisis, was motivated by moral and political considerations as much as by Service and strategic interests. He took very seriously his position within the Royal Family, the governing class and the Navy and, therefore, pushed his opposition to MUSKETEER as far as he could without prejudicing these interlocking positions. The fact that Mountbatten did not resign over Suez was of considerable importance for the Navy when he successfully defended its interests during the Sandys Defence Review in 1957/58.

Patrick Dean is remembered as the man who accompanied Donald Logan, assistant private secretary to the Foreign Secretary, Selwyn Lloyd, to the second Sèvres meeting. Yet, as Scott Lucas informs us, this memory of Dean is unfortunate because it distracts attention from his real importance as an essential liaison during the crisis. He was not only Superintending Under-Secretary of State of the Permanent Under-Secretary of State's Department and Chairman of the Joint Intelligence Committee, which linked the Foreign Office, the military and MI6. But he also bypassed official channels and passed on messages to the secret services from the Prime Minister. Dean's story, as Lucas makes clear, was part of a much larger and more important catalogue of chaos and fragmentation within Whitehall which led to the pursuit of several foreign policies during Suez. Moreover, MI6's persistent and, some might argue pernicious, influence led straight to the disaster of November 1956. Given the continued closure of the files of the Secret Service, its role at Suez has been largely ignored or underrated by historians. But Scott Lucas's account of Dean's essential role in propping up the shaky structure of policy-making casts important new light on the muddle that allowed MI6 to operate outside 'official' policy.

Tony Shaw shows that coincidence, combined with the closed nature of the British governing elite, placed Sir Alexander Cadogan, one of the most distinguished civil servants of his generation, in a uniquely wide-ranging position during the Suez Crisis. During the dispute he operated in three apparently autonomous, but ultimately antagonistic, spheres: as Chairman of the English-Speaking Union's Commonwealth Current Affairs Unit, as a government director of the Suez Canal Company and as Chairman of the BBC's Board of Governors. Further complications arose from his close friendship with Eden dating from the interwar appeasement years. Tony Shaw demonstrates that Cadogan's overall impact on Suez lay more in the sphere of presentation of government policy than in its actual formulation. While this by itself might not have shaped the course of events, it helps to shed light on the public dimensions of the crisis. It also raises another question relating to the scope for influence offered to those officials who were relative outsiders during the dispute.

As Chris Brady points out, the policy-making role of Sir Donald Logan, assistant private secretary to Selwyn Lloyd, was negligible but his place in the history of Suez is considerable. Logan was a man of genuine integrity who was present at an important moment in British history: the collusion meetings at Sèvres in late October 1956. He has told his story without embellishment and if only for this reason it is worth including him in this study. But he is also of interest because of his refusal to blow the whistle on Eden and the Prime Minister's deceptive statement to Parliament on 20 December 1956. Logan epitomises the practical and realistic image of the British civil servant at this period.

Sir Roger Makins was in the unique position for a British official of viewing the initial stages of the crisis from Washington, where he was British Ambassador until 11 October, and its later stages from London, after he became Joint Permanent Secretary of the Treasury on 15 October. The role he played in the Suez Crisis, therefore, is of particular interest to historians. Makins's main duties as Ambassador during the early stages of the crisis were to keep on good terms with the Eisenhower Administration, conveying British policy to them, and to explain US policy to London without losing the confidence of the Eden government. The main thrust of Makins's advice as Joint Permanent Secretary of the Treasury throughout the rest of the Suez Crisis was the need to secure US support for an International Monetary Fund (IMF) loan for Britain and other financial and economic measures to avert the looming disaster for sterling and the economy. It was as a result of his transatlantic contacts that the British government eventually secured vital financial and economic support, in return for withdrawing from Egypt. Saul Kelly shows that Sir Roger Makins's involvement in the Suez Crisis clearly demonstrated his belief in the vital importance for Britain of the 'alliance' with the United States, which should only be overridden in the last resort.

Sir Pierson Dixon, British Ambassador to the United Nations during Suez, had one of the most onerous tasks of all British officials during the crisis. He had to defend Britain's use of force against Egypt in the UN, a forum in which Britain had few supporters, even though he was often kept 'in the dark' about the real aims of Eden's policy. Edward Johnson examines in detail Dixon's defence of that policy during the week of military operations which began with the Israeli invasion of Egypt on 29 October and ended with the ceasefire on 6 November. After the ceasefire, as Edward Johnson shows, he and Selwyn Lloyd tried unsuccessfully, due to US and UN opposition, to link the terms for the despatch of the UN force to British withdrawal and clearance of the Canal. Although Dixon later claimed that the Anglo-French action at Suez was 'a miscalculation and a mistake', at the time he did what he could to defend it publicly, while warning privately of the serious consequences for Britain of ignoring the UN. The personal effect of all this was 'the severest moral and physical strain he had ever experienced'.

A great deal of criticism has been levelled by historians at Sir Ivone Kirkpatrick for his role in the Suez affair. As Permanent Under-Secretary at the Foreign Office he was a key player in the development of policy and one of the few who had an overview. He was a solid supporter of Eden's policy towards Egypt. Ann Lane has identified the two overweening concerns which shaped Kirkpatrick's approach to the crisis. The first was his interpretation of Soviet foreign policy, which he believed to be aimed at challenging Britain's position in the Middle East. Greatly influenced by contemporary ideas on the nature of a totalitarian state's foreign policy, Kirkpatrick believed that Britain should firmly resist the Soviet threat. His view of Soviet aims was connected with the second major influence on his thinking: his experience of the rise of Hitler in the 1930s. He was determined that Britain should not again make the mistake of appeasing dictators and that the latter's ambitions should be effectively discouraged at the first opportunity. His belief that Nasser was such a dictator combined with his concern at Soviet aims in the Middle East to frame his approach to the Suez Crisis. As Ann Lane shows, he was staunch in his support of Eden's adoption of the Rhineland analogy and encouraged him to exorcise the ghosts of the 1930s. In the final stage of the crisis Kirkpatrick was outmanoeuvred as the Suez operation became increasingly determined by military considerations. But his defence of British actions to his senior officials went beyond the call of loyalty to ministers.

The conclusion by John Young places Whitehall and the Suez Crisis within the long-running debate about the influence of officials on British foreign policy. Young's analysis corrects the rather one-dimensional view of Suez as a moral dilemma for British officials. For, 'despite their qualms and questions, they also helped pave the way for the use of force'. The conclusion assesses how the Whitehall machine worked during the Suez Crisis, and the importance of personalities and personal links and their effect on the functioning of the system and allows us, for example, to look afresh at the motives of the Prime Minister, Anthony Eden, in treating his advisers as he did.

It will not be possible until the full release of the files of the Joint Intelligence Committee and MI6 to form a complete picture of how Whitehall functioned during the Suez Crisis; rumours that the most sensitive secret intelligence material was destroyed soon after the event may even make this task difficult. But this study, by looking at the roles of a wide range of advisers and shedding light on less well-discussed facets of the affair, contributes to our greater understanding of Whitehall, British policy-making and the Suez Crisis.

ACKNOWLEDGEMENT

The editors wish to thank the Institute of Contemporary British History, in particular Peter Catterall, Virginia Preston and Gill Staerck, for their support of the conference held at the University of Westminster in December 1996, papers from which form the basis of the present volume. We also wish to acknowledge the contributions of Professor Geoffrey Warner and Professor John Young as chairs and commentators at that conference. The editors and contributors also thank those policy makers, politicians, civil servants and military men who have given freely and patiently of their knowledge and time to the apparently endless stream of historians working on Suez.

All archival references are to material held at the Public Record Office, Kew unless otherwise stated. Crown copyright material in the Public Record Office is reproduced by permission of the Controller of Her Majesty's Stationery Office.

NOTES

1. See for example, W.S. Lucas, *Divided We Stand* (London: Hodder & Stoughton, 1991) and K. Kyle (London: Weidenfeld & Nicolson, 1991) *passim*.
2. P. Hennessy, *Whitehall* (London: Secker & Warburg, 1989), pp.163–4.
3. P. Hennessy and M. Laity, 'Suez – What the Papers Say', *Contemporary Record*, Vol.1, No.1 (Spring 1987), pp.2–3.
4. H. Thomas, *The Suez Affair* (London: Weidenfeld & Nicolson, 1967), pp.40, 139.
5. J. Charmley, *Churchill's Grand Alliance: The Anglo-American Special Relationship 1940–1957* (London: Sceptre, 1995), p.330; P. Dixon (ed.), *Double Diploma, The Life of Sir Pierson Dixon, Don and Diplomat* (London: Hutchinson, 1968), pp.264, 277–8.
6. A. Nutting, *No End of a Lesson. The Story of Suez* (London: Constable, 1967); P. Gore-Booth, *With Great Truth and Respect* (London: Constable, 1974), pp.228–32
7. L. Johnman, 'Defending the Pound: The Economics of the Suez Crisis, 1956' in A. Gorst, L. Johnman and W.S. Lucas (eds), *Postwar Britain, 1965–1964* (London: Pinter, 1989).
8. Hennessy, *Whitehall,* p.167.
9. Ibid., p.168.

Alternatives to Nasser: Humphrey Trevelyan, Ambassador to Egypt

MICHAEL T. THORNHILL

On Tuesday 30 October 1956, the day of the Anglo-French ultimatum to Egypt, Britain's Embassy in Cairo began destroying its papers. This emergency procedure was last enacted in 1942 as German tanks approached Alexandria from the Western Desert. There was no time to separate the secret material from the rest and the Embassy furnace was soon found to be inadequate for the task. Half a dozen steel cages were erected on the lawn next to the Chancery building and each was filled with blazing documents. Passing and repassing files, Embassy staff formed a chain to replenish the bonfires. Ash drifted across the surrounding neighbourhood.[1] At 9:00 p.m., Britain's Ambassador to Egypt, Humphrey Trevelyan, met with President Nasser to explain his government's demands, which had been issued by the Foreign Office that afternoon.[2] With composure, Nasser rejected the ultimatum and stated that it amounted to a threat of unprovoked aggression.[3] 'Whatever one thinks of him,' Trevelyan later observed, Nasser's 'prompt and decisive refusal required courage'.[4] No restrictions were placed on the Embassy until noon on Friday 2 November, when the compound was sealed by Egyptian police. Electricity and telephone lines were also cut.[5] From this point on, Trevelyan and his staff observed the 'war' from the Embassy roof. Apart from the sounds of rifle practice in the day and unexplained small-arms fire in the night, the spectacle consisted of anti-aircraft shells bursting over Cairo West airport. On 10 November, four days after the ceasefire, the Embassy internees were taken by train to the Libyan border.[6]

In subsequent years, Trevelyan never disguised his opposition to the Anglo-French-Israeli invasion, describing it as a 'lamentable muddle'.[7] The central theme in his biographical account of the episode, published in 1970, was that he and his advisers repeatedly warned against intervention in Egypt's internal affairs, and that the Embassy was neither informed nor consulted about the on-going military preparations.[8] While it was true that the Cairo Embassy was not told of the war plot hatched at Sèvres,[9] the assertion of general ignorance is deeply misleading. Owing to the destruction of Embassy records at the start of the war phase of the crisis, the release of government papers in 1987 (under the 30-year rule) did little to alter the impression left by Trevelyan. Historians instead concentrated on aspects of the crisis where the archival evidence was abundant. Only with regard to intelligence materials were questions raised about what was missing from the documentary record.[10] Nevertheless, in Scott Lucas's *Divided We Stand* and Keith Kyle's *Suez*, both published in 1991, a picture began to emerge of a more extensive role for Trevelyan's Embassy in 1956.[11] This picture concerned the search for an alternative government, which was to take office after Nasser was toppled from power. However, both authors saw the Embassy's input as secondary to that of Britain's Secret Intelligence Service (MI6).

This analysis contends that, during 1956, the imperial practice of making and breaking Egyptian governments was conducted much as it had been in the past. In other words, the main channel for manipulating Egyptian politics remained the British Embassy in Cairo. It alone had the long-standing contacts with politicians of the constitutional era, many of whom were expected to be suitably embittered by four years of exclusion from political life following the Free Officers' seizure of power in 1952. These contacts were not with Trevelyan but with his advisers, Cairo careerists steeped in the legacy of Cromer, Lloyd, Lampson, *et al*. By examining the structures and officials behind the Ambassador, this analysis seeks to offer a more nuanced assessment of the Embassy's role in Suez. The evidence is admittedly fragmentary for reasons already mentioned. However, if the effect is to shift attention from MI6 plotting, which is usually unverifiable, and instead locate the crisis in the wider context of British *imperium* in Egypt, some good will have been done.[12]

Trevelyan arrived in Cairo in August 1955 following a spell as chargé d'affaires in Peking. Although his only previous experience in the Middle East was as counsellor in Baghdad 1948–50, he was nevertheless well versed in Asian nationalist movements having served in the Indian Political Service in the 1930s. From the start, Cairo was a difficult posting. The Anglo–Egyptian Defence Agreement of October 1954, whereby Britain agreed to evacuate its 80,000-strong garrison from the Suez Canal Zone base, had done little to improve relations. The brief honeymoon period after the settlement was soon interrupted by Nasser's attacks on the Baghdad Pact. As Foreign Secretary, Anthony Eden steered the 1954 settlement through the Cabinet despite considerable frontbench and backbench opposition. He was therefore particularly sensitive to any Nasser-inspired complications in the Middle East after he became Prime Minister in April 1955 and so took a personal interest in all Egyptian matters. The effect was to severely limit Trevelyan's scope for diplomatic manoeuvre.

By March 1956, Eden had come to the conclusion that the maintenance of Britain's Middle Eastern interests demanded the removal of Nasser from power. The Czech arms deal, the failure of the Anglo-American sponsored peace talks between Israel and Egypt (project ALPHA), and the continuing radio propaganda against the Baghdad Pact all proved to be too much for the Prime Minister. The breaking point was King Hussein's dismissal of Sir John Glubb as head of Jordan's Arab Legion on 1 March. By the end of the month, Eden had persuaded the Eisenhower administration of Nasser's permanent opposition to Western interests and the upshot was a joint covert plan – codenamed OMEGA – aimed at weakening Nasser's domestic position, while isolating him in the Arab world.[13] Thus, even before the nationalisation of the Suez Canal Company, Britain, with American support, had embarked on a policy of destabilising Nasser. Trevelyan's Embassy necessarily played an important role in implementing this policy.

For 70 years, the manipulation of Egyptian politics had been an essential function of the British Embassy in Cairo. Indeed, so much so that the Residency (as the Embassy was called before the Anglo–Egyptian Defence Treaty of 1936) was itself an integral part of Egypt's state-executive. Sir Miles Lampson, a distinguished predecessor of Trevelyan, likened the situation to a three-legged stool. The three components were the Palace, the Wafd (Egypt's leading nationalist party during the constitutional years, 1923–52) and the Residency.[14] But as Trevelyan realised during the March discussions, this analogy had long since lost its relevance. The monarchy and the political parties, including the Wafd, had been swept away after the military coup of July 1952. Moreover, the Embassy's influence had always rested on the ability of British forces to occupy and control the Nile Delta. Yet one of the main reasons why Britain agreed to the evacuation of the Suez base was because the military chiefs believed that a sustainable occupation of Cairo, Alexandria, and Port Said was no longer possible even with 80,000 troops in the Canal Zone.[15]

Consequently, the tenor of Trevelyan's advice throughout 1956 was that nationalist extremism would be the lasting result of old-style interference in Egypt's internal affairs. This approach was first articulated in the wake of the Czech arms deal when the Foreign Office asked for an Embassy assessment on the desirability of removing Nasser. In a memorandum dated 2 December 1955, Trevelyan replied that the alternatives were another 'military *junta* perhaps more hostile to the West or a civilian government which would quickly become [the] Wafd and might be extreme nationalist in policy'.[16] In an accompanying letter, Trevelyan requested that he be summoned home for an interview with the Foreign Secretary before any such policy was embarked upon. The Ambassador was clearly anxious about the growing hostility of officials in London.[17] An assurance was subsequently given by the Foreign Office that 'no decisive action' would be taken against Nasser 'without the fullest consultation with all concerned'.[18] In March 1956, Trevelyan's increasing concern over the British government's mood was such that he asked to see recent Cabinet papers on the Egyptian issue.[19] The irony in this was that it was Embassy reporting that persuaded London to see Nasser as irretrievably hostile.

Since November 1955, Trevelyan had been receiving highly secret reports from a source believed to be close to Nasser. These reports indicated that the Egyptian leader was planning to attack Israel and that he was getting ever closer to the Russians.[20] Trevelyan passed on the intelligence material to London but was deeply uneasy about its effect on decision-makers. This came to a head in late March when the Foreign Office appraised him of measures being drawn up to destabilise Nasser. After consultations with his senior staff, including the Embassy's Minister, Ralph Murray, and the Oriental Secretary, Trefor Evans, Trevelyan sent a ten-page dispatch marked 'Top Secret and Personal' to Sir Ivone Kirkpatrick, the Permanent Under-Secretary in the Foreign Office. Its premise was that the crystallising approach did not take full account of all the elements in the situation or of the consequences which were likely to follow from the proposed action. The main conclusion was highly prescient: 'We can no longer put pressure on Egypt with the same ease as hitherto now that British troops are no longer in the country and the Communists are ready for their own purposes to support Nasser and relieve him from our pressure.' The Ambassador ended by warning that a 'tough policy which did not come off would leave us far further back than we were before'.[21]

Trevelyan's dispatch also doubted the long-term commitment of the United States to hostile measures against Nasser, especially if open-ended military and financial obligations were involved.[22] Again, the irony in the situation was that it was Embassy information which persuaded America – and in particular the CIA – that Nasser, their protege since the military coup four years earlier, had turned against the West.[23] Not all the CIA's operatives were happy with this shift, and the first stirrings of American objections were heard in April owing to loose anti-Nasser talk in Whitehall. Trevelyan demanded that greater discretion be observed or the policy really would have no chance of success.[24] It was perhaps fortunate for Anglo-American planning that Egypt recognised the People's Republic of China in mid-May. As the CIA liaison officer in London later observed, Nasser had trodden on the US Secretary of State's 'most sensitive corn'.[25] While Nasser's action may well have saved OMEGA from falling at the first hurdle, Trevelyan was nevertheless perceptive in questioning Washington's stomach for all aspects of the operation.

Although the absence of documentation prevents a detailed assessment of the Embassy's role in OMEGA, an examination of the original memorandum of 28 March 1956 allows inferences to be made over the areas of involvement. The basic strategy was to isolate Nasser both domestically and internationally. Working over a period of many months, there was to be a gradual squeeze on the Egyptian economy in order to ferment popular disatisfaction with the military regime. In the meantime, black propaganda radio broadcasts would seek to drive a wedge between Egypt and the other Arab states, and in particular Saudi Arabia.[26] The Embassy's Information Department would have helped supply the raw material for disinformation purposes, while the Oriental Secretariat advised on tactics. Nasser's confidante, Mohamed Heikal, has since written that the hostile propaganda campaign concentrated on Nasser's supposed ambitions to topple the old feudal regimes of the Middle East and centralise the region's oil production for Egyptian – and by extension Soviet – ends.[27]

Operation OMEGA was co-ordinated by a number of different agencies in the British and US governments and was not an exclusive MI6–CIA project. In Britain, its implementation was routinely carried out by desk-level officials in the Foreign Office's African Department (under which Egypt was subsumed). These officials were in regular consultation with the staff at the British Embassy in Cairo.[28] Trevelyan himself was never enamoured with OMEGA and he did his best to keep it from slipping into open hostility with Egypt. On 1 May, for instance, he suggested that Britain and the US should give the green light to the Aswan Dam project. His reasoning was that the offensive measures against Nasser would not then be interpreted as hostile to the Egyptian people.[29] Despite Trevelyan's personal views, the Embassy was still expected to play a central role in the implementation of OMEGA. Except for the crucial fact that the last British troops left Egyptian soil on 13 June in line with the 1954 Agreement schedule, none of this was particularly new to Anglo–Egyptian relations. Indeed, the history of the 74-year 'Temporary Occupation' was characterised by informal methods of intervention in Egypt's internal affairs. This is worth spelling out because the same policy-making machinery was adapted to meet the special circumstances of the full-scale crisis following the nationalisation of the Suez Canal Company. The key difference in policy after 26 July was timing, with Eden no longer prepared to pursue a long-term strategy of ousting Nasser. Immediate results were demanded.

Trevelyan's last meeting with Nasser before the Suez Crisis was on 19 June; they did not meet again until the day of the British ultimatum.[30] Eden instructed Trevelyan to avoid anything resembling negotiations with Nasser's government.[31] It was clear that the Cairo Embassy was tainted by its past advocacy of diplomatic solutions, not least during the recent base negotiations. Although the Ambassador had changed since then, many of the Embassy officials remained in place. These included the head of the Oriental Secretariat, Trefor Evans, and John Hamilton, the long-serving political advisor. Eden (at least when his notorious temper flared up) also had doubts about Trevelyan himself. In early 1956, for instance, he scribbled on a telegram from Cairo that the Ambassador seemed 'very gullible'.[32]

Denied a diplomatic role in the crisis, Trevelyan had to content himself with a stream of telegrams down-playing Britain's ability to install a lasting alternative government to Nasser. Trevelyan later summarised the content of his Embassy's dispatches during this period.

> We commented that Nasser would fight if attacked and would block the Canal. It should not be difficult to defeat the Egyptian Forces, but the difficulties would start after that. The Egyptians would organise guerrilla warfare and it would be difficult for us to disengage without long and widespread operations against guerrillas organised by Nasser or, if he had fallen, by his proclaimed successor. No government set up by the occupying Forces would last. Only a government untainted by collaboration with the British could hold its position.[33]

Another direct preoccupation of the Embassy was the safety of British and foreign nationals in Egypt in the event of an Anglo-French invasion. The advice to London was as follows:

> Whatever was done, we should not endanger the lives of the large non-Egyptian population in Cairo, Alexandria and on the Canal. A breakdown of internal security in the cities might have most serious consequences for Egyptians and others, for which we should bear a heavy responsibility. There was the political aspect. The British and French could not continue their occupation indefinitely. They would have to leave again.[34]

Eden was well versed with these arguments having used most of them himself to persuade a reluctant Cabinet to accept the 1954 Suez Base Agreement.[35] He now simply chose to ignore them. 'Tell him to cheer up!,' he minuted on one of Trevelyan's telegrams warning of prolonged guerrilla warfare.[36] Trevelyan's later assessment of Suez was that 'Eden had been ill and his judgement had been affected'.[37]

Whatever Trevelyan's personal reticence about military action, his Embassy was still obliged to advise London on the Egyptian personalities who might be encouraged to form a successor government. A formal request for information was made on 8 September, in a letter to Trevelyan from Adam Watson, the head of the Foreign Office's African Department. Prior to this date, the matter had been under 'general review'.[38] The query was prompted by Ralph Murray, who was still officially the Minister at the Cairo Embassy (that is, second in charge) but who had been based in the Foreign Office since April.

Although the Foreign Office *List* makes no mention of any secondment to London during 1956, it is reasonable to assume that he was heavily involved in the black propaganda aspects of OMEGA. In 1948, Murray had been the founding head of the Foreign Office's secret anti-communist propaganda section, the innocuously named Information Research Department.[39] With the onset of the crisis, Murray's experience in Egypt, together with his intelligence background, moved him to the centre of Whitehall planning. It was in his capacity as senior Foreign Office representative on the Egypt Official Committee (EOC) that he requested information on the possible alternatives to Nasser.

The EOC was the body linking the military and political aspects of invasion planning. At its inaugural meeting on 24 August, the chairman, Cabinet Secretary Norman Brook, stated that the committee's main task was 'to determine the broad principles which should govern the handling of civil affairs in Egypt in the event of military action'.[40] Several important points were made at this meeting. First, that 'there were good reasons to believe that, given the defeat of the Egyptian Army and the collapse of the Nasser regime, a successor government could be formed'. Second, that the maintenance of law and order 'would be enhanced if the function headquarters, in or near Cairo, of such Nasser agencies as Army Intelligence, the Liberation Rally and the National Guard could be eliminated at an early stage of Allied military action'. Third, that 'it would be better to accept the risk of a breakdown in central government [meaning the administrative machinery], and to improvise a remedy at the time, than to assemble a standby organisation now'. And fourth, that the allied forces would have to have food supplies in waiting 'to guard against the possibility that famine conditions might temporarily arise'.[41]

Murray's insightful work as the Egyptian expert on the EOC was soon noticed at the highest levels. On 19 September, as a result of a staff conference chaired by Eden at 10 Downing Street, he was appointed Political Advisor to the Allied Commander-in-Chief, General Keightley, to take effect from the start of military operations.[42] The Political Advisor was to be responsible for arranging the formation of a successor government, after which he would act as a liaison between it and Keightley.[43] Murray was acutely aware of the sensitivity of the appointment and he requested that the French be kept in the dark for as long as possible because any leaks would render his return to Egypt as Minister impossible.[44] Murray's pivotal role in this process meant that the British Embassy in Cairo had an influential voice at the heart of proceedings.

Murray's own thinking on the possible alternatives to Nasser was first outlined in a minute dated 22 August. 'It will be an ungrateful task', he wrote, 'to assume office on British bayonets and some difficulty may be experienced in finding competent Ministers. A large number of formerly prominent and able figures, not necessarily of marked party affiliation, are extremely dissatisfied with the present regime, however, and there is reason to hope that some of them may come forward immediately'.[45] This assessment reflected Murray's two years experience as Minister in Cairo, which included a spell as chargé d'affaires, prior to his secret secondment to London in 1956. After the failure of the 1946 negotiations, Britain's Embassy in Cairo had developed a formula which held that any lasting settlement in Anglo–Egyptian relations must be a cross-party affair. The 1936 Defence Treaty was viewed as the model in this respect. If this was not the case, opposition parties would seek to out-bid each other with anti-British nationalist agendas thereby creating an unstable political environment. While the Free Officers' consolidation of power after 1952 meant that this formula was obsolete at the signing of the 1954 Agreement, the desire to topple Nasser in 1956 reaffirmed its relevance.

Trevelyan responded to the African Department's request for the names, addresses, and telephone numbers of suitable Egyptian personalities by the most secure means possible. Trefor Evans, the expert on such matters, made a special journey to London to advise Murray and the EOC in person.[46] The organising principle of his advice was to include as many of the *ancien regime* parties as possible. In practice, this meant co-opting prominent personalities (party machines had been dismantled after the 1952 revolution) into a 'national' government.[47] It was also accepted that a successor administration would have to reflect the post-1952 role of the army in Egyptian politics, hence the desire to bring on board disaffected elements from the armed services. This latter requirement tied in with the need for internal security and stability after Nasser's fall. For obvious political and military reasons, Britain did not want to initiate another long-term military commitment in Egypt. Furthermore, a broad-based government which was not dependent on a single person stood a better chance of survival against Nasser's threat that any puppet leader would be assassinated within days or even hours after taking office.[48]

The former Egyptian president General Mohamed Neguib was a key element in Britain's planning for a successor government. Neguib had been the figurehead for the military junta between 1952 and 1954, yet real power was exercised behind the scenes by the younger officers led by Nasser. Aware of his popularity with the Egyptian masses and encouraged by an ambitious wife, Neguib decided in the spring of 1954 to demand responsibilities commensurate with his presidential office. The ensuing internal power struggle was resolved in Nasser's favour after public utility workers were brought on to the streets to demonstrate against Neguib's policy of reconstituting the political parties. This was the first time organised labour in Egypt had been deliberately and effectively used for political purposes.[49] The British Embassy in Cairo had regarded Neguib as a calming influence on the younger officers. It was this moderation, together with his ability to carry with him important sections of the army, which made the former president a vital component in the post-invasion civil affairs planning.[50] Hence, from early August onwards, Britain's black propaganda radio broadcasts called upon the Egyptian people to return 'honest General Neguib' to public life so that he could lead Egypt back to constitutionalism.[51] When MI6 officers met with Egyptian dissidents in France at the end of August, Neguib was identified as the likely president in a successor government.[52]

As in several previous crises (most notably with the Abdin Palace incident in 1942), the Cairo Embassy turned to the Wafd in 1956 to help secure Britain's imperial interests.[53] The Wafd was Egypt's largest political party during the constitutional era and it alone contested all seats in parliamentary elections. Egypt's smaller parties tended, for the main part, to be splinter groups from the Wafd and none could compete on a national basis with the parent party.[54] Consequently, if free elections were called, the Wafd could be assured a parliamentary majority. This powerful domestic constituency meant that the Wafd's backing for an agreement was essential for it to have any lasting worth. In 1946, the collapse of the Bevin–Sidqi Protocol under the weight of opposition criticism reaffirmed this lesson. Consequently, when Britain wanted to renew defence talks with Egypt in 1949, Embassy officials acted as intermediaries between Wafdists and the Palace to assure the latter that the Wafd supported the monarchy. This was a necessary preliminary step for King Farouk to call free elections, which he did in early 1950 resulting in the expected Wafd victory.[55] Buffetted by mounting domestic difficulties, the new Wafd administration opted for playing the nationalist card against the continuing British occupation. Matters came to a head in October 1951 when Prime Minister Mustapha al-Nahas abrogated the 1936 Defence Treaty. The ensuing Abrogation Crisis brought about Britain's last major intervention in Egypt's internal affairs prior to 1956. The aim of toppling the Wafd government was achieved in January 1952, but only after widespread anti-Western rioting in Cairo.[56] Four and a half years later, British officials were willing to forgive and forget past Wafd misdemeanours in the interests of destroying the Nasser regime. As the Cairo Embassy well understood, the viability of a successor government would hinge on popular support and eventually a democratic veneer, and this meant including senior Wafdists in a successor administration.[57]

In this respect, Salah al-Din was the most obvious candidate for Britain's requirements. First, he commanded (or had done before the Wafd Party was outlawed) the backing of the middle tier of Wafdists, the *effendi* class of lawyers and government officials, aged in their forties and the backbone of the party apparatus after the Second World War. This faction was clearly more credible in 1956 than the '1919' cronies, many of whom had grown rich from landownership and who were in their sixties and seventies.[58] Salah al-Din had approached Nasser a few days after the military coup in 1952 offering to form a young and clean Wafd with a view to acting as the political arm of the Free Officers' movement. Nasser declined the offer.[59] A similarly pristine programme, however, was what British officials desired in 1956. Another reason for Salah al-Din's suitability was his impeccable nationalist credentials. As Foreign Minister in the last Wafd administration, he had been the architect of the populist anti-British policy.[60] His inclusion in a successor government would therefore help offset its inevitable stooge image. In August 1956, the Foreign Office received reports that Salah al-Din was in contact with a group of dissident officers known as 'The Partisans of the Right'. Their platform of returning Egypt to constitutional rule appealed to Salah al-Din and he agreed to accept the premiership if it became available. Although Britain's connections with this group are not known, it is perhaps significant, as Keith Kyle points out, 'that its programme included the improvement of Anglo–Egyptian relations and the cancellation of trade agreements with the Soviet Union, China and Czechoslavakia'.[61]

The non-Wafdist personalities identified by British officials included Ali Maher and Ahmed Mortada al-Maraghi. Maher was especially well known to the Embassy, having held Cabinet posts in the 1920s and 1930s before becoming prime minister in 1936 and 1939–40. His dismissal in 1940 and his internment two years later for pro-Axis sympathies came at Lampson's lordly insistence. Maher held the premiership on two more occasions both in 1952, first in the month-long administration which came on the heels of the Wafd's dismissal on 27 January and then as a short-lived political front for the military junta between 23 July and 6 September.[62] In September 1956, Maher signalled to British officials that he had the names of an embryonic cabinet 'in his pocket'.[63] Although this claim was taken with a pinch of salt, Maher was seen as a suitable candidate for a senior ministerial position.[64] As for al-Maraghi, his great strengths were his experience, albeit brief, as Minister of Interior and his reputation for being tough on corruption.[65] The Interior Ministry was the main cog in Egypt's administrative machine. Ralph Murray and the other officials concerned with civil affairs in Egypt after the invasion were highly conscious of the need to keep Egypt's administrative machinery in working order. The last thing they wanted was for the British and French invasion forces to set up a full military government.[66]

Trevelyan played no first-hand part in these intrigues. It would in any case have been counter-productive for him to do so because he was elaborately watched by the Egyptian security forces. The Ambassador was also guarded for his own benefit, Cairo being the location of Sir Lee Stack's murder in 1924 as well as Lord Moyne's assassination in 1944.[67] Nasser seemed to think, moreover, that the British government might even stage an incident against their own Ambassador to create a provocation in order to justify military action.[68] Trevelyan wrote in his memoirs that the Embassy 'could not comment on plans about which we were not told'.[69] Yet the reality was that the Embassy was involved in a range of activities connected with destabilising Nasser.

One of the main themes of the propaganda war, for instance, was that Britain's quarrel was not with the Egyptian people but with Nasser alone. To this end, the Embassy's Press Secretary, John Tull, gave daily briefings and guidance to journalists. On 17 August, the *Daily Express* correspondent in Cairo, Donald Edgar, wrote a belligerent article against Nasser in which he made direct reference to Tull's off-the-record comments. This implicated the Embassy in a serious breach of diplomatic etiquette, embarrassing Trevelyan and angering Nasser.[70] Nasser responded that same day by granting interviews to three senior correspondents, including Tom Little of the British-owned Arab News Agency and John Slade-Baker of the *Sunday Times*. Slade-Baker consulted with Terence Garvey, the Head of Chancery in the Embassy, over appropriate questions for the meeting. It was during this interview that Nasser made the threat that so worried Trevelyan. Recalling how Samson pulled down the pillars of the temple in Gaza burying himself and everyone else in the ruins, Nasser stated that he would do the same if Britain and France attacked Egypt.[71] Edgar received his come-uppance a week later when he was lured into an Egyptian security service trap and expelled from the country.[72] Three other journalists were also expelled around this time after they tried to penetrate the house where General Neguib was being kept in *residence forcée*. Neguib was subsequently removed to a secret location, probably in southern Egypt.[73]

Trevelyan's Embassy was also directly implicated in covert operations involving the banned Islamic 'extremist' group, the Moslem Brotherhood. In late August, a spy-ring headed by James Swinburn, the Cairo manager of the Arab News Agency and a former professor at Cairo University, was rounded up.[74] According to Heikal, the arrested men had been trying to encourage Islamic militants to riot in the main Egyptian cities, possibly to provide an excuse for foreign intervention *á la* 1882. Two diplomats, J.B. Flux and J.G. Gove, were expelled for their involvement in the affair.[75] Flux was an old hand in the Embassy having served in Cairo since 1919. His official position was First Secretary for Commercial Affairs, but in truth he was one of the key sources of intelligence on Egypt's internal political scene. This was evidenced on his return to London when he went straight to the centre of the Foreign Office machinery concerned with finding an alternative to the Nasser regime.[76]

Despite this setback to Britain's intelligence network in Egypt, Embassy officials continued to believe that rioting, whether secretly encouraged or not, remained a real possibility. On 13 September, Slade-Baker recorded in his diary a conversation he had with Evans and Hamilton. The latter, he wrote, made the point that 'the country was not solidly behind the regime'. The entry continues: 'Both Trefor and Hamilton think that if there are any demonstrations and the police open fire and kill say fifty people or so there will be wide-spread counter-revolutionary movements throughout the country, particularly at Tanta which is full of fanatics.'[77] It will be recalled that the strategy of fermenting anti-government disturbances had been successfully deployed three years earlier against the Iranian leader Mossadeq. It was also possible that Britain's secret contacts with the Moslem Brotherhood stemmed from a mutual desire to see Nasser assassinated. *Ikhwan al Muslimin* had a history of assassination tactics, including the the murder of Prime Minister Mahmud al-Nuqrashi in 1948.[78]

During 1956, there were two approaches within the British Embassy in Cairo to the problem of Nasser's regime. There was Trevelyan's approach which warned against intervention in Egypt's internal affairs, whether via the covert methods of OMEGA or through the outright use of military force. The likelihood either way was that a new chapter would be added to the emotional anti-British history of Egypt. Trevelyan believed that the increased difficulties of dealing with successor governments, let alone the problem of disengagement if an invasion was attempted, would be to the lasting detriment to the British–Egyptian connection. He put this case one last time to the Foreign Office on 24 October, ironically enough the day the Protocol of Sèvres was initialled.[79] A more pragmatic approach was adopted by Trevelyan's senior Embassy advisers. Policy implementation rather than high policy itself was their primary concern. The Oriental Secretariat, Chancery, and Information Office all had specific tasks to carry out and the response of the officials concerned was efficient, expert, and loyal. The Embassy's Minister, Ralph Murray, seconded to the Foreign Office for much of the year, was particularly effective in getting Embassy advice heard and acted upon. This was evident in the policy of trying to install a multi-party successor government drawing upon discontented elements from across the political spectrum. The only grumbles of discontent within the Embassy came later and these related to the circumstances of the collusion with Israel.[80] The administrative structures behind the Ambassador were thus an integral part of the British government's military and political preparations in 1956. On the crucial question of finding an alternative government to the Nasser regime, policy was formulated much as it had been in the past. This gave due emphasis to the experience and expertise of the British Embassy in Cairo, while also allowing for specialist input from the Foreign Office's African Department and the Assistant Under-Secretary in charge of Middle Eastern affairs. The EOC, which was grafted on to this process a month into the crisis, ensured that Embassy advice was acted upon in wider Whitehall planning for post-invasion civil affairs in Egypt.

NOTES

1. H. Trevelyan, *The Middle East in Revolution* (London: Macmillan, 1970) p.116; Middle East Centre Archive, St Antony's College, Oxford, J.B. Slade-Baker Diaries, 26 Sept.–23 Nov. 1956.
2. The Foreign Office presented the communiqué to the Egyptian Ambassador in London at 4.25 p.m. GMT. An 'emergency' telegram containing the text was wired to the Cairo Embassy at 5.14 p.m. PREM 11/1105, FO to Trevelyan, 30 Oct. 1956.
3. PREM 11/1105, Trevelyan to FO, 30 Oct. 1956.
4. H. Trevelyan, *The Times*, 6 July 1978, p.14. This reference is contained in a review of Selwyn Lloyd's *Suez 1956: A Personal Account* (London: Jonathan Cape, 1978).
5. Trevelyan, *Middle East in Revolution*, p.117.
6. Ibid., pp.116–26.
7. Trevelyan, *The Times*, 6 July 1978, p.14.
8. See Trevelyan, *Middle East in Revolution*, passim.
9. On collusion, see A. Shlaim, 'The Protocol of Sèvres, 1956: Anatomy of a War Plot', *International Affairs*, Vol.73, No.3 (1997), pp.509–30.
10. The papers of the Cairo Embassy are preserved as FO 141. Files from 1952–56 were destroyed on 31 Oct.–1 Nov. 1956. Earlier, non-active, records were deposited in the Foreign Office Library and are now open for inspection at the Public Record Office.
11. See W.S. Lucas, *Divided We Stand* (London: Hodder & Stoughton, 1991) and K. Kyle, *Suez* (London: Weidenfeld & Nicolson, 1991).
12. For an assessment of MI6's role, see R. J. Aldrich's review article, 'Intelligence, Anglo–American Relations and the Suez Crisis, 1956', *Intelligence and National Security*, Vol.9, No.3 (July 1994), pp.544–54; also, T. Bower, *The Perfect English Spy: Sir Dick White and the Secret War 1935–90* (London: Mandarin, 1995), pp.189–202. In this chapter, MI6's activities are considered only when they overlapped with Embassy business.
13. Lucas, *Divided We Stand*, pp.104–15; Kyle, *Suez*, pp.99–103.
14. For an overview of Britain's imperial position in Egypt, see M.E.Yapp (ed.), *Politics and Diplomacy in Egypt: The Diaries of Sir Miles Lampson 1935–1937* (Oxford: Oxford University Press, 1997), pp.6–15.
15. M.T. Thornhill, 'Britain and the Egyptian Question, 1950–54', Unpublished D.Phil, Oxford, 1995, pp.200–1.
16. FO 371/118832/JE1015/1, Trevelyan to Shuckburgh, 2 Dec. 1955.
17. Ibid.
18. FO 371/118832/JE1015/A, minutes by Kirkpatrick and Shuckburgh, 9 Dec. 1955.
19. FO 371/118862/file, Watson to Trevelyan, 22 March 1956; also FO 371/118862/JE1053/20G, Watson to Trevelyan, 6 April 1956.
20. FO 371/121726/VR1073/118G, Trevelyan to Shuckburgh, 8 March 1956; and FO

371/118869/JE1071/31G, Shuckburgh to Makins, 19 March 1956. These reports show that the Foreign Office regarded the source as an Embassy contact. Lucas, on the other hand, emphasises MI6's input, cf. Lucas, *Divided We Stand*, pp.109–25.

21. FO 371/118862/JE1053/34G, Trevelyan to Kirkpatrick, 26 March 1956.
22. Ibid.
23. FO 371/118869/JE1071/31G, Shuckburgh to Makins, 19 March 1956. On the development of CIA contacts with the Free Officers, see Miles Copeland, *The Game of Nations* (London: Weidenfeld & Nicolson, 1969).
24. Kyle, *Suez*, p.101; also, W. Eveland, *Ropes of Sand: America's Failure in the Middle East* (London: Norton, 1980), pp.168–89.
25. C. L. Cooper, *The Lion's Last Roar: Suez 1956* (London: Harper & Row, 1978), p.92.
26. Lucas, *Divided We Stand*, pp.111–12.
27. Mohamed H. Heikal, *Cutting the Lion's Tail: Suez Through Egyptian Eyes* (London: Corgi,1988 ed.) p.118.
28. See file FO 371/118862, especially JE1053/31, Trevelyan to Watson, 5 May 1956; JE1053/31A Trevelyan to Watson, 8 May 1956; and JE1053/31G, Watson to Trevelyan, 15 May 1956; also Lucas, *Divided We Stand*, pp.116–25.
29. FO 371/118862/JE1053/32, Trevelyan to Watson, 1 May 1956.
30. Trevelyan, *Middle East in Revolution*, p.114.
31. Ibid., p.96.
32. FO 371/121650/VQ10316/21, Trevelyan to Foreign Office, 2 Feb. 1956.
33. Trevelyan, *Middle East in Revolution*, p.105.
34. Ibid. p.106; also FO 371/118832/JE1015/45, Trevelyan to Foreign Office, 30 Aug. 1956; FO 371/118832/JE1015/47, Trevelyan to Foreign Office, 19 Sept. 1956.
35. See especially Chapter 6 in Thornhill, 'Britain and the Egyptian Question', pp.164–99.
36. PREM 11/1099, Trevelyan to Foreign Office, 15 Aug. 1956.
37. H. Trevelyan, *Public and Private* (London: Hamish Hamilton, 1980), p.56.
38. FO 371/118997/JE11924/61G, Watson to Trevelyan, 8 Sept. 1956. The last specific request for names was made in Oct. 1955. See FO 371/118997/ JE11924/61G, minute by Murray, 4 Sept. 1956.
39. Historians, Library and Records Department, Foreign and Commonwealth Office, *IRD: Origins and Establishment of the Foreign Office Information Research Department, 1946–48*, (London: FCO, 1995), pp.1–5.
40. CAB 134/1225, EOC (56) 1st mtg., 24 Aug. 1956.
41. Ibid.
42. CAB 134/1217, minutes of Prime Minister's Staff Conference, 19 Sept. 1956; also FO 371/118997/JE11924/74G, minute by Kirkpatrick, 20 Sept. 1956. Murray's IRD experience would also have been an important factor in the appointment. One of the most innovative aspects of the military planning was the emphasis placed on psychological warfare, the aim being to encourage opposition elements to take the initiative in toppling Nasser and seizing power. This was naturally seen as preferable to British forces marching on Cairo and establishing a successor regime themselves. See CAB 134/1225, 27 Sept. 1956: 'Organisation for Psychological Warfare,' note by Norman Brook.
43. An early enunciation of this role was made at the first meeting of the EOC. The details of the Political Advisor's instructions underwent many drafting stages, cf. the EOC's minutes in CAB 134/1225.

44. FO 371/118997/JE11924/74, minute by Murray, 20 Sept. 1956; on Britain's reluctance to associate too closely with France regarding Egyptian civil affairs, see CAB 134/1216, EC (56) 22nd mtg., 27 Aug. 1956.

45. FO 371/118996/JE11924/40G, minute by Murray, 22 Aug. 1956; a polished version of this document was circulated to the Egypt Committee as EC (56) 28, under Foreign Secretary Selwyn Lloyd's name.

46. FO 371/118997/JE11924/61G, Trevelyan to Watson, 15 Sept. 1956.

47. Adam Watson to author, 15 March 1997. Unfortunately, the actual minutes of Evans's meetings while in London have been retained under the Official Secrets Act.

48. FO 371/118832/JE1015/47, Trevelyan to Foreign Office, 19 Sept. 1956; see also, Trevelyan, *Middle East in Revolution*, p.87.

49. J. Gordon, *Nasser's Blessed Movement: Egypt's Free Officers and the July Revolution* (New York: Oxford University Press, 1992), pp.127–56; T. Little, *Egypt* (London: Ernest Benn Ltd., 1958) pp.225–36; and Thornhill, 'Britain and the Egyptian Question', pp.175–82.

50. In 1954, the armoured cavalry units had backed Neguib in his power struggle against Nasser; Little, *Egypt*, p.231.

51. Kyle, *Suez*, p.152.

52. Lucas, *Divided We Stand*, pp.193–94.

53. Adam Watson to author, 15 March 1997. The Foreign Office was also aware that Wafdists had been in touch with Neguib shortly before the nationalisation of the Suez Canal Company; see various minutes at FO 371/118832/JE1015/42. On 15 Nov., Kirkpatrick minuted that Britain favoured the Wafd 'not on any ideological grounds', but because they were 'the only people likely to succeed in overthrowing Nasser', see FO 371/118833/JE1015/72, note of conversation between Kirkpatrick and Gazier, 15 Nov. 1956.

54. See J.J. Terry, *The Wafd 1919–52: Cornerstone of Egyptian Political Power* (London: Third World Centre for Research, 1982).

55. Hoda Gamal Abdel Nasser, *Britain and the Egyptian Nationalist Movement, 1936–52* (Reading: Ithaca Press, 1994) p.204; and R. Vitalis, *When Capitalists Collide: Business Interests and End of Empire in Egypt* (Berkeley and Los Angeles: California University Press, 1995), pp.172–3.

56. Thornhill, 'Britain and the Egyptian Question', pp.44–67.

57. It is noteworthy that when President Sadat relaxed Egypt's laws on political parties in the 1970s, the Wafd was the first of the *ancien regime* parties to re-emerge.

58. On the internecine and generational feuding during the Wafd's last administration, see J. Gordon, 'The False Hopes of 1950: The Wafd's Last Hurrah and the Demise of Egypt's Old Order' in *International Journal of Middle Eastern Studies*, Vol.21, 1989, pp.199–202.

59. US National Archives, R[ecord] G[roup] 59, 774.00/7-3152, Caffery to State Department, 31 July 1952; RG 59, 774.00/8-752, Caffery to State Department, 7 Aug. 1952; FO 371/96932/JE1052/393G, minute by Bowker, 30 July 1952.

60. Thornhill, 'Britain and the Egyptian Question', p.20.

61. Kyle, *Suez*, p.150.

62. Thornhill, 'Britain and the Egyptian Question', pp.92–96.

63. FO 371/118832/JE1015/50, minute by Flux, 29 Sept. 1956.

64. Ibid.; also, minute by Wilton, 29 Sept. 1956; these minutes were approved by Ralph Murray.

65. Thornhill, 'Britain and the Egyptian Question', p.73; al-Moraghi was one of the Egyptian politicians who met with MI6 officers in southern France in late August, see Kyle, *Suez*, p.211.
66. This was a running theme in EOC meetings, cf. the minutes contained in CAB 134/1225.
67. Their respective positions were Governor-General of the Sudan and Minister Resident in the Middle East.
68. Trevelyan, *Middle East in Revolution*, p.94.
69. Ibid., p.105
70. Slade-Baker Diaries, 17 Aug. 1956, p.1482; also FO 371/118833/JE1017/16/ 56G, Trevelyan to Ross, 6 Oct. 1956.
71. Slade-Baker Diaries, pp.1481–83.
72. He was approached by a man claiming to be a member of a dissident group of senior Army officers plotting the overthrow of Nasser, Slade-Baker Diaries, 25 Aug. 1956, p.1491.
73. Ibid., 26 Aug. 1956, pp.1491–92; also, Trevelyan, *Middle East in Revolution*, p.110.
74. Hugh Thomas notes that the arrests may have been prompted by a tip-off from the Russians, who were receiving intelligence material from the traitor George Blake. See H. Thomas, *The Suez Affair* (London: Pelican ed., 1970) p.70, footnote.
75. Heikal, *Cutting the Lion's Tale*, p.169.
76. It was one of Flux's contacts, for instance, who passed on the information that Ali Maher was willing to form a successor government; see footnote 63.
77. Slade-Baker Diaries, 13 Sept. 1956, p.1515.
78. C. Tripp, 'Egypt 1945–52: The Uses of Disorder', in M. Kolinsky and M.J. Cohen (eds), *Demise of the British Empire in the Middle East* (London and Portland, Or: Frank Cass, 1998) p.128. There was also a Moslem Brotherhood attempt on Nasser's life in 1954, but this may have been staged by the authorities to justify a crackdown on the organisation. R. Mitchell's *The Society of Muslim Brothers* (London: Oxford University Press, 1969) remains the most illuminating history on this subject during the 1950s.
79. FO 371/118997/JE11924/92G, Trevelyan to Ross, 24 Oct. 1956.
80. Middle East Centre Archive, St. Antony's College, Oxford, Monroe Papers, John Hamilton interview with Elizabeth Monroe, September 1959. Hamilton commented that 'the French and Jews upset the "real plan"' and that 'the British envisaged an operation that would end with a collapse *á la* Mussadiq'.

'A Modern Major General': General Sir Gerald Templer, Chief of the Imperial General Staff

ANTHONY GORST

> The old adage should be recalled that war is the continuation of policy when other means have failed. This implies straightaway a relationship between Government and the Armed Forces whereby the latter are required to act within the policy established by the former...it must however remain the duty of the Government to provide a clear political aim and consistent direction and Force Commanders have the right to expect this in order that operations can be planned for its achievement.[1]

It is perhaps surprising that in the extensive literature covering Britain and the Suez Crisis in 1956 the role of the British military remains comparatively under-researched.[2] This is all the more remarkable given that much of British diplomatic policy during the summer and autumn of 1956 was *de facto* shaped by the timings and requirements of the military operation. Norman Brook's 'timetable' of mid-August, for example, prepared just before the first London Conference convened, represented a clear acknowledgement of the inter-action between the diplomatic, political and military spheres by attempting to synchronise the timings of military actions, notably the sailing of assault convoys, with the timings required by diplomatic consider-ations.[3] It is difficult to fully appreciate the evolution of British policy towards Egypt without an understanding of how the military response formulated by the British military influenced the course of British diplomacy in the summer and autumn of 1956 and *vice versa*.[4] The Chief of the Imperial General Staff General Sir Gerald Templer, was a pivotal figure in the British military establishment yet, like many senior British military figures, his personality, role and influence remains comparatively obscure; in contrast to the vivid pen-portraits and biographies of, for example, Eden, Lloyd and Macmillan, many of the military figures remain sketchy ciphers, their characters and motivations unclear.[5]

On 19 November 1956 Templer delivered an appreciation of the recent military operations against Egypt concluding that 'of course we were right – plumb right' to launch Operation MUSKETEER. In a bullish, if somewhat perverse, interpretation Templer argued that Britain had 'stopped quite a big war in the Middle East' and 'halted the march of Russia through the Middle East and onto the African continent'. Furthermore, Britain had succeeded in revealing the inadequacies of the United Nations 'as an instrument for solving world problems' and had 'forced…the United States to adopt some form of Middle East policy'. These remarkable results had been brought about by an 'incredibly complicated operation [that] was carried out in a manner of which the country can be proud…when history is written, it may well be considered a classic'.[6] Speaking only two weeks after the cease-fire in Egypt, Templer was no doubt in part conscious of the possible effect of his words on both morale in the Army and wider public opinion. In later life Templer was to modify his views, concluding that

> If History deals faithfully with those in military command the names of Generals Charles Keightley [Allied Commander-in-Chief, Operation MUSKETEER] and Hugh Stockwell [Land Force Commander, Operation MUSKETEER] will go down as two men who carried out their task splendidly *in the face of great political interference in military plans* (italics added for emphasis).

This impatience with politics and politicians was both characteristic of the man and symptomatic of the frustrations that he and the British military experienced in the long-drawn-out events of 1956. Templer, however, remained convinced that Britain had been right to launch Operation MUSKETEER and equally convinced that the armed forces had played their part as well as could be expected within the constraints imposed upon them.[7]

While Templer, and indeed the other Chiefs of Staff, may not have initiated British government policy towards Nasser's nationalisation of the Canal in July 1956, because Eden and much of the Cabinet, their political masters, were inclined towards a forceful response from the very beginning of the crisis, arguably Templer, the most 'hawkish' of the Chiefs, played a key role in shaping the manner of Britain's military response in the summer and autumn of 1956. His influence on British military policy at critical stages in the crisis, particularly in the July to August period, must therefore be examined closely. This is no easy task as Templer was averse to the keeping of voluminous files, and the CIGS papers at the Public record Office for this period are rather thin, consisting of little more than collections of telegrams and papers, with few annotations by Templer. Moreover, while Templer's own papers, held at the National Army Museum, are relatively full for some periods of his life, those for his term of office as CIGS, and particularly those for the Suez period are disappointingly thin.

Templer is perhaps best known as the architect of British success in the counter-insurgency war against Communist guerrillas in Malaya where he held the combined posts of High Commissioner and Director of Operations from 1952 to 1954. In the Second World War Templer had had a 'good war', beginning as a battalion commander of the Royal Sussex Regiment; he rose to be the youngest Lieutenant-General in the British Army before being severely wounded in Italy. On his recovery post-war, Templer served briefly as Director of Civil Affairs in the British Military government of Germany before joining the War Office in London, initially in 1946 as Director of Military Intelligence, later, in February 1948, becoming Montgomery's Vice Chief of the Imperial General Staff. On his return from Malaya, Templer was denied the prestigious command of the British Army on the Rhine, instead bringing his Malayan experience to bear on the deliberations of the Swinton Committee into colonial security and intelligence on which he served in the first half of 1955.[8] Appointed CIGS in September 1955, his chief concern and pre-occupation were the constant discussions about the shape and size of the army within Britain's overall defence policy and defence budget. Although there is a natural temptation to assume that Suez was the only pre-occupation of the British Chiefs of Staff (COS) in the summer of 1956 these debates, predominantly about manpower and money, would continue all through that momentous year: the normal business of the COS continued to occupy the bulk of their time both in Committee and, to a lesser extent, in the Service Ministries.

While Templer appeared on the surface to be almost a caricature of the bluff soldier, dressing in the inevitable pin-stripe suit and bowler hat while in 'mufti' in Whitehall, a contemporary profile characterised Templer as 'a man who lives on his nerves and "gets there" by quickness of thought, intelligence and sheer guts'.[9] Given to explosions of temper often expressed in earthy language – exemplified by his comment to Mountbatten, 'Dickie, you're so crooked that if you swallowed a nail you'd shit a corkscrew'[10] – his formidable exterior concealed a more subtle if acerbic character: another contemporary observer characterised him as 'an awkward cuss, but he was so good it didn't matter'.[11] Templer had learnt several lessons during his time in Malaya which he was to apply as CIGS; principal amongst these was that modern warfare was not simply about the clash of arms on the battlefield but had to be fought 'on the social, economic and political fronts as well'. Templer strongly believed that 'you can't defeat communism just with bullets, bayonets and bombs.'[12]

As CIGS, the professional head of the British Army, Templer sat on the regular meetings of the COS. This body, charged with providing military advice about Britain's strategic aims and stance to the Cabinet, was in the summer of 1956 in a state of some flux. In the first place the COS was bedding down a new organisation with a new post, Chairman of the Chiefs of Staff (CCOS) occupied by Marshal of the Royal Air Force, William Dickson, interposed over the heads of the CIGS – the Chief of the Air Staff (CAS) Air Chief Marshal Dermot Boyle and the First Sea Lord Admiral Lord Louis Mountbatten. This reorganisation, designed to provide clearer advice to Ministers and to reinforce the relatively weak position of the Minister of Defence, had been resisted by Templer who feared a dilution of the roles of the individual service heads and potentially that of the COS Committee itself. The original proposals of Eden and Lloyd were therefore amended so that the CCOS was not to be 'the Chief Military Adviser to the Government' but would simply be 'Chairman of the Chiefs of Staff Committee and Chief of Staff to the Minister of Defence'.[13]

It has been argued that this new configuration enabled Eden to exert undue influence on Operation MUSKETEER using Dickson as his conduit to Keightley and the MUSKETEER planning team, bypassing the COS Committee.[14] Templer himself however stated unequivocally that the COS 'attended all or nearly all the Cabinet and Defence Committees concerned and also the more frequent meetings of that inner circle of Cabinet [the Egypt Committee] which dealt with the matter closely'.[15] This rather overstates the case; the COS were not necessarily present at all the key Cabinet meetings; the Defence Committee had little if any input on policy formulation during the Suez Crisis, nor did the COS attend all the Egypt Committee meetings. However, it is clear that the COS were consulted on all the key military issues, including the problematic objective of the operation, in the summer and autumn of 1956, with the probable exception of collusion.

The bedding down of the new COS organisation was not helped by the fact that the incompatibility of the individual Chiefs, particularly Mountbatten and Templer, led to a good deal of friction in COS meetings: through much of 1956 the CCOS Dickson was ill and unable to mediate between these two dominant personalities.[16] Other contemporary Whitehall insiders have argued Templer was probably the most able of the COS in the summer 1956, a fact which, together with his forceful personality and the distrust with which Mountbatten was held in some circles, allowed Templer a strong position within the COS.[17]

Templer's involvement in the events which led to the Suez Crisis began soon after his installation as CIGS with the ill-fated 'Templer Mission' to Jordan in November 1955. Despite considerable experience of the Middle East, including a tour of the area with General Keightley the Commander in Chief Middle East Land Forces (CinCMELF) in the summer of 1955 to meet the leading politicians in the area, Templer's visit to Jordan has been characterised as a 'diplomatic disaster'.[18] The abrasive Templer – an observer recalled him 'shouting and punching the table' – was probably not the right choice to undertake the delicate task of moving the Jordanians closer to the Baghdad Pact and away from Egyptian influence. Indeed, the collapse of the Jordanian government and the swift deterioration in political stability in Jordan can in some measure be attributed to the Templer mission.[19] Despite this rather unhappy experience, it was to be Templer, together with elements within the Foreign Office, who defended Britain's 'forward strategy' in the Middle East, built around the Baghdad Pact, from his fellow COS in the Spring of 1956.[20] Templer had growing doubts about the utility of Jordan as an ally, particularly the effectiveness of the Jordanian Arab Legion, but, despite reacting predictably badly to the sacking of General Glubb ('Glubb Pasha', the British Commander of the Jordanian Arab Legion) by King Hussein, in March 1956,[21] Templer still held that 'it was essential that we should give all possible support to Iraq, and if Jordan was lost to us, there was a very grave danger that Iraq might go too. For this reason we could not abandon Jordan'.[22]

Templer did, however, take the opportunity, to shift the responsibility for the subsidies to Jordan from the War Office budget to that of the Foreign Office.[23] The significance of Templer's defence of the Baghdad Pact, built round Iraq with the possibility of strengthening through the accession of Jordan, became steadily apparent with the nationalisation crisis. One of the driving forces behind the progressive hardening of British policy towards Egypt in the spring and summer of 1956, in addition to the threat posed by Nasser's actions to more traditional British interests, was the threat to the West's Cold War alliance in the Middle East, which Britain had done so much to foster, the Baghdad Pact.[24]

On the news of the nationalisation of the Suez Canal Company reaching London on the evening of 26 July 1956, Templer was along with the other COS summoned to an after-dinner meeting by the Prime Minister to discuss Britain's military options in the light of this surprising development; it is clear that at this meeting Eden was inclined towards a rapid military response.[25] However, the COS were successful in firmly restraining any ministerial, and particularly Prime Ministerial, enthusiasm for a *coup de main* by lightly armed airborne or commando forces. This hare was started inadvertently by Mountbatten with his suggestion that the Mediterranean Fleet could sail to Cyprus, pick up the Royal Marine Commandos and land them at Port Said under an air umbrella provided by carrier-based air cover. Mountbatten himself then quashed this scenario as impractical and dangerous as it would leave the 1200 Marines exposed to Egyptian counter-attacks.[26] Templer was even more determined that if an operation against Egypt was to be undertaken then it should be mounted properly using the maximum amount of conventional forces at Britain's disposal. His assertion that the army would take at least six weeks to assemble an invasion force in the Middle East was decisive in committing Britain to a long haul in the confrontation with Egypt.[27]

Despite criticisms, made with hindsight given the lack of resistance mounted by Egyptian forces in the first week of November 1956, that the COS were over-cautious and that their plans represented over-insurance against a repetition of the Arnhem disaster of the Second World War, this was in fact founded on sound military considerations.

In the summer of 1956 Britain simply lacked the flexible and mobile quick-response forces, including amphibious assault shipping, to mount a *coup de main* in the face of Egyptian forces equipped with high quality Soviet bloc supplied equipment, some of it, particularly aircraft, more modern than that of the British forces, and possibly stiffened by foreign technicians and advisers.[28] For Templer the application of overwhelming force was the *sine qua non* of any military operation against Egypt. A constant concern for Templer and Keightley was the lack of administrative and logistical facilities in the Middle East for sustained offensive operations by the army; Britain, Templer felt, therefore had to build up forces in the area slowly and methodically before releasing them for a short, sharp campaign to overwhelm Egyptian defences.[29]

Fortuitously, the Joint Planning Staff (JPS) had recently undertaken an appreciation of 'limited war against Egypt' as part of a defence Policy Review barely one week before the nationalisation of the Canal. Ominously this paper warned that a conventional limited war with Egypt would be 'protracted and expensive' and that 'it would be prudent and, in the long run, economical to be able to deploy overwhelming force from the outset.' In order to defeat the Egyptian army of some 80,000 men, excluding frontier and security forces, organised in two Infantry Divisions, seven Infantry Brigades and two Armoured Groups deploying some 600–700 tanks, seize Port Said and capture the major airfields in the Canal Zone would involve Britain deploying at least three divisions plus a Parachute Brigade Group supported by at least three aircraft carriers. Moreover, to neutralise the Egyptian Air Force would require the commitment of eight Medium Bomber, two Light Bomber and eight Fighter squadrons.[30] Interestingly, discussion of this paper at the COS on 24 July had seen Templer and Mountbatten assuming different positions to those they were to take only two days later when the contingency became real. While Templer thought 'the forces required were too heavy in relation to the likely opposition', only one division would be needed for the battle, the remaining two being used 'to administer the country and the Canal while a political solution was being examined', Mountbatten argued that 'a force commander responsible for the operation...could not risk an assault on too light a scale. Under-insuring in the force requirements would be fatal.' The 'Limited War' paper was referred for re-drafting to bring out Templer's point that 'the forces required were based on the worst case'.[31]

The 'Outline Plan' produced by the JPS in London, in response to the Cabinet's authorisation 'to prepare a plan and timetable for military operations should they prove unavoidable', was based heavily on the 'limited war paper' of the previous week and proposed

> a concept of operations based on poising a ring of forces within striking range of Egypt. When this was sufficiently far advanced, an ultimatum will be issued failing acceptance of which a maritime blockade and air action will be instituted and – if this is still necessary – an assault will be made on the northern end of the canal and a threat posed to Alexandria.

Bomber forces and fighter squadrons could be concentrated in the area relatively quickly; however the problem was the provision of an amphibious lift for the commando assault forces – it would take at least until the middle of September before the necessary landing craft could be taken out of mothballs and despatched to join the Amphibious Warfare Squadron at Malta. This stately plan, which could, rather unkindly perhaps, be characterised as a 'mini-OVERLORD' was approved by the Egypt Committee on 2 August 1956.[32] It was not to survive long as the newly appointed Force Commanders, notably General Stockwell, were unhappy with the poor facilities offered by the proposed landing area, Port Said, and instead, with their planners, many of them former MELF staff, proposed HAMILCAR, an operation aimed at Alexandria.[33]

Fortunately, this new objective chimed with the war aim articulated by the Egypt Committee on 30 July 1956: 'While our ultimate purpose was to place the Canal under international control, our immediate objective was to bring about the downfall of the present Egyptian Government.' This somewhat confused war aim was to cause no little problem for the military planners and some friction between the politicians and the military. An assault on Port Said might secure the Canal but would do little to bring down Nasser, while an attack on Alexandria was closer to the seat of the Egyptian government in Cairo but was far removed from the scene of the Crisis, the Canal. At one point, when Mountbatten asked for clarification of the political objective of the proposed military operations Eden told him that 'he would have no interference from the COS on political matters'. Keightley was also to be the victim of Eden's irascibility.[34]

By 7 August Harold Macmillan, the Chancellor of the Exchequer, was arguing that Alexandria should be the target as this was more 'directly related' to the 'real aim' of overthrowing Nasser's government.[35] MUSKETEER was therefore recast by the Force Commanders, using HAMILCAR as the basis, as an amphibious and airborne assault on Alexandria. Presented by the COS to the Egypt Committee, the compelling argument was 'this might not be the quickest way of carrying out the object which we were given... [but] the more rapid reaching of Cairo might well result in an earlier fall of the Egyptian government'.[36] The question of where the operation against Egypt should be launched, Port Said or Alexandria, and the question of the primary objective – securing the Canal or toppling Nasser – was not, however, to go away: as the Commander of the British 2 Corps was to later note, 'the planning stages of MUSKETEER suffered from the lack of a consistent political direction.'[37]

In pursuit of these dual objectives, Templer added a refinement to military planning in early August 1956 and imposed his distinctive style onto British military plans and operations against Egypt by adding a psychological warfare element onto the rather traditional plans put forward by the JPS and refined by the MUSKETEER force commanders and planning staff. Drawing on his Malayan experience in which propaganda and psychological warfare had been closely integrated with military operations, Templer showed himself to be a very modern general with his emphasis on targeting the morale and will to resist of Egypt while attempting to separate Nasser and his government from the support of the Egyptian population. The psychological warfare element of MUSKETEER has hitherto proved difficult to pin down with several Ministry of Defence and Service Ministry staff and military planners expressing in interview some degree of mystification as to its origins and doubts as to its efficacy.[38] However, following the release of previously retained documents under the 'Open Government Initiative' it is possible to trace the evolution of the psychological warfare element of MUSKETEER. It is clear that this was an integral part of operational planning almost from the start and that the driving force behind this was General Templer. On 2 August he produced a memorandum on the place of psychological warfare in operations against Egypt. After surveying the existing bodies and mechanisms for psychological warfare, Templer suggested that

[an] essential part of the possible future operations is a

comprehensive psychological warfare plan. This could be broadly divided in three phases:

Phase 1 An all out attack on Egyptian morale, combined with some action to restrain other Arab states

Phase 2 (If military operations commence) An all out attack on other Arab states de-bunking Egypt, combined with some action to disrupt any resistance in Egypt

Phase 3 Rehabilitation

Templer concluded, however, that 'this plan could not be successfully carried out by any of the committees in existence'. He suggested that

> What is wanted as a matter of urgency is a high-powered official committee to deal with psychological warfare in all its aspects in respect of the proposed operations. The Foreign Office, the Colonial Office, the Treasury, the Commonwealth Relations Office and the three Services are all concerned and must be included.

This note was taken by the COS the same day: Templer's colleagues strongly supported the plan and invited him to put it to the Egypt Committee.[39] Anthony Head, the Secretary of State for War quickly presented Templer's case for the establishment of a committee to co-ordinate psychological measures in Operation MUSKETEER to the Egypt Committee. The result, following discussions with the Foreign Secretary and the Foreign Office, was the establishment in mid August of the Information Co-ordination Executive headed by Rennie (the head of the Information Research Department of the Foreign Office) which worked to an advisory committee made up of representatives of the Commonwealth Relations Office, the Colonial Office, the Ministry of Defence, the Chiefs of Staff, SIS, the BBC and the Cabinet Office.[40] The COS representative was to be the Director of Forward Planning.

Based in London, the Information Co-ordination Executive was to be responsible for overall control of propaganda and psychological warfare in connection with MUSKETEER: in theatre, the psychological warfare element was to be pursued by a team headed by a Director of Psychological Operations, Brigadier Bernard Fergusson (a former colleague of Templer's in Malaya). The psychological warfare programme was to take some time to evolve and, in any case, was not fully implemented due to the unforeseen circumstances in which MUSKETEER was eventually to be launched. As Keightley later noted:

> Very great emphasis had been laid upon the importance of psychological warfare in the operations as originally planned but when the operations started at 10 hour notice on a quite different basis to that which we had planned, our psychological warfare team was naturally unprepared for this change…the fact that the operations were set, in the event, in a completely unexpected framework nullified his [Fergusson's] efforts.[41]

However, the campaign was to include both 'black' and 'white' radio broadcasts, voice aircraft, leaflets as well as more overt measures such as air raids against targets that would affect Egyptian morale.[42]

Templer did not, however, believe that propaganda and psychological warfare alone could achieve Britain's objectives. He continued to argue that an invasion and occupation of key areas in Egypt was necessary to secure Britain's aims: this can be clearly seen in his reactions to the next phase of military planning. By early September 1956 a new military plan was needed as the provisional 'D-Day' had moved back from 15 September to 25 September 1956 due to the extended negotiations arising out of the London Conference and could not in any case be held beyond 6 October 1956 because of the onset of adverse weather conditions in the Mediterranean.[43] Moreover several individuals, notably Mountbatten, the First Lord of the Admiralty, Lord Hailsham, and Keightley himself, were concerned by the likely level of Egyptian casualties if an assault on Alexandria was launched with a preliminary naval bombardment and air strike.[44]

Keightley and the Force Commanders therefore formulated MUSKETEER (REVISE) which reverted to Port Said as the objective for the operation. A more fundamental change, however, was the use of air attacks and psychological warfare to create 'a situation which will lead to a breakdown of Egyptian resistance to Western Operation of the Suez Canal and enable Allied forces to secure the Canal Zone'. The operation would begin with an intensive air bombardment to destroy the Egyptian Air Force and would be followed by attacks against military and economic targets alongside intensive psychological warfare broadcasts to isolate Nasser from the Egyptian population. Only after these first two phases were complete would Anglo-French forces land at Port Said, occupy the Canal Zone before moving on Cairo.[45]

Although MUSKETEER (REVISE) offered a number of advantages, not least a halving of the lead-time required from authorisation to the beginning of operations to eight days, Templer was concerned 'whether economic, air and naval action…could achieve capitulation and such complete disintegration of the Egyptian Army as to make land fighting unnecessary.' Moreover, Templer was worried about the reliance on an air offensive to break Egyptian morale as 'it was impossible to prove the validity of assumption. If it was by any chance false, our position, both military and political would be extremely difficult'. If a landing at Port Said did prove necessary, Templer predicted heavy damage would be caused to the city. Templer's doubts were shared by both Stockwell and General Beaufre (the French Deputy Land Commander). For Templer psychological warfare was simply an adjunct, albeit an important one, to military operations and he continued to believe that ultimately an invasion would be necessary to reverse the nationalisation of the Canal.[46]

Once MUSKETEER (REVISE) had been accepted by the Cabinet, the role of the COS subtly altered: with a concept of operations that seemed to meet both the immediate and long-term political objectives of the Egypt Committee, the COS became less concerned with strategic planning and more concerned with the assembly of equipment and the movement of forces to the Middle East. While the Force Commanders and their planning staffs fine-tuned the MUSKETEER (REVISE) plans, Templer and the War Office became far more concerned with making forces available for commanders on the spot.[47] For the War Office this was a relatively complicated task for a good deal of the specialist equipment and personnel had to be taken from the reserve and transported to bases in the Mediterranean and Middle East; even the paratroop battalions, Britain's 'intervention' force, required re-training and the provision of extra equipment.[48]

This change in the role of the COS was reinforced by the fact that the emphasis from the middle of September moved to the diplomatic arena with Britain faced with, in rapid succession, Dulles's Suez Canal Users Association, the Second London Conference and, eventually, the referral of the Suez Canal dispute to the United Nations. However, the COS were not idle in this holding period; rather they began to assess the long-term implications of Nasser's actions for Britain's position in the Middle East. It is clear that the strains and frustrations of the previous two months were beginning to tell on the COS. Templer noted, for example, with some degree of asperity when discussing the terms of reference for a study of threats to Britain's overseas interests, 'if an examination of this sort had been carried out earlier, the Services would have had suitable plans in existence and would have been better prepared to meet the Suez emergency.'[49] More seriously, the strained relations in COS meetings between Mountbatten and Templer worsened still further, with on one occasion, according to Ziegler, Templer calling Mountbatten 'yellow'.[50]

For the COS, the situation in the Middle East in October 1956 became more rather than less complicated; the attack by Israel on a Jordanian police post introduced a new variable into the volatile situation in an especially acute form. The British military were now faced with a situation where, for approximately ten days, there was the distinct possibility that Britain could be involved in a war with Israel in defence of Britain's obligations to Jordan. While the MUSKETEER forces could be used to carry out Operation CORDAGE, a war plan for operations against Israel, and indeed air and naval forces were put on alert against Israel, Britain could not undertake MUSKETEER and CORDAGE simultaneously.[51] This nightmare situation was ultimately resolved in a most unexpected fashion: a fundamental part of the Sèvres negotiations which turned Israel into Britain's temporary *de facto* ally in the Middle East was an agreement that Israel should attack Egypt rather than Jordan.[52] There is a degree of confusion about when the British military were informed of collusion with Israel; the very fact that such confusion exists suggests that the British military were not formally told about this dramatic change of alignment in the Middle East which, to say the least, had implications for MUSKETEER in terms of its timing, the circumstances in which it would be launched and the conduct of operations. Certainly, many military figures, including Templer, could tell that something was in the wind and made *ad hoc* arrangements accordingly but the Cabinet seem to have decided to exclude the British military, with the exception of Mountbatten, from the circle of those privy to the information. That this did not have dire military consequences can be ascribed to the success of the Israeli military operations in the Sinai, the fact that British forces in the Middle East had been moved and brought to readiness for CORDAGE and the fact that MUSKETEER (REVISE) could be adapted and mounted at comparatively short notice, though at some cost to the effectiveness of the psychological warfare plan.[53]

With the launching of Operation MUSKETEER, Templer's reaction was one of relief, telling Dick White, the head of SIS, 'Thank God we're off…if anybody tries to pull us back now, I'll have his balls.'[54] However, Templer was to be disappointed for, although the preliminary air strikes against the Egyptian Air Force were successful, the enforced hiatus between the beginning of MUSKETEER and the landing of the Anglo-French forces at Port Said, while the assault convoys made their way from Malta, allowed world opinion expressed at the United Nations to interfere with the conduct of operations. On 4 November 1956 the COS discussed the timing of the planned parachute operations in MUSKETEER (Operation TELESCOPE, the dropping of British and French paratroops to seize Gamil airfield and bridges south of Port Fuad in advance of the seaborne assault) in relation to the United Nations General Assembly discussions. Dickson considered that 'it might be best to postpone the operation', pointing out the political difficulties in which Britain might find itself at the United Nations if the operation was launched 'accompanied by preliminary fire support if the Egyptians had agreed to cease hostilities'. At this threat to tailor military operations to meet political considerations Templer flared up, arguing vehemently that 'the Commander in Chief had already gone to the limit in risking the lives of his own forces, in order to save the lives of Egyptian civilians'. Templer argued that

> HMG [should] accept the complete cessation of all hostilities throughout Egypt and Israel at once except at Port Said where a cease-fire could be accepted at 12 noon on 5 November 1956. It should be made clear that an airborne operation would take place in Port Said. If his colleagues agreed, the COS could advise the Government to accept the military risks of this early warning of their military intentions but must add that their proposals assumed that there would be no restriction on the follow-up by air and sea.[55]

This proposal, which was not in the end adopted, illustrates not only Templer's impatience for political interference in military operations that might cost the lives of British servicemen but also his willingness to gamble militarily to secure political and diplomatic objectives. For Templer, as for many British military figures, the

Cabinet's acceptance of a cease-fire on 6 November 1956 with military operations only half completed and with the MUSKETEER forces dangerously exposed in Port Said was frustrating. For the remainder of November and December 1956 Templer was deeply concerned with the inter-related questions of the creation and insertion of a United Nations Force and the withdrawal of the MUSKETEER forces while still maintaining a degree of readiness should renewed hostilities with Egypt break out.[56]

How then can the role of Templer during the Suez Crisis be assessed? The shortcomings of MUSKETEER were not the fault of either Templer or his fellow chiefs. The slow mounting of MUSKETEER was the result of a lack of conventional forces, caused by constraints on defence expenditure and a concentration on the nuclear deterrent in the 1950s, and was compounded by the delays enforced by diplomatic activity which were themselves the result of Britain's inability to intervene quickly. The lesson that Templer and the army drew from MUSKETEER was the necessity to have available mobile forces which could intervene in a trouble spot, such as Jordan in 1958, quickly and decisively.[57]

If Templer and his fellow Chiefs can be criticised it is for accepting political aims for MUSKETEER from the Cabinet and Egypt Committee that were confused and probably not achievable, even if Templer's psychological warfare plan had not been rendered ineffective because of the conditions under which MUSKETEER was eventually to be launched. Templer, however, admired Eden, as a politician and an individual, and was fundamentally in agreement with his assessment of Nasser. Moreover, as a good soldier Templer believed his role was not to 'bellyache' but to accept his orders and carry out his job to the best of his ability. This did not stop him from concluding in later life that 'the outcome [of the Suez Crisis] disgusted me with the conduct of public affairs in this country, whether on the Cabinet level or in the House of Commons.'[58]

NOTES

1. WO 288/79, Commander 2 Corps 'Operation MUSKETEER, Lessons and Recommendations', undated.
2. The standard work remains R. Fullick and G. Powell, *Suez: The Double War* (London: Hamish Hamilton, 1979): the 1990 re-issue of this volume did not, however, make use of the 1956 records available at the Public Record Office from January

1987. J.A. Sellers, 'Military lessons: The British Perspective' in S.I. Troen and M. Shemesh, *The Suez-Sinai Crisis 1956: Retrospective and Reappraisal* (London: Frank Cass, 1990) is an operational history.

3. CAB 134/1217, EC(56)19, 14 Aug. 1956.
4. See for example A. Gorst and W.S. Lucas, 'Suez 1956: Strategy and the Diplomatic Process' in *Journal of Strategic Studies*, Vol.11, No.4, Dec. (1988), pp.391–436.
5. In part this is a result of the nature of the sources available for the study of the formulation of British military policy in 1956. The records of the Chiefs of Staff Committee (COS), for example, contain the bare bones of discussion in these regular meetings. They are *not* verbatim transcripts and very often contain little more than notes of the decisions reached while points raised in discussion are not necessarily attributed to particular individuals.
6. WO 216/909, 'CIGS Appreciation of Suez', 19 Nov. 1956.
7. J. Cloake, *Templer, Tiger of Malaya. The Life of Field Marshal Sir Gerald Templer* (London: Harrap, 1985), p.355.
8. Ibid. and Michael Carver, 'Sir Gerald Templer', Lord Blake and C.S. Nicholls (eds), *Dictionary of National Biography, 1971–80* (Oxford, OUP, 1986) p.836.
9. National Army Museum, Templer Papers 7410-29-6, 'Profile of General Sir Gerald Templer' by Lt-General Brian Horrocks, *Sheffield Telegraph*, 25 April 1955.
10. P. Ziegler, *Mountbatten* (London: Collins, 1985), p.528.
11. Cited in Cloake, *Templer*, p.338.
12. Templer Papers, 7410-29-1, 'Speech by the High Commissioner to the Legislative Chamber', 19 March 1952; Templer Papers 7410-29-2, 'Speech to the Alamein re-union dinner', 22 Oct. 1954.
13. Cloake, *Templer*, pp.337–8, and B. Jackson and D. Bramall, *The Chiefs: The Story of the United Kingdom Chiefs of Staff* (London: Brassey's, 1992), pp.295–6.
14. F.A. Johnson, *Defence by Ministry* (London: Duckworth, 1980) p.48; Cloake, *Templer*, p.350
15. Cloake, *Templer*, p.354.
16. Jackson and Bramall, *The Chiefs*, p.298.
17. Interview with Sir Frank Cooper by A. Gorst and W.S. Lucas, 1989.
18. W.S. Lucas, *Divided We Stand: Britain the United States and the Suez Crisis* (London: Hodder & Stoughton, 1991), p.76.
19. K. Kyle, *Suez* (London: Weidenfeld & Nicolson, 1991), pp.90–93.
20. Gorst and Lucas, 'Suez 1956', pp.392–4.
21. E. Shuckburgh, *Descent to Suez* (London: Weidenfeld & Nicolson, 1986), p.342.
22. DEFE 4/85, COS (56)104, discussed at COS(56) 31st mtg., 13 March 1956.
23. DEFE4/86, COS(56) 45th mtg., 1 May 1956.
24. R. Ovendale, *Britain, the United States and the Transfer of Power in the Middle East, 1945–1962* (London: Leicester University Press, 1996), pp.140–78.
25. Gorst and Lucas, 'Suez 1956', p.399.
26. Kyle, *Suez*, p.138; Lucas, *Divided We Stand*, p.143; Gorst and Lucas, 'Suez 1956', p.400. Some of the confusion surrounding the use of Commando forces to seize Port Said as soon as possible has been caused by, in Kyle's judicious phrase, Mountbatten's 'habit of improving the historical record'.
27. Kyle, *Suez*, p.138; Jackson and Bramall, *The Chiefs*, p.298.
28. Gorst and Lucas, 'Suez 1956', p.396–9; Grove, *Vanguard to Trident: British Naval Policy since World War II* (Annapolis , Naval Institute Press, 1987), pp.183–4.

29. See for example, DEFE 4/89, COS (56) 73rd , 80th and 83rd mtgs., 27 July 1956, 14 Aug. 1956 and 23 Aug. 1956.
30. DEFE 4/88, JP(56)125(F), 18 July 1956.
31. DEFE 4/88, COS(56) 71st mtg., 24 July 1956.
32. CAB 128/30 Pt.II, CM(56)54, 27 July 1956; DEFE 4/89, JP(56)135(F), 31 July 1956, discussed at COS (56) 76th mtg., 1 Aug. 1956.; CAB 134/1216, EC (56) 9th mtg., 2 Aug. 1956.
33. Sellers, 'Military Lessons', pp.25–8.
34. Ziegler, *Mountbatten*, p.540; Gorst and Lucas, 'Suez 1956', p.412.
35. CAB 134/1216, EC(56)3rd mtg., 30 July 1956; CAB 134/1217, EC(56)8, 7 Aug. 1956 discussed at CAB 134/1216, EC(56) 11th mtg., 7 Aug. 1956.
36. CAB 134/1217, EC(56)15, 10 Aug. 1956 discussed at CAB 134/1216, EC(56) 14th mtg., 10 Aug. 1956.
37. WO 288/79, Commander 2 Corps 'Operation MUSKETEER, Lessons and Recommendations', undated.
38. Liddell Hart Centre for Military Archives, King's College London, Suez Oral History Collection. Interviews with Sir Frank Cooper, Brigadier Hunt and Sir Richard Powell.
39. WO 216/907, note by CIGS 'Psychological Warfare', 2 Aug. 1956; DEFE 4/89, COS (56) 77th mtg., 2 Aug. 1956.
40. CAB 134/1216, EC(56) 9th and 10th mtgs., 2 and 3 Aug. 1956.
41. DEFE 11/137, COS(57)220, 11 Aug. 1957.
42. Kyle, *Suez*, p.238–240; Lucas, *Divided We Stand*, p.192.
43. DEFE 11/138, SD12(56)1(F), 9 Sept. 1956.
44. Gorst and Lucas, 'Suez 1956', p.412.
45. CAB 134/1217, EC(56)43, 6 Sept. 1956.
46. DEFE 4/90, COS(56) 89th and 90th mtgs., 6 Sept. and 9 Sept. 1956; Fullick and Powell, *The Double War*, p.58.
47. Interview with Brigadier Hunt, 1989.
48. Gorst and Lucas, 'Suez 1956', p.401.
49. DEFE 4/90, COS(56) 97th mtg., 9 Oct. 1956.
50. Ziegler, *Mountbatten,* p.541.
51. Gorst and Lucas, 'Suez 1956', pp.419–21.
52. Kyle, *Suez*, pp.565–7.
53. Kyle, *Suez*, pp.339–42; Lucas, *Divided We Stand*, pp.251–3; Gorst and Lucas, 'Suez 1956', pp.422–4.
54. Cloake, *Templer*, p.352.
55. DEFE 32/5, COS(56) 111th mtg., 4 Nov. 1956.
56. DEFE 4/92, COS(56) 112th, 117th and 118th mtgs., 7, 14 and 16 Nov. 1956.
57. See, for example, P.J. Darby, *British Defence Policy East of Suez 1947–1968* (London: Oxford University Press, 1973), Chapters 4 and 5.
58. Cloake, *Templer*, p.354.

Playing the Role of a Cassandra: Sir Gerald Fitzmaurice, Senior Legal Advisor to the Foreign Office

LEWIS JOHNMAN

When the news of Nasser's nationalisation of the Suez Canal Company reached Eden, the Prime Minister was hosting a dinner in honour of King Feisal of Iraq. At the impromptu meeting which convened to discuss the nationalisation, the Lord Chancellor, Lord Kilmuir, a guest at the dinner, recounts in his diaries that he had 'got over the point…that it was wrong in international law to endanger the international control of an international waterway and that the company had been treated as an international entity…'[1] This seems to have laid the ground for two themes which would recur throughout the crisis. First, the government's willingness to take its legal advice from the Lord Chancellor and his office, thereby ignoring the more usual channels of legal advice – the offices of the Attorney-General and Solicitor-General who took their advice from the departmental legal officials. Second, a stress on the 'internationalisation' of the Canal which conveniently avoided the fact that the government had a very weak case over the nationalisation. On the day following the dinner, 27 July 1956, the Cabinet accepted that:

> we should be on weak ground in basing our resistance on the narrow argument that Colonel Nasser had acted illegally. The Suez Canal Company was registered as an Egyptian company under Egyptian law; and Colonel Nasser had indicated that he intended to compensate the shareholders at ruling market prices. From a narrow legal point of view, his action amounted to no more than a decision to buy out the shareholders. Our case must be presented on wider international grounds. Our argument must be that the Canal was an important international asset and facility,

and that Egypt could not be allowed to exploit it for a purely internal purpose.[2]

But even this rationalisation in Cabinet was in advance of any considered opinion by the Law Officers.

The issue was to be debated in the House of Commons and the legal advisers were asked to brief the Foreign Secretary, Selwyn Lloyd. This brief boiled down to six somewhat flimsy points. The threat of force to keep British and French subjects working was a breach of international law and by implication meant that the Egyptians would be incapable of operating the Canal and thus discharging their obligations under the 1888 Convention of Constantinople. The Convention itself was entered into on the basis of a company jointly operated by Britain and France, which had over the years acquired an international character and that nationalisation of such a company was, in itself a breach of international law.[3] Sir Gerald Fitzmaurice, the Senior Legal Adviser at the Foreign Office since 1953, who had joined the Foreign Office Legal Department in 1929, was directly involved in drawing up the brief for Lloyd; while the legal advisers made the best of their case, Fitzmaurice conceded to the Attorney-General, Sir Reginald Manningham-Buller, that:

> the fundamental legal difficulty in the Suez Canal case is that although the Egyptian Government are committing a number of illegalities, none of them amount, at any rate at present, to a direct breach of the Suez Canal Convention, and therefore they do not help us on the central issue on which we are seeking to base ourselves.[4]

These were reservations with which the Attorney-General and the Solicitor-General, Sir Harry Hylton-Foster, fully concurred.[5]

Despite this weakness the government did require a legal case, especially if there was to be a resort to force. Eden had given early indication of this in a letter to the US President, Eisenhower, arguing that 'we should not allow ourselves to become involved in legal quibbles...we must be ready, in the last resort, to use force to bring Nasser to his senses'.[6] What alarmed Fitzmaurice and other Foreign Office legal advisers, however, was the heavy lobby briefings of the press in the first week of August by the Prime Minister's press secretary, William Clarke, and the head of the Foreign Office News Department over Britain's willingness to use force.[7] This, allied to incoming

Foreign Office telegrams from Tripoli which suggested that Libya was being considered as a base for military operations against Egypt, brought from Fitzmaurice a warning to Harold Beeley, who was then chairing the official inter-departmental committee, the Suez Canal Sub-Committee of the Cabinet's Official Committee on the Middle East, that:

> We are already on an extremely bad wicket legally as regards using force in connection with the Suez Canal. Indeed, whatever illegalities the Egyptians may have committed in nationalizing the Suez Canal Company, these do not in any way, as things stand at present, justify forcible action on our part, and such a justification could only arise, if at all, from some further and much more drastic step on the part of the Egyptian Government amounting to a closure of the Canal, or at any rate, a definite refusal or impeding of passage through it.[8]

Fitzmaurice's view was stiffened a few days later when he was approached to provide a legal justification, in the light of a military occupation of Egypt, for the establishment of military courts and administration. After rehearsing a range of theoretical situations, Fitzmaurice concluded that 'there would be no legal basis for any such action on our part'. He then went to the nub of the issue exposing his 'feeling' that it had been generally believed that the Egyptians would sooner or later do something which did breach the 1888 Convention and provide the pretext for military intervention. Now, however:

> I think we must…face the fact that in all probability we shall not be offered this pretext, and I think, therefore, we must give some thought to how the legal aspects of the matter are to be presented if we carry an armed intervention into effect purely and simply on the basis that the Canal must be internationalized, or rather, I think we must face the fact that we shall be unable to make out a legal case. The repercussions of such a situation may well be very serious, and may be very lasting and far-reaching. They are, for instance, quite certain to affect our position in the United Nations, and almost every question that will arise in the forthcoming United Nations Assembly, extremely adversely. In saying all this, I have no wish to intervene on policy matters, but I am bound to point out what is involved from the legal point of view.[9]

The Sub-Committee's brief for the first London Conference reflected some of this input arguing that all aims could be pursued 'without resort to military action' and that military action would not only damage wider political relationships and the Commonwealth, but the very settlement of the Canal dispute which the British government was seeking.[10]

The problem, of course, was that pursuit of the issue by legal means alone, if it were successful in internationalising the Canal, could not possibly achieve Eden's primary objective of 'undoing Nasser'. It was the twin aims of Eden's policy – internationalisation of the Canal and the overthrow of Nasser – which caused confusion and consternation amongst the legal advisers, and according to the Lord Privy Seal, Rab Butler, caused many Cabinet members to be 'muddled by this duality of purpose'.[11] Exactly at which point Eden decided, if indeed he did, to narrow the circle of legal advice is uncertain but it does seem clear that he and, by extension, Lord Kilmuir were only interested in legal advice which would prove the nationalisation illegal and provide a justification for intervention. The Lord Chancellor's Office, therefore, seized upon a letter in *The Times* of 11 August 1956 from Professor A.L. Goodhart of University College, Oxford. Citing standard legal textbooks, Brierly's *The Law of Nations* and Oppenheim's *International Law: Peace*, and legal precedent such as the case of the Cherokee Nation vs. Southern Kansas Railroad Company, of 1890, Goodhart's conclusion was manna for the Lord Chancellor's Office. Goodhart noted that:

> it has been said that under modern international law force must never be used except to repel a direct territorial attack. This view cannot be accepted, as the use of force is not so limited; thus, for example, a State may take all necessary steps to protect the lives of its citizens abroad. Similarly it may use force to protect a vital national interest which has been imperilled. In such a case it is the State that has altered the status quo by the use of force which is guilty of aggression.[12]

While Fitzmaurice was prepared to draft papers for the First London Conference making the best case against the nationalisation, as he commented, the papers were 'designed to shake the view of some Delegations that the Egyptian action was unquestionably lawful' but, that as things stood, it did not 'afford legal justification for the use of force'.[13] With the failure of the London Conference, however, and with the Canal continuing to operate smoothly, the justification for the use of force remained elusive.

Following the London Conference the British government considered referring the dispute to the Security Council of the United Nations. Even here the government's hopes were to be rudely dashed by the advice of its UK Permanent Representative at the UN, Sir Pierson Dixon, who correctly diagnosed that such an approach was 'designed to give colour to military intervention by France and ourselves'.[14] As Dixon read the UN situation: ' it is quite out of the question to extract from the Security Council a good vote on a resolution designed to justify subsequent use of force, particularly force exerted by two nations without further reference to the United Nations'.[15] In this he was supported by Fitzmaurice who commented that:

> It is very difficult to get it into the heads of people in this country that the Security Council is not an institution for settling disputes, or even for doing justice between nations, but an institution for preventing or stopping wars…The argument that by going to the Security Council we have done everything possible and that the Security Council having proved itself impotent, we are now justified in going ahead on our own, may well appeal to public opinion in this country, but the argument is based on a misconception of the real functions of the Security Council.[16]

As a covering memo from I.T.M. Pink, the Superintending Under-Secretary at the United Nations Department of the Foreign Office, to the Permanent Under-Secretary at the Foreign Office, Sir Ivone Kirkpatrick, dryly noted, 'the assembly of considerable forces in the Mediterranean cannot be kept secret' and that if during a Security Council debate a military operation against Egypt were to be launched then 'the tables would immediately be turned upon us in the Security Council and we should be faced with a resolution deploring the use of force and enjoining HMG and the French Government to refrain from using force and settle the problem by peaceful means'. The initiative would, therefore, 'have become a boomerang'.[17] Accordingly the government decided, at this stage, not to approach the UN and the US Secretary of State, John Foster Dulles, promulgated the idea of the Suez Canal Users Association (SCUA).

As the public and diplomatic focus moved from the First London Conference to SCUA, the focus among the legal advisers revolved around an extraordinary series of exchanges between Fitzmaurice and Sir Ivone Kirkpatrick, who as Selwyn Lloyd later commented, 'throughout ...[the crisis]... knew everything'.[18] Kirkpatrick, it would seem, if not exactly trying to convince Fitzmaurice at the personal level as to the use of force, was attempting to wring from him a legal justification for armed intervention. Kirkpatrick based his case not on any legal precedent, although the clear desire for a legal justification remained paramount, but rather on the political and moral reasons for supporting force. To Kirkpatrick's view, which was stated policy, 'that force would only be used in the last resort', Fitzmaurice neatly turned the Hitler analogy around, arguing that this had been typical of Hitler's tactics; if his objectives were achievable by negotiation well and good, if not, the doctrine of force as a last resort was invoked and as Fitzmaurice put it, 'is not our position exactly the same and the argument just as specious?' The Hitler analogy itself was rudely dismissed with the Egyptians having shown 'no liking for military adventures and certainly no capacity for it', and indeed, on the last occasion on which this had been put to the test, the nascent state of Israel had 'wiped the floor with them'. To the accusation that Nasser had brought the issue upon himself by the arbitrary nationalisation of the Canal, Fitzmaurice did concede some ground but argued that this did not justify 'taking the law into one's own hands and acting as one's own policeman, judge and executioner'. He then turned to the 'lifeline and jugular vein' argument which had been much touted during the crisis and found that this too was a somewhat desperate argument. Nasser had neither closed nor restricted passage through the Canal and force could hardly be justified 'in order to keep open a canal which...remains open and seems likely to continue so'. Even the 'jugular vein' argument boiled down to a variant of what might happen at some future unspecified date and in some unspecified set of circumstances and afforded no justification 'apart from reasons of prestige and UK internal politics'. Nor did action because it was demanded by public opinion move Fitzmaurice because, as he rightly forecast, the government was 'seriously underestimating the strength of feeling which will manifest itself against the use of force' and which cut 'right across party alignments'. Fitzmaurice concluded that:

Even if some 'incident' can be provoked, I am afraid that matters will by then have gone so far that no-one will credit its genuineness and it will appear mere pretext. Our preparations will have been such that we shall not be able to escape the charge of having launched a deliberate and prepared attack.

The result would be the loss of 'all our moral influence in the UN' and the government left entirely reliant 'on political justifications' for its actions.[19] Kirkpatrick was probably unsurprised by both the arguments and the strength of feeling in Fitzmaurice's memoranda. As an 'insider' he hedged, citing the American intervention in Guatemala, in 1954, and he re-invoked the Hitler analogy by pointing out that 'we were reluctant to slap Hitler down because he was so strong and now we're reluctant to stop Nasser because he's so weak'. It reminded Kirkpatrick of the German Generals, who would not revolt when the war was going well because it would be of little use, but applied the same logic when the war was going badly. Was it not, he asked, 'all escapism...any excuse so as not to take the plunge?' While he could agree with Fitzmaurice that the issue was a 'matter of sentiment rather than reason', in that world opinion compelled Britain to accept the Egyptian coup while opposing a retaliatory coup based on similar arguments, as he saw it the problem remained 'should we resolve to perish gracefully because opinion thinks that this is what we should do?'[20]

As SCUA gathered momentum the issue of whose legal advice was acceptable became more focused. Even before the SCUA scheme was accepted by the Cabinet, however, grounds for rejection had been provided by Lord Kilmuir. Dulles's interpretation of Article 8 of the 1888 Convention was that this gave the users all of the rights which they required; they could, therefore, effectively club together and manage the Canal if Egypt refused to accept the proposals for the internationalisation of its operation. Kilmuir's interpretation of Article 8 was that it gave only signatories to the Convention – not users – any rights, and that the rights were limited to drawing to the attention of the Egyptian government 'any event threatening the security or free passage of the Canal'. The Convention, however, contained no provision for sanctions if the Egyptian Government failed to act. Kilmuir then touched, albeit briefly, on the fact that it had been the British who had steadfastly resisted all previous moves in the direction of internationalisation, an uncomfortable point, which Kilmuir avoided in his conclusion, arguing that: 'while the Convention of 1888 imposes clear obligations on Egypt there is nothing in it which gives the users of the Canal any such rights as Mr Dulles suggests and that the Convention can be enforced only by economic or physical pressure and, in the last resort, by force'.[21] Thus, well before Dulles's famous remarks about 'not shooting our way through' and the scheme having 'no teeth in it', the legal ground had been prepared as to why the scheme was unworkable and why it could be rejected. SCUA, arguably, was just one more step towards justification for 'the last resort'.

In essence, Kilmuir was asserting the doctrine of necessity. Broadly, this held that if every conceivable legal means of self-preservation had been exhausted and the very existence of the State was still in danger, the State was justified in having recourse to such a means of self-preservation, even though it would otherwise be unlawful. The burden of proof in such cases lay with the party which invoked the plea of necessity.[22] But, as Fitzmaurice saw this:

> The last resort argument is only a valid one if you have a legal case for using force in the last resort. Otherwise, it avails nothing, and only serves to bring out the fact that you are not prepared to give up your objective even if it means, in the last resort, using force to obtain it. In short, you postpone your aggression as long as possible, but you are ready to commit it if necessary.[23]

He then took the unusual step of writing to the senior legal adviser in the Lord Chancellor's Office, Sir George Coldstream. Fitzmaurice appealed, through Coldstream, to the Lord Chancellor that whatever the political and economic justifications for using force in Egypt, there was no legal justification. Attacking Egypt on the ground that the nationalisation was illegal was itself illegal, a breach of the UN Charter and a simple act of aggression. The justification of getting rid of Nasser was no better in that it was based on the perception that he might, in the future, harm Britain's interests. As Fitzmaurice noted 'the Lord Chancellor will know from his recollections of the Nuremberg Tribunal within what very narrow limits the doctrine of necessity affords a legal justification for the use of force'. He concluded that:

> we do not seem to have anything approaching the sort of case which would bring us within the doctrine of necessity...All this seems to me to build up not merely to the absence of a legal

case...but also, which is much worse, to an exceedingly bad moral position, or at least one that will be so regarded by a very large section of world opinion...In their present mood, HM Government may think that they do not much mind about general opinion. But will they still feel the same after the event, when it may be too late.[24]

Strong as this was, it was unlikely to move Kilmuir who, as early as 31 July, considered Fitzmaurice's views as being 'to the country's disadvantage'.[25]

Coldstream duly passed Fitzmaurice's letter, which he termed 'courageous and important', to Kilmuir but it appears to have fallen on fallow ground.[26] On 12 September Kilmuir mounted a robust defence of the government's position in Parliament.

Is it not plain that in such circumstances States which are party to the agreement, in the fulfilment of their international obligations, have not only the right but a positive duty to take such steps as may be necessary to compel the delinquent to fulfil his international obligations?...Every neglect of an international legal duty constitutes an international delinquency, and the injured State can, subject to its obligations of pacific settlement, through reprisals or even war compel the delinquent State to fulfil the international duties.[27]

Kilmuir was thus pushing the government's constant line that because Nasser's nationalisation of the Suez Canal Company was illegal, although even this was of dubious veracity, the right to use force remained an option. Even so, the Lord Chancellor did not seem to have kept abreast of precedent as it had developed in international law. Delinquency on the part of a state created liabilities of a civil rather than a criminal nature and the punishing of such was not within the jurisdiction of other states. Criminal delinquency could only be defined as crimes against humanity or peace and as Fitzmaurice observed 'Nasser's present actions could not be brought within that category'.[28] Citing the interpretation of American international lawyer, Quincy Wright, of Article 51 of the UN Charter, he stated that: 'Preventative war, when the danger is any degree speculative or remote, constitutes aggression under this conception, and under the Charter any preventative war initiated by a government on its own responsibility is aggression'.[29] But, as the British government prepared to take the Suez case to the Security Council of the UN, Fitzmaurice's rationalisations were ignored.

By the end of September, the Second London Conference on SCUA had closed, the British and French had referred the dispute to the United Nations Security Council and Eden and Lloyd had been in discussion with the French in Paris. Even the referral to the Security Council gave Fitzmaurice some cause for concern, as had the first attempt, given his rationalisation that the role of the various branches of the UN was widely misunderstood. As he quite correctly pointed out, there was nothing in the Charter of the UN that even implied that a function of the Security Council was to force members to respect their international obligations. The primary function of the Security Council was to maintain or restore international peace and security and it was only as a lower function of this primary duty that the Security Council could engage in dispute settlement as such. Indeed, under the terms of the Charter, the Security Council could be requested to intervene but even then could only make recommendations. As the situation stood, therefore, the only specific duty which the Security Council could discharge was to maintain or restore peace and that, so far, it had 'not failed in that duty'.[30]

Again, this was to little avail. Lloyd's address to the Security Council on 5 October reflected Kilmuir's advice, and ignored Fitzmaurice's, but did not go quite as far as asserting last resort.[31] But, as Fitzmaurice wrote to Francis Vallat, the law officer attached to the United Kingdom Delegation to the United Nations, what Lloyd was asserting was merely 'an aggravation of the original illegality but no more'.[32] Here, however, the urbanity of the normal civil servant, given the strain that must have been felt by the narrowing of the decision-making and policy-advising circle, began to crack. In the final paragraph, Fitzmaurice wrote as such:

> I should be grateful if you would address a minute to the right quarter in the above terms. Perhaps the simplest thing would be if you were to quote what I have said verbatim as coming from me. It should be seen by an Under-Secretary and also by Kirkpatrick. If there were any way of conveying it through the Private Secretaries at No.10 I should like this to be done. It might not be a bad thing to send a copy to Dobson at the Lord Chancellor's Department, as it is more than likely that it is in that quarter that the Prime Minister obtains his advice.[33]

The message could be no clearer: the ordinary channels of communication were blocked and Eden was prepared only to accept advice that suited his case. Thus in the immediate wake of the Chequers meeting, which spawned the Sèvres agreement, when the Minister of State at the Foreign Office, Sir Anthony Nutting, recommended that Fitzmaurice should be brought in 'on a matter which involved taking the law into our own hands', Eden's response was that 'Fitz is the last person I want consulted. The lawyers are always against our doing anything. For God's sake, keep them out of it. This is a political affair.'[34] Although as Fitzmaurice had already pointed out on numerous occasions even the politics of the case, never mind the legality, were weak. Keeping the lawyers 'out of it', at least in terms of the Law Officers, as the Sèvres agreement developed, became effectively the policy as the decision-making network was drawn even tighter in an effort to prevent the collusion becoming known.

The exceptional situation was confirmed by a letter from the Attorney General, Manningham-Buller, to the Lord Chancellor, Kilmuir. The Attorney-General's office had been charged with preparing a memorandum on the legal position with regard to the use or threat of force by the UK should the Security Council fail to take effective action. But as the Attorney-General noted, 'things appear to be moving so fast' that 'I feel under some obligation to inform the Prime Minister of the views of the Law Officers pretty soon'. The Lord Chancellor's office had recently attempted to use the Kellogg-Briand Pact of 1928 as a justification for the use of force but as the Attorney-General pointed out, by signing the Pact, the UK government had 'condemned recourse to war for the solution of international controversies' and that the solution of all disputes 'should never be sought except by pacific means'. As Manningham-Buller concluded: 'the only force used by Nasser up to date was in relation to the seizure of the Canal Company's property in Egypt. We do not think that the use of that force would now justify the use of force by us.'[35] Clearly then the vast weight of legal opinion was firmly against armed intervention and the use of force and this attested to the further narrowing of legal advice as the Sèvres collusion was hatched.

In preparation for the intervention, the Lord Chancellor produced a Top Secret memorandum on the Use of Force which, as a note between the Secretary at No.10 and the Lord Chancellor's Office made clear was very restricted; noting that the Lord Chancellor's memorandum was being sent in fair copy, the No.10 Secretary, Cairncross, commented that 'there are only three more copies which we are keeping for the time being'.[36] The attempt to find any form of pretext which would stand as a legal justification had taxed the Lord Chancellor's office in the extreme and Kilmuir had settled on a variant of the doctrine of necessity, the doctrine of self-defence. In Kilmuir's rationalisation this held that it was clearly within the latter doctrine to forcibly resist any attempt to annex national territory by invasion. It was, therefore, by extension at least, justifiable in international law that international territory annexed by invasion was covered by the same doctrine. Furthermore the Security Council was powerless to act if the use of the veto denied it any measure for righting the wrong. Kilmuir argued that:

> In the present case the Suez Canal Company was an international body and its concession the basis of the international character of the Canal as expressly admitted by Egypt in the preamble to the 1888 Treaty. By purporting to nationalise the Company and so terminate the concession, Egypt has been guilty of a breach of the obligations implicit in that Treaty, with the effect that the foundation of the international character of the Canal departed. From the moment of Colonel Nasser's first speech the Canal was changed from an international waterway to a national possession to be used for purposes of national policy. Just as the Rhineland was re-militarised, the Canal was de-internationalised. Egypt, by her invasion of the rights of the signatory powers under the Convention of 1888, has been guilty of a crime of aggression against those powers.[37]

Force, less the point be missed, was justified to rectify this situation.

Even the Attorney General struggled to make much of this, arguing that international territory encompassed areas such as Trieste and trust territories, but did not extend to the Suez Canal which the UK had recognised as an integral part of Egypt; thus there was 'no basis for the argument that the forcible seizure of the Company's assets constituted such an attack on international territory as would justify the use of force by the states prejudiced by it'. Without the blocking of the Canal or the restriction of passage through it, 'the threat or the use of force would be a plain infringement of our obligations under the Charter'.[38] By the day of the Anglo-French air attacks on Egypt, 31

October, Fitzmaurice was concluding that the Anglo-French action amounted to military invasion and occupation despite the fact that it was Egypt that was the victim of the attack by Israel. As Fitzmaurice saw it, 'legally, it is impossible to see how this can be justified merely on the basis of an Egyptian refusal to clear out of a large zone of their own territory, and in the face of Israeli attacks.' Worse still, in Fitzmaurice's eyes, Britain had had to use its veto, for the first time in its membership of the UN, to prevent Britain and France being condemned for their actions and additionally had vetoed another resolution 'the result of which would have been to direct the Egyptians and Israelis to do the very thing we were in effect calling upon them to do, namely to stop the hostilities, and thus to secure our professed aim of preserving the Canal from war damage'.[39]

On 1 November, with the sitting of the House of Commons suspended in disarray, the bombing of Egyptian airfields and the UN General Assembly meeting, the arguments over the legal case came to a head. Fitzmaurice, having been given 'a brief sight of the legal paper on the basis of which I understand the government have been acting', metaphorically tore it to shreds. Using force, Fitzmaurice reasoned, to protect the lives of one's citizens abroad only arose when the danger came from the local government or where such government had lost control. The existence of armed hostilities with Israel did not justify intervention by Britain and, indeed, the main danger to British lives in Egypt appeared to come from British armed intervention. With regard to the supposed right to intervene to protect property abroad, Fitzmaurice was even more caustic, claiming that 'no such right under present-day international law existed'. Furthermore:

> where is the British property in question? The Suez Canal is not British property, nor is the Suez Canal Company as such, though we may own some shares in it. All we have is an interest in the matter arising from our passage rights under the Suez Canal Convention. This is quite a different thing... the doctrine that interests, even vital interests, in another country, confers a right of armed intervention there, is precisely the doctrine which the United Nations Charter was intended to negative.

The decision, Fitzmaurice argued, was political and had 'no legal justification'. Citing a Foreign Office telegram to Amman, Jordan, which informed the British Ambassador that 'HMG are advised on the highest legal authority that they are entitled under the Charter to take every measure open to them within and without the United Nations to stop the fighting and to protect their nationals and interests which are threatened by these hostilities', Fitzmaurice disassociated the legal advisers from the advice. Then, in a veiled swipe at the narrow channel from whence the government's legal advice had come, he noted that the highest legal authority normally meant the Law Officers of the Crown, the Attorney-General and Solicitor-General, who 'constitutionally have the ultimate, and sole ultimate responsibility as legal advisers to the Crown and hence to the government of the day'.[40] As of 1 November 1956, the highest legal authority had not been consulted.

When copies of Fitzmaurice's memoranda reached the Lord Chancellor's Office, Sir George Coldstream penned a hurried note to Lord Kilmuir, who was due to speak in the House of Lords in defence of the government's actions. Noting that Fitzmaurice's minute was 'wholly unhelpful' Coldstream told Kilmuir that it was his 'duty to show it to you at once, *because it may have currency among other Ministers*'.[41] Despite a strong defence by Kilmuir in the House of Lords on 1 November, just how exposed the government's position had become was attested to by the fact that Lord McNair, the ex-President of the International Court, felt compelled to write to Kilmuir. Point by point, McNair stripped Kilmuir's case to the bone. There was no authority in international law for the armed intervention of a neutral state in a conflict between two other states to protect the nationals or property of the neutral state. Nor was there any precedent in international law for armed intervention to protect freedom of passage through a canal or other international waterway. As to the 'new – and the novel – ground for intervention put forward by the Prime Minister...namely, the right to prevent the conflagration from spreading', there existed no legal basis. This could only apply if the UK was acting on a mandate from the UN which had already been negated by a Resolution calling upon Britain to stop its intervention. There was no legal justification for attempting to impose a buffer zone between the two warring parties; indeed, the letter and spirit of the UN Charter expressly forbade the arrogation of such power to an individual state or states, unless under the authority of the UN as a collective measure. Not only had Britain not sought such authority, it had concealed its intentions from the UN and attempted to present it with a fait accompli. Turning to Kilmuir's main argument, the doctrine of self-defence, McNair was equally scathing. Even allowing Kilmuir the wide latitude he had claimed in his speech, the final determination of the matter lay with the 'competent international authority', the UN General Assembly, which had instructed Britain to desist from its intervention. His conclusion was blunt:

> our intervention is illegal... if the question of its legality should come before the International Court (as might well happen upon a request by the Assembly or the Security Council for an Advisory Opinion – in which case no consent to the jurisdiction by us would be required), we should most certainly have to expect judgement against us.[42]

Although the Lord Chancellor's Office set about constructing a brief for Kilmuir by way of a reply there is no record in the files of any answer being sent.

The final debacle, at least as far as Fitzmaurice was concerned, came early in November as the British and French pressed on with their attack. Fitzmaurice took the unusual step of circulating a complete disclaimer throughout the Foreign Office Legal Department. He asserted that the legal advisers had been consistent in their advice as to the illegality of intervention; some of the memoranda and minutes to this effect had been seen by the Foreign Secretary; and at least one had gone before the Egypt Committee which meant 'that it was seen by the principal Ministers concerned'. However:

> The Prime Minister has...taken his advice on the matter from the Lord Chancellor, and virtually all the legal arguments which the government have put forward, and which I have constantly queried, have emanated from that quarter... With regard to the latest developments and the decision to embark on Anglo-French armed intervention in Egypt, neither the legal advisers here nor the Law Officers were consulted, and the first that was heard about it was the Prime Minister's statement in Parliament the day before yesterday.[43]

All of which left the Law Officers wondering whether they should resign. The situation also raised grave difficulties for the legal advisers at home and abroad, and indeed, raised constitutional questions. Fitzmaurice was standing as a candidate for re-election to the International Law Commission of the United Nations but in the present circumstances 'could hardly expect to get more than a dozen votes' and Vallat was to sit on the European Human Rights Convention where 'the United Kingdom position…is bound to be seriously prejudiced'.[44] Given the amount of international work which the legal advisers did, Fitzmaurice pressed Kirkpatrick for leave to state that the government's action had been entirely political and that the legal advisers were not responsible for the legal advice. Furthermore, the situation raised grave constitutional issues, and that:

> although our action in Egypt may happen to be in accordance with your [Kirkpatrick's] views and policies, the way in which the matter has been handled on the legal side, with the regular legal channels of advice by-passed and the government acting on private advice from the Lord Chancellor without the legal advisers here or the Law Officers even knowing what advice is being given, is, on any normal and long-term view, detrimental to the proper functioning of the Foreign Office.[45]

Worse, outside the UK, Fitzmaurice asserted, no one had heard of the Lord Chancellor as an office, or understood his position; while it was true that the Lord Chancellor sat in the Cabinet and could be asked for his advice, this was tendered on a personal basis as an eminent lawyer, not because his office invested him with any official function to do so. The Lord Chancellor did not sit in the Cabinet as a Law Officer of the Crown, or as a general adviser to the government, but as the head of the judiciary and ministerial head of the department which ran the administrative aspect of the machinery of justice and the officer who presided over the House of Lords. Whereas the government had a perfect right to ask for legal advice from any quarter it wished, they could not constitutionally assert that they had acted on legal advice from the highest quarter as 'the Lord Chancellor is *not* higher than the Law Officers'.[46] The by-passing of the normal channels of legal advice, Fitzmaurice asserted, 'always leads to trouble' and the position of the legal advisers had been rendered impossible due to the fact that 'the Cabinet and the Prime Minister were proceeding independently on the basis of private advice tendered by the Lord Chancellor', as such, 'the Law Officers…have an absolutely unanswerable case over not having been consulted'.[47]

In conclusion, therefore, what can be said about the influence of Fitzmaurice on policy making within the crisis? The answer is easy:

nothing. What this contribution does demonstrate is further clear evidence of the way in which the decision-making and policy-making circle was narrowed during the crisis to the point where only those supportive of Eden's ultimate objectives were 'in the know'. Across Whitehall the normal channels of communication were blocked and the Prime Minister and Cabinet seem to have struck an attitude of either ignoring, or not wishing to receive, any advice which could possibly act as a brake on their determined course of action.[48] As it was with ignored Treasury advice, so it was with ignored legal advice: the advice proved correct and the Suez hawks were proved wrong. Fitzmaurice may have had no wish to play the role of Cassandra[49] but what should be borne in mind is that Fitzmaurice, like Cassandra, was right, and being right, was ignored.

NOTES

1. Kilmuir Papers, Churchill College, Cambridge. KLMR 1/5, Desk Diary 1956, entry for 26 July 1956.
2. Quoted in D. Carlton, *Britain and the Suez Crisis* (Oxford: Blackwell, 1988), p.133.
3. LCO2/5760, 'Suez Canal. Legal Opinion of the Lord Chancellor, the Law Officers and the Legal Adviser to the Foreign Office', 31 July 1956.
4. FO 800/747, Fitzmaurice memo, 2 Aug.1956.
5. Ibid., Manningham-Buller to Fitzmaurice, 2 Aug. 1956.
6. Carlton, *Suez Crisis*, p.114.
7. K. Kyle, 'Britain and the Crisis, 1955–1956', in W.R. Louis and R. Owen (eds), *Suez 1956: The Crisis and its Consequences* (Oxford: Clarendon, 1991 ed.), pp.113–14.
8. Quoted in Carlton, *The Suez Crisis*, p.114.
9. FO 800/748, Fitzmaurice to Caccia, 13 Aug.1956.
10. K. Kyle, *Suez* (London: Weidenfeld and Nicolson, 1992 ed.), p.186.
11. Lord Butler, *The Art of the Possible* (London: Hamish Hamilton, 1971), p.189.
12. LCO2/5760, 'Letter to *The Times* by A.L. Goodhart', 11 Aug. 1956.
13. FO 800/748, Fitzmaurice to Rae, 17 Aug. 1956.
14. Ibid., Dixon memo, 24 Aug. 1956.
15. Ibid.
16. Ibid. Fitzmaurice memo, 24 Aug. 1956.
17. FO 371/119174/JE14214/21, Pink to Kirkpatrick, 24 Aug. 1956. I am very grateful to Dr. E.J. Johnson for drawing my attention to this reference.
18. Selwyn Lloyd Papers, Churchill College, Cambridge, SELO 6/145, Lloyd to Hugh Thomas, 31 Aug. 1966.
19. FO 800/748, 'Suez Canal and the Use of Force', memoranda from Fitzmaurice to Kirkpatrick, undated, but probably between 31 Aug. and 4 Sept. 1956.
20. FO 800/748, Fitzmaurice to Kirkpatrick, 4 Sept. 1956, handwritten annotation by Kirkpatrick.

21. LCO 2/5760, Kilmuir to Eden, 6 Sept. 1956.
22. FO 800/747, unsigned Foreign Office memorandum on 'The Doctrine of Necessity', 4 Sept. 1956.
23. FO 800/747, Fitzmaurice to Pink, 7 Sept. 1956.
24. FO 800/747, Fitzmaurice to Coldstream, 6 Sept. 1956.
25. Kilmuir Papers, KLMR 1/5, Desk Diary 1956, entry for 31 July 1956.
26. LCO2/5760, Coldstream to Kilmuir, 7 Sept. 1956.
27. FO 800/747, quoted in Fitzmaurice to Manningham-Buller, 17 Sept. 1956.
28. Ibid.
29. Ibid.
30. FO 800/747, Fitzmaurice to Coldstream, 25 Sept. 1956.
31. S. Lloyd, *Suez 1956: A Personal Account* (London: Jonathan Cape, 1978), pp.271–5.
32. FO 800/747, Fitzmaurice to Vallat, 9 Oct. 1956.
33. Ibid.
34. A. Nutting, *No End of a Lesson: The Story of Suez* (London: Constable, 1967), p.95.
35. LCO2/5760, Manningham-Buller to Kilmuir, 12 Oct.1956.
36. LCO2/5760, Cairncross to Rankin, 22 Oct. 1956.
37. LCO2/5760, Kilmuir memo, 15 Oct. 1956.
38. FO800/747, 'Paper by the Attorney General' undated, but certainly between 22 and 31 Oct. 1956.
39. LCO2/5760, Fitzmaurice to Dobson, 31 Oct. 1956.
40. FO800/747, and LCO2/5760, Fitzmaurice to Kirkpatrick, 1 Nov. 1956.
41. LCO 2/5760, Coldstream to Kilmuir, 1 Nov. 1956; emphasis in the original.
42. LCO2/5760, McNair to Kilmuir, 4 Nov. 1956.
43. FO800/747, Fitzmaurice memo, 1 Nov. 1956.
44. FO800/747, Fitzmaurice to Kirkpatrick, 5 Nov. 1956.
45. Ibid.
46. Ibid.; emphasis in the original.
47. Ibid.
48. For the manner in which Treasury advice on the likely economic impact of armed intervention at Suez was dealt with c.f. L. Johnman, 'Defending the Pound: The Economics of the Suez Crisis, 1956' in A. Gorst, L. Johnman and W.S. Lucas (eds) *Postwar Britain 1945–1964: Themes and Perspectives* (London: Pinter, 1989), pp.166–79.
49. FO 800/748, Fitzmaurice to Kirkpatrick, undated, handwritten memorandum, probably between 31 Aug. and 4 Sept. 1956: 'I have no relish for playing the role of a Cassandra'.

The Mandarins' Mandarin: Sir Norman Brook, Secretary of the Cabinet

KEITH KYLE

Sir Norman Brook, who had already been Secretary of the Cabinet for nine years at the time of the Suez Crisis, was described by his successor, Lord Trend, as being in appearance 'correct, sober and unostentatious... He discouraged informality in greeting and address; and his manner was one of rather intimidating reserve.'[1] A mandarin's mandarin, his greatest strength was said to lie in his skill in reconciling diverse, conflicting and often ramblingly expressed views within a few pungent sentences. 'He thought things out with extreme thoroughness and care,' wrote another colleague, Lord Bridges, at his death. 'He was never hasty or impatient; he avoided declaring himself a strong adherent of particular lines of action.'[2] To his anonymous obituarist in *The Times* he:

> was a man of immense authority. The first impression was of size, with a head that was large even for such a heavy frame and a calm gaze from heavy-lidded eyes. Then came the quiet, rather slow voice. At the start it might seem casual, even lethargic. But this illusion was dispelled as his voice took on a cutting edge and he shaped the words on which he wished to pivot his thoughts. He was a pianist of some distinction, an enthusiastic golfer and a carpenter of great talent.[3]

Two tasks in particular Brook regarded as vital – to keep the Cabinet in step, especially its senior Ministers, and to preserve continuities. For instance, when the Conservative government under Winston Churchill took over from Labour in 1951 Brook had taken pains to convey the news, unwelcome to many including the Prime Minister, that the course of decolonization in West Africa was irreversible, that the Gold Coast (Ghana) was set on the road to independence with full Commonwealth membership, with Nigeria following on behind. Addressing Sir Winston on 1 December 1954 he had written, 'I recognise that this policy may be unpalatable to you...However much we may sigh for the past, we have to live in the present – and to plan for the future.'[4]

Brook did not see that future as being in terribly secure hands given Churchill's established heir, Sir Anthony Eden. When the Cabinet Office staff were discussing over lunch the succession to Churchill, it was common ground that, for reasons alike of health and of temperament Eden was unlikely to last a full Parliament as Prime Minister. The consensus that R.A. Butler would be the ultimate beneficiary was breached only by the Cabinet Secretary. Speaking last, he quietly opted for Harold Macmillan.[5]

William Clark, on joining the staff at 10 Downing Street as Anthony Eden's Press Secretary in October 1955, found Brook much preoccupied, as was Sir Edward Bridges, the Head of the Civil Service, by the tensions between Eden and these two possible heirs, and tensions also between these two.[6] On 6 February Clark noted in his diary that over lunch with Brook, 'We discussed a bit glumly how we could reconcile some of the Eden–Butler–Macmillan splits.' The Cabinet, they decided, had 'blundered around quite a bit recently', not, as the press alleged, because Eden could not make up his mind but because he made it up too quickly without full consultation.[7]

In April 1956 when, following Glubb Pasha's dismissal by the King of Jordan and the stoning of the Foreign Secretary, Selwyn Lloyd, on a visit to Bahrein, Eden was talking about rushing troops into Kuwait, Bahrein and other Gulf spots to save the rulers from their subjects, Brook chose to re-circulate Eden's own Cabinet memorandum of 1953. This had argued that, 'In the second half of the twentieth century we cannot hope to maintain our position in the Middle East by the methods of the last century.' Making specific reference to the use of British troops for political purposes Eden had then said, 'Our strategic purposes in the Middle East can no longer be served by arrangements which local nationalism will regard as military occupation by foreign troops.' The Prime Minister was not amused by the reminder. His Principal Private Secretary wrote to Brook, 'I wish I could say that the PM received your views with delight or appreciation.'[8]

That Eden was quite capable of putting down the most distinguished public servants with asperity was evident from his rebuke to Bridges, recorded by Clark, ' Well, Edward, I suppose I've got to try to save this country while you traitors try to break it down in every way you can. Poor old England! Poor old England!'[9] At the height of the Suez crisis he berated the Chief of the Air Staff in a manner that astounded the latter's private secretary, listening in.[10] But Brook always seemed to retain his confidence. In July, a few days before Suez broke, it was announced that in the autumn he would succeed Bridges on retirement as Head of the Civil Service, while combining this post with that of Cabinet Secretary. He was to share the title of Permanent Secretary to the Treasury with Sir Roger Makins, who was coming home from the Washington Embassy.

Once Nasser had seized the Suez Canal Company on 26 July 1956 Brook became the focal point of all relevant decisions. Not only was he keeping the minutes of the Cabinet and of its Egypt Committee, presided over by the Prime Minister, which handled the crisis on a day-to-day basis until the last days when it really mattered, but he was also already the chairman of the long-running Defence (Transition) Committee [D(T)C] of senior civil servants from the ministries concerned with Britain's response to any threat of war.[11] This committee of 20 or so persons was called into session as soon as the crisis started and met 29 times in the course of its duration, mostly working to the Egypt Committee. Its composition varied; there were a number of Permanent Secretaries but the Foreign Office, for example, sent the chairman of the Joint Intelligence Committee, Patrick Dean.

The minutes of the committee's first meeting are still withheld – they undoubtedly had to do with the application of the War Book. This had been the pride and joy of the great Cabinet Secretary and Secretary of the Committee of Imperial Defence in the First World War and between the wars, Lord Hankey. Hankey's work for the CID in 1912–14 – ensuring that everyone in the bureaucracy should know, just by looking it up, what needed to be done in a transition from peace to war – had been much acclaimed, and after the war he had been out to ensure that the lessons then learned should not be lost.[12] The War Book was consequently invaluable again in 1939. In the post-war period and particularly since 1949–50 Brook and his assistants had been, in the spirit of Hankey, much involved in cajoling departments, with somewhat mixed results, to keep up their own War Books as well as to contribute to the government one.[13]

The great majority of files about the government War Book, like the record of the first session of the D(T)C on Suez, are still withheld. But it appears from what has been released that it was 'constantly being amended at four monthly intervals' to keep up with war planning and that its use 'when there is a threat of war' was contemplated in three stages: the first, activated by the Prime Minister alone, involved the committee in reviewing War Book measures in the light of a particular situation; the second which was a precautionary stage and the third which was the war stage both required Cabinet decision.[14] We know that the War Book in 1956 had 16 numbered chapters on, for instance, machinery of government, treatment of enemy shipping and aircraft, fuel and power supplies, shipping and ports, and treatment of information.[15] By reference to the War Book Brook could immediately inform Ministers what wartime regulations were still in force and what need there might be for primary legislation or Orders-in-Council under the royal prerogative.

To double check Brook told all departments on 17 August that Ministers wished urgently to know whether there would be any need to seek fresh powers when Parliament was to be recalled for a special session in ten days' time. (Like many Suez dates, this one slipped). The next meeting of the D(T)C was for this purpose thrown open to all heads of department, including those had not hitherto been included.[16] But, in the case of Suez, as Tom Dibble remarks in 'Consequential Matters...', his valuable MA thesis which I have consulted with advantage, 'The core dilemma for the D(T)C...was how to employ machinery officially designed for a state of war while not actually wanting to admit being in one.'[17]

Brook told the second meeting of the D(T)C on 31 July that, 'There was no reason to suppose that the Egyptians were either capable of running the Canal effectively or of setting aside resources for its necessary development to carry increased international traffic in the future.'[18] The decision of the Cabinet to use force as a 'last resort' would, he said, require one division to deal with Egypt and two further divisions to maintain law and order and keep the country and the Canal under control.

The question naturally arose as to what powers the government could call on in peacetime to provide for this supposed 'last resort'. General Templer, the Chief of the Imperial General Staff, had asked for the requisitioning of shipping. Brook told him that the Ministry of

Transport's requisitioning powers had been withdrawn but fortunately the Royal Prerogative could be called in aid.[19] At the Committee's third meeting on 31 July it was reported that an Order-in-Council had been drafted to give the Transport Ministry the powers it required. The public were not to be told about this, but Brook proposed in a memorandum to Ministers on the Egypt Committee on 21 August that if the validity of any requisition was challenged the position could be made all right retroactively by an indemnity bill.[20]

However there were evidently limits to the usefulness of this device. In the same memorandum Brook opposed Templer's request for powers to direct labour on the grounds that the Defence Regulations had expired and he warned the Egypt Committee of the dangers of going for press censorship as Winston Churchill had urged. From the point of view of military security, he said, there was no advantage in exercising control over information unless it applied to foreign newspapers also, which would require complete postal and telegraphic censorship, while as for controlling comment strong political objections were to be anticipated. Complete censorship could be imposed on Cyprus and Malta, being colonies.[21]

Brook also found it necessary to point out the implications that flowed from the ministerial decision not to describe any military action as a 'war'. For instance, the prerogative power of internment applied to *enemy* aliens. But if there were no 'state of war' there could be no 'enemies'. Similar difficulties would arise over detention of enemy ships and aircraft, seizure of contraband, and so forth. Force commanders would rather naturally want to know how far in these circumstances they could exercise the rights of a belligerent. Brook's solution was an empirical one – let the force commanders say what they wanted to do and then in each case it could be seen whether and how a justification could be worked out for this under international law.[22]

On 12 August Brook told Clark that he was warning the Prime Minister that the idea of using force was becoming increasingly unpopular. 'How do you do it in this age? Call together Parliament, send in the troops and get a positive vote of perhaps forty-six in Parliament and a vote against you in the UN? It just isn't on.' Bluff would only work until the armada sailed; then 'we are committed because it can neither turn back nor sit offshore.' Clark quoted him as saying, 'Our Prime Minister is very difficult. He wants to be Foreign Secretary, Minister of Defence and Chancellor.'[23]

On 14 August Brook, notwithstanding any private misgivings, sought to supply, on Eden's instructions, a disciplined framework for the Egypt Committee's approach to Suez, co-ordinating the military, political and diplomatic timetables. The London Conference was to meet on 16 August for one week; Parliament should be reconvened for 27 August for two days to endorse the results of the conference; then, one week from 30 August to 5 September would be allowed for the receipt of any Egyptian counter-proposals and for their subsequent rejection; the assault force would sail from Britain on 7 September; and the air bombardment of Egypt would begin on 17 September, followed by the sea-borne landing on the 20th.

However, when the question of timetables came up in the Egypt Committee, there was an outburst of protest from the Minister of Defence, Sir Walter Monckton, the most dovish member of the committee, which Eden and some other ministers such as Home and Lennox-Boyd found profoundly unsettling. Monckton had been unable to endure hearing the Chancellor of the Exchequer, Harold Macmillan, talking of the date of this 'last resort' operation as if it were already a settled matter and had lashed out. Other ministers afterwards wrote hastily to reassure the Prime Minister that they were on his side. Brook weighed in with a four-page handwritten note to Eden designed to calm him down. He skilfully drew from divided counsels the common ground that 'we cannot afford to let Nasser get away with this – for, if he succeeds, we lose our oil and, with it, our standard of life in this country, not to mention our position in the Middle East and our influence as a World Power.' Differences arose, he contended, because ministers varied in the extent to which they felt that, before resorting to force, Britain must show that she had exhausted all other methods. Some might even require 'some further provocative act by Nasser' before they would be satisfied.

Brook advised Eden not to 'put the [full] Cabinet at the final fence too soon'; he was doubtful whether there was a sufficient consensus that the 'final resort' had been arrived at. He even hazarded a guess about which way individual ministers would go if they were put prematurely to the test. He wrote down the names of six of them, including Monckton and R.A. Butler – generally considered to be the Deputy Prime Minister though he did not hold the title – who would want to postpone resort to force 'until all else has been tried or until Nasser provides us with a good occasion, whichever happens earlier', and to these he added the name of Edward Heath, the Chief Whip. Rather strangely he put queries against the names of two Ministers: the Lord Chancellor, Lord Kilmuir, who was providing Eden with arguments for the legitimacy of the use of force in contradiction to the opinions of his official legal advisers, and Heathcoat Amory, a conscientious, rather unassertive Minister of Agriculture, who was quite definitely a dove. Apart from these and three 'unknown quantities', Brook thought that the rest would be 'pretty solid'.

He also pointed out what a cleverly advised Nasser might be prompted to do. He might send a reply to the plan of the London conference that was 'somewhere between acceptance and rejection' and then offer to negotiate a new Treaty. The impact of this on world opinion (and on 'middle opinion' at home) would need to be carefully assessed before asking the full Cabinet to pronounce on the use of force.[24]

Hitherto Brook had made use of the D(T)C as the instrument for keeping senior officials of the other ministries on board and ensuring swift co-ordination rather than following the more normal bureaucratic procedure of creating a more narrowly composed Official Committee to match the Cabinet's Egypt Committee. For a wide range of activities he continued to do so. It was only on 24 August, when the crisis had already been going for a month, that Brook presided in his rooms in the Cabinet Office over the first meeting of the Egypt (Official) Committee, whose minutes, called the Darracott file after the name of its secretary, were specially concealed after the event to prevent their falling into the hands of a perhaps unsympathetic successor government.[25] Initially it was set up with a limited purpose: to provide policy guidance in the event of military operations against Egypt over the handling of civil affairs; other tasks were later added.

Operational objectives, Brook explained at the first meeting, were 'to destroy the Egyptian Army, to bring down the Nasser Government and to control the Suez Canal...' Happily the Foreign Office reported that, 'There were good reasons to believe that, given the defeat of the Egyptian Army and the collapse of the Nasser regime, a successor Government could be formed which would be able to maintain law and order...' The chances of this would be much improved if the headquarters, in or near Cairo, of such 'Nasser agencies' as Army Intelligence, the Liberation Rally and the National Guard could be eliminated at an early stage by military action.

Thus, thankfully, the British and French would not, except as a very last resort, have to assume responsibility for the central government of Egypt. They would aim to spend the minimum time in or preferably outside Cairo while a 'co-operative' government was being installed and then move on to the Suez Canal. A memorandum from the Foreign Secretary to the Egypt Committee suggested, 'We might hope to stay in Cairo no more than a day or two.' There would not be need for anything openly entitled an Administration of Occupied Enemy Territory, 'which would, incidentally, carry with it a legal and moral obligation to feed the population.'[26] The Brook Committee therefore assumed, on Foreign Office guidance, that, 'On the basis of past experience, the Egyptian administrative machine would continue to function with something approaching its normal state of efficiency despite a change of Government.' Military control over the civil authorities therefore needed to be catered for in advance only in respect of the Canal zone.[27]

The most frustrating task for Brook and his fellow-mandarins turned out to be the attempt to draw up the Commander-in-Chief's political directive. The first draft submitted to the Official Committee by the Foreign Office assumed, according to the then prevailing plan, an assault landing at Alexandria followed by a march to Cairo, whereupon the instructions of the Political Adviser, Ralph Murray, formerly Minister at the Cairo Embassy, would be to 'bring about the formation of a new Egyptian government which will disavow Nasser's policies, undertake the pacification of the country, order co-operation with Allied forces and be ready to negotiate an international regime for the Suez Canal.'[28] But the change of strategy in mid-September, by which the Alexandria landing was abandoned, the principal assault on Egypt was to be from the air and the landing of a much smaller force at Port Said was to take place only when organized resistance was seen to be at its last gasp, rather altered the context of the directive.

Once more it fell to the Cabinet Secretary to draw up a timetable, starting at D-14 with a warning to British subjects in Egypt and then the evacuation of British civilians including the unfortunate Suez Canal Base contractors on D-10 and D-9. It provided for the movement of French aircraft and paratroops to Cyprus on D-10 and British aircraft to Malta and Cyprus on D-8, then an official warning to shipping to avoid Egyptian waters and to civil aircraft to avoid flights over Egypt on D-3, and ended up with the ultimatum on D-1 and the start of the air offensive on D-Day.[29] With this strategy (code-named MUSKETEER REVISE and bearing the motto *Nec Tenui Ferar Penna,* 'And may I not be borne on a fragile wing'), no date was mentioned for the sailing of the expedition from Malta or its landing at Port Said since this was to depend on the judgement of when the back of Egyptian resistance had been broken. This was an arrangement, insisted on by the military, that clearly left Eden unhappy.

The timetable was put to a Chiefs of Staff conference at Chequers, attended by the Prime Minister and General Sir Charles Keightley, the Allied Commander-in-Chief designate, on 24 September. The next day Sir Norman Brook reported to the Egypt Committee about the major unhappiness of General Keightley about the pressure he was getting from 'Ministers' (in other words the Prime Minister) to hasten the landings. Sir Charles wanted it spelt out clearly in his political directive that 'the whole basis of the plan is that sufficient time will be allowed for the air action…so that resistance will have crumbled before any landing is made in Phase Three.' Unless this were done, Brook had been told, the bombing of oil and communications targets would not have made themselves fully felt, propaganda would not have built up effective popular pressure and the Egyptian Army would not have been destroyed. Above all, Brook said, the Nasser government might still be in power. This meant that, if Nasser's overthrow was still to be a principal aim, they must be prepared to keep up the air attacks and propaganda during Phase Three until his regime crumbled or 'send a force to Cairo to overthrow his Government and enable a successor regime to be established'. The only trouble about that would be that the draft directive did not provide for this contingency 'since the forces made available for the present plan would not be adequate for that purpose'. Keightley might find himself administering the Canal area in the face of a hostile Egyptian government.[30]

The passage whose drafting most perplexed Brook's official committee, until the rush of events at the end of October ensured that no political directive was ever issued, was the one concerning the Syrian airfields. The British rightly had predicted that Nasser might send the pick of his air force to the airfields of other Arab states. But one of these, Syria, was within a few minutes' flying time of the desperately overcrowded airfields on Cyprus. The Chiefs of Staff said that the amount of damage that could be inflicted by a flank attack from Syria might jeopardise the whole operation 'and that this risk must be eliminated at all cost'. Keightley wanted the directive to give to him the option of striking Syrian airfields pre-emptively if the danger seemed imminent. The Foreign Office held out for the Cabinet to have the last word.[31]

Ironically one passage which appeared in all versions of the directive and gave no trouble at all was the section concerning Israel:

> It is possible that Israel may take advantage of the situation and attack Egypt... It is politically most important that...there should be no association or appearance of association between your forces and Israeli forces. HMG and the French Government will declare appropriate areas of Sinai and Egypt west of the Canal...to be combat areas and issue a warning that any land, sea or air forces found in these areas not belonging to the forces under your command will be held to be enemy forces.[32]

It is one of the myths of Suez that the civil service was excluded throughout from the secret planning of the expedition against Egypt. But the crisis as a whole should not be confused with the desperate last days of it. For most of the time, civil servants who had clearance to receive documents code-named TERRAPIN (admittedly a strictly limited class) were fully in the picture and in the driving seat for the detailed planning for the use of force. Of no one was this more true than Sir Norman Brook, with his two committees – Defence (Transition) which continued to meet throughout the crisis and was the focal point for co-ordinating the reports of more specialized groups, and Egypt (Official) – on top of his being secretary of the Cabinet and of the Egypt Committee.

There was from the beginning a certain ambiguity about the role of the Egypt Committee. As Brook put it to the Prime Minister on 13 September,

> The Committee has come to perform two different functions: (a) In relation to the political handling of the Suez question, it acts as a sort of Inner Cabinet...; (b) It supervises the military preparations and plans... If it were not in being this work would be done by the Defence Committee.[33]

The Egypt Committee's membership, though initially small with six ministers, was in practice very flexible and in the aggregate quite large in the effort to fulfil both functions.

Brook's minute just quoted was designed to meet a practical situation. At the stage that had been reached in the gradual process of integrating the armed services there was a Minister of Defence but also still individual Service Ministers. Sir Walter Monckton, with his civilian background, pleasant wartime experience of Egypt and dovish outlook, was the Minister of Defence and the only Service Minister originally designated for the Egypt Committee. By contrast Anthony Head, the Secretary of State for War, had been a wartime brigadier and Director of Plans for Amphibious Operations and was on 18 October to replace Monckton as Minister of Defence. It was scarcely surprising that from the outset of the crisis Eden should have found in Head a more congenial policy adviser and should have encouraged him to attend Egypt Committee meetings. But this discrimination was increasingly resented by Lord Hailsham and Nigel Birch, the political chiefs of the Admiralty and the Air Ministry and neither of them known for possessing a long fuse. It was Brook's task to put it to the Prime Minister that 'some dissatisfaction' was to be expected if the situation were allowed to continue. His suggestion, which was promptly accepted, was that since all three Service Ministers would have had 'virtually a right to sit' on the Defence Committee, had that been allowed to operate normally, and since it would be 'hardly feasible' to separate the two functions of the Egypt Committee, now they should all join in future meetings, so long as this were done 'unobtrusively'.[34]

That did not in fact do Hailsham and Birch much good, since the Egypt Committee was not consulted about the final operation. There were no meetings minuted after 17 October, the day after Eden's critical trip to Paris, until 1 November, after the die had been cast.[35] The Egypt Committee was not in fact suitable for the 'Inner Cabinet' function when it came to the type of operation that was plotted and embarked on between these two dates. Only for this last phase were members of the bureaucracy almost totally excluded and normal records of meetings not kept; nevertheless, one of the few exceptions was Brook. He was for example present (as was Sir Richard Powell, the Permanent Secretary at the Ministry of Defence) at the Chequers meeting on 21 October which despatched Selwyn Lloyd to meet the Israelis and the French at Sèvres and he was there when he reported back.[36]

As Cabinet Secretary he recorded in vivid phrases the full Cabinet's approach to the actual application of force. And it was his melancholy task to round up any written evidence of collusion with the Israeli attack on Egypt and destroy it. There is therefore no direct account of Sèvres in the papers in the Public Record Office. However, in one copy only of Brook's minutes for 23 October is to be found a single reference to 'secret conversations which had been held in Paris with representatives of the Israeli Government.'[37] Those words are omitted from all other copies that were distributed.

The completely changed storyline mapped out by the Protocol of Sèvres had to be welded onto the existing MUSKETEER strategy (by then they had stopped using 'Revise') under conditions of the utmost secrecy. Brook's timetable went by the board (as did the Suez contractors' chances of escape). At noon on Sunday, 28 October, the day before the Israeli assault on Egypt, the air task force headquarters at Episkopi in Cyprus assumed control over all offensive aircraft and the force commander was then told that it was already D-3 by the timetable. At 3.30 p.m. on 30 October, just one hour before the ultimatum was to be delivered, Brook told the members of the D(T)C what was happening and added, not surprisingly, that ministers had decided to take no action for the time being on the political directive.[38]

When the Suez archives were opened to researchers in 1987 most were surprised at the clarity and candour with which Brook had recorded the critical exchanges in the series of Cabinet meetings beginning on 25 October and ending on 6 November. As to his own views, he usually kept them to himself but William Clark recorded that when on 5 November he discussed his own resignation with Brook the latter remarked that 'he realised that no intelligent man could support the policy.'[39]

On the same day, to the astonishment of colleagues who had expected him to be too preoccupied elsewhere, Brook turned up at a party. 'I've seen a good many cock-ups in my time,' he remarked, 'but I have never seen anything like this. So I thought I might as well go out and have a drink.'[40]

In October 1956, just as the Suez story was approaching its climax, Sir Edward Bridges' retirement took effect. As had been announced in July, Brook then reached the peak of his profession when he added the headship of the Home Civil Service to his existing duties as Cabinet Secretary and began to share the official leadership of the Treasury with Sir Roger Makins. Makins was to give full-time economic advice while Brook was to look after administration. It was characteristic of the atmosphere in which the policy of collusion was conceived that, despite the post Makins had held in Washington and the post he was taking up, nothing whatever was said to him about what was going to happen until the day before the Israeli attack when he was informally let into the secret by the Chancellor, Harold Macmillan. He instantly obtained permission to consult with Brook, because he saw at once the dimensions of the problems in Anglo-American relations that were about to arise. Brook worked closely with him to save the Nato alliance and to enlist American help to stabilize the position of sterling.[41]

In the weeks that followed the cease-fire at Port Said and the departure of Eden for a rest in Jamaica, Brook's massive calm was an immense asset as he worked to put the pieces of British government and policy back together. 'You display colossal patience through all these crises,' wrote James Stuart on leaving the Cabinet in January 1957, 'I can't think how you control yourself.'[42] He carefully rationed the amount of information supplied to Eden in Jamaica so as to discourage any tendency to try to control policy from across the water and he sought to counter Eden's mounting inclination to heap all the blame for the Suez fiasco on the United States. 'The last six months have been grim indeed and I owe so much to you for making it possible to live and fight through them,' Eden wrote to him after he had given up the struggle to retain the Premiership. 'I was wrong, though,' he went on, 'in underestimating the American – or rather the Ike-Dulles – hostility. I suppose they had always wanted us out of the Middle East, or at least Dulles did. I was warned of this years ago when the Republicans came in, but I did not believe it. Now I do.'[43]

Brook would never have expressed himself about the United States in this way. He agreed with Selwyn Lloyd in deploring 'the strong anti-American bias throughout' the first draft of Eden's memoirs in 1959, when they both read them,[44] and had done his utmost to preserve the intimate links with the transatlantic ally in the days when they were most under strain. He stood for the permanent government of Britain, while striving to supply an efficient machine for the policies of those elected politicians for the time being in charge. Never was the task of reconciling these two objectives fraught with such difficulty and strain. Brook had the qualities to survive.

Following the precedent of Hankey, the press liked to label Norman Brook (who on being raised to the peerage became Lord Normanbrook) as 'the man of secrets'. The Public Orator at Oxford said in 1961, 'As far as state secrets are concerned he out-does the God of Silence.' A certain *frisson* was felt, therefore, when, at his death, he was found to have left a 'locked diary' to his widow. But when his papers were released at the Bodleian Library in June 1997 its contents were not among them.[45]

NOTES

1. Lord Trend, 'Brook, Norman Craven, Baron Normanbrook,' E.T. Williams and C.S. Nicholls (eds.), *Dictionary of National Biography 1961–1970* (Oxford: OUP, 1981) p.142.
2. Bodleian Library, Sir Norman Craven Brook Papers, Bridges note undated.
3. *The Times*, 16 June 1967.
4. D. Goldsworthy (ed.), *British Documents on the End of Empire: The Conservative Government and the End of Empire 1951–1957. Part II Politics and Administration* (HMSO, 1994), doc.193; PREM 11/1726, Brief by Sir N. Brook for Sir W. Churchill, 1 Dec. 1954.
5. Interview with Dr Ehrman (Historian, Cabinet Office 1948–56), Aug. 1998.
6. William Clark, *From Three Worlds* (London: Sidgwick & Jackson, 1986), p.151.
7. Bodleian Library, Clark Papers, diary entry 6 Feb. 1956.
8. PREM 11/1457, Brook to Eden, 14 April 1956, Bishop to Brook, 15 April 1956.
9. Clark, *From Three Worlds*, p.160.
10. R.J. Penney in *RAF Historical Society, Proceedings*, 3, 1987, pp.32–3.
11. Though there was some fluidity of membership the departments normally represented were the Treasury, Foreign Office, Ministry of Transport, Ministry of Defence, Commonwealth Relations Office, Ministry of Labour, Ministry of Fuel and Power, Cabinet Office and Chiefs of Staff Committee.
12. S. Roskill, *Hankey. Man of Secrets Vol II 1919–1931* (London: Collins, 1972), pp.405–6.
13. CAB 21/3426, Hewison to Plumer, 22 April 1949; CAB 21/3426, Griffiths memo, 15 Aug. 1950. The Treasury admitted in 1950 that 'we rather belatedly are now preparing the first revision of the Treasury War Book since 1939.' The year after Suez the Board of Trade was protesting that: 'Until we have clearer guidance as to the assumptions of a future war it is impossible for us to say with any confidence what the steps will be. It is in any case very likely that we shall find it difficult, even once the economic assumptions have become clearer, to set out for the purpose of the War Book the kind of action we should take.' CAB 21/3431, Stevens to Blake, 27 Sept. 1957.
14. CAB 21/3426, Griffiths memo, 15 Aug. 1950.
15. CAB 21/3421. There was a seventeenth chapter, which was unnumbered, that dealt with foreign information.
16. CAB 21/3542, Brook memo, 17 Aug.1956.
17. T. Dibble, '"Consequential Matters…" A study of the Defence (Transition) Committee during the Suez Crisis of 1956', p.10. I am very grateful to Dibble for the chance to read his unpublished thesis, which supplements my own research on a number of points.
18. The management of the Suez Canal was in any case scheduled to revert to Egypt in 1968 and there had been before the seizure of the Canal Company considerable

anxiety as to whether the company's poor relations with the Egyptian government would stand in the way of the widening and deepening of the Canal which the oil industry required in the last years of the concession.

19. CAB 134/815, D(T)C(56) 2nd mtg., 27 July 1956.
20. CAB 134/1217, EC(56)30, 21 Aug. l956; CAB 134/815, D(T)C(56) 3rd mtg., 31 July 1956.
21. CAB 134/815, D(T)C(56) 5th mtg., 7 Aug. 1956.
22. CAB 134/815, D(T)C(56) 10th mtg., 24 Aug. l956.
23. Clark, *From Three Worlds,* pp.171–2.
24. PREM 11/1152, Brook to Eden, 25 Aug. l956.
25. The file, now to be found in the PRO at CAB 134/1225 contains a note to this effect.
26. PREM 11/1100, ff 304–6, 'Egypt: Military Planning.' Memo from Foreign Secretary, 28 Aug. 1956.
27. CAB 134/1225, EOC(56) 1st mtg., 24 Aug. l956.
28. CAB 134/1225, 'Draft Political Directive to the Allied Commander-in-Chief'; see also CAB 134/815, D(T)C(56)16th mtg.
29. PREM 11/1104, COS(S)(56) 5th mtg., 24 Sept. 1956.
30. FO 371/118997/JE11924/76, draft note by the Egypt (Official) Committee, 24 Sept. l956 and JE11924/76C, Powell to Brook, 25 Sept. l956; CAB/134/1217, EC(56)53, 25 Sept. 1956.
31. ADM 205/136; FO 371/118997/JE l1924/76C and JE11924/79; CAB 134/1217, EC(56)53.
32. CAB 134/1217, EC(56)53, 25 Sept. l956.
33. PREM 11/1089B, Brook to Eden, 13 Sept. l956.
34. PREM 11/1089B, EC(56)1, 28 July 1956; Brook to Eden, 13 Sept. 1956; De Zulueta to Hunt, 14 Sept. 1956. I owe these references to Dr. Christopher Brady.
35. Hailsham (and perhaps Birch) were in fact told what was afoot shortly in advance of the Israeli attack. 'Up to that point,' he has said, 'I had been deliberately kept in the dark by higher authority.' He added on 10 Jan. 1981 that he had been 'very put out by the deception.' G. Lewis, *Lord Hailsham* (London: Jonathan Cape, l997), p.157.
36. S. Lloyd, *Suez 1956. A Personal Account* (London: Jonathan Cape, 1978), pp.180–85.
37. CAB 128/30, CM(56) 72nd mtg., 23 Oct. 1956.
38. CAB 134/815, D(T)C(56) 16th mtg., 30 Oct., l956.
39. Clark, *From Three Worlds,* p.210.
40. Ehrman interview, Aug. 1998.
41. Interview with Lord Sherfield (Sir Roger Makins), 1990.
42. Bodleian Library, Brook Papers, Stuart to Brook, 21 Jan. 1957.
43. Brook Papers, Eden to Brook, 16 Jan. l957.
44. FO 800/728 file.
45. Brook Papers.

In the Know?
Sir Gladwyn Jebb: Ambassador to France

CHRISTOPHER GOLDSMITH

Most historical accounts of the Suez Crisis have touched on the involvement of Sir Gladwyn Jebb, Britain's Ambassador to Paris from 1954 to 1960, often pointing out that he felt it necessary to draw up a memorandum about events in case there was an official inquiry. These accounts have tended to concentrate on the events following the Ambassador's exclusion from the Franco-British ministerial meetings in the middle of October 1956, where the British Prime Minister Anthony Eden and his Foreign Secretary Selwyn Lloyd took the decision to accept the French Challe plan for collusion with Israel against Egypt. Certainly this aspect of Jebb's involvement in the crisis has much to tell us about the position of officials in government decision-making at this stage. Nevertheless, it is also important to recognise that Jebb had been deeply involved in developing a common Franco-British approach to the nationalisation of the Suez Canal Company and that, from the beginning, this was an approach that was based on a joint military operation against Nasser.

Before examining Gladwyn Jebb's role in the Suez Crisis, it is useful to establish a picture of his career and personality. He entered the Foreign Office in 1924 after obtaining a First in History at Oxford. His talents were quickly recognised and in 1929 he was appointed as Private Secretary to Hugh Dalton, Under-Secretary of State at the Foreign Office in the Labour government. After the change of government in 1931, Jebb went to the Rome Embassy for four years, where his main responsibilities were reporting on economic and commercial matters. When he came back to London this experience was put to good use in the newly-formed Economic Section of the Foreign Office, where he worked for three years before becoming

Private Secretary to two Permanent Under-Secretaries, Sir Robert Vansittart and Sir Alexander Cadogan. In the early years of the Second World War he was Diplomatic Advisor to Hugh Dalton at the Special Operations Executive, but this proved to be a low point in his career. A victim of political and Civil Service infighting, he returned to the Foreign Office under a cloud and was put to work on planning British policy for the post-war period. Suddenly he was in his element, drafting plans for what were to become the International Monetary Fund and the United Nations. With the arrival of Ernest Bevin as Foreign Secretary, Gladwyn Jebb became a senior policy advisor, playing an important role in the shaping of Britain's position in the post-war world. His final posting before the Paris Embassy was as Britain's Permanent Representative on the UN Security Council, where he gained some public notoriety for his successful advocacy of the Western position during the debates on the Korean War.

By July 1956 Jebb had been in post as Ambassador to Paris for slightly more than two years. He had viewed his appointment to one of the 'big three' posts as something of a disappointment, as he had hoped for and still coveted the position of Permanent Under-Secretary at the Foreign Office.[1] His abilities as an original policy maker, who could be relied on to draw up a lucid scheme at short notice, were fully recognised, although he himself admitted that he sometimes got it wrong. He was also an effective negotiator, receiving great praise from the Belgian statesman Paul-Henri Spaak for his successful management of the first General Assembly of the United Nations. However, his manner could be somewhat disconcerting, with Jebb himself saying that it was not his 'strong point to be terribly nice to people or to think up little schemes on how to get round difficult points'.[2] He had a tendency to be rather pompous and self-important, while even friends like Harold Nicolson or Hugh Dalton could describe him as 'rude and disagreeable' or 'much colder and more cynical' than his Canadian contemporary, Lester Pearson.[3] This mixture of characteristics would seem to have made Jebb an unlikely candidate for a senior ambassadorship, but he was a competent administrator, an effective orator and made a success of his stay in Paris.[4] A greater barrier to his further promotion was his 'somewhat abrasive' relationship with Anthony Eden, which led to his effective isolation from the heart of the policy-making process.[5] Eden, renowned for his knowledge and skill in foreign affairs, preferred to be the dominant figure in the Foreign Office, even after he assumed the premiership.

Although there had been successful co-operation between Britain and France over the Geneva Conference and German rearmament in 1954, this had proved to be a false dawn as far as any revival of the Entente Cordiale was concerned. Indeed, before President Nasser's announcement of the nationalisation of the Suez Canal on 26 July 1956, Middle Eastern affairs had been a considerable cause of tension between the two countries. Regardless of their stated adherence to the framework established in the Tripartite Declaration of May 1950, the British and United States governments had in practice increasingly excluded the French from policy discussions about the region. The Eden government's promotion of the Baghdad Pact, as a means of bolstering British influence in the region after the military evacuation from the Suez Canal Zone in 1954, had provoked criticism from the Quai d'Orsay, both in private and public. On the other hand, the Foreign Office was increasingly concerned about the level of arms transfers from France to Israel. By the spring of 1956 tensions between the two countries had reached such a pitch that Eden called the French 'our enemies in the Middle East'.[6] Part of the explanation of the French attitude was rooted in their concern about the implications for traditional French interests in the Levant of British support for Iraq. Although Jebb and other Foreign Office officials could question how important these interests were to the French, neither French politicians nor officials had forgotten their eviction from the region at the hands of the British immediately following the Second World War. Nevertheless, John Beith, the Head of Chancery in Paris, identified the heart of the problem:

> We are faced with the dilemma which is really the essence of policy in this matter, i.e. 'Bring the French in or accept French criticism and possibly obstruction'. A good deal of the present unsatisfactory French attitude can be traced to our inability to consult them, in the fullest sense on one occasion or another.[7]

This was a problem that the British government seemed unwilling to face up to and Franco-British friction continued to build throughout the first six months of 1956.

Eventually the Socialist French Foreign Minister Christian Pineau was invited to visit London at the end of July to discuss a range of Middle East questions. British Embassy officials in Paris reported that

Pineau had expressed particular concern at the withdrawal of funding from the High Aswan Dam project, fearing that it might drive the Egyptians further into the Soviet sphere.[8] Once the news of Nasser's reaction had broken, France and the United Kingdom found common cause against Egypt. Pineau arrived in London on 29 July 1956 and made it clear that his government supported the adoption of an aggressive policy. His discussions with Eden and Lloyd ignored the differences of the previous 18 months and concentrated on 'how best to play the hand' and laying out a timetable for action. They also agreed that any diplomatic initiatives would only 'fill the gap' until military preparations were completed.[9]

Gladwyn Jebb's initial response to nationalisation was much the same as many of his colleagues. He recalled in his memoirs: 'I was among those who favoured, in principle, some kind of direct action to bring the Canal back under the control of the Company, always provided that we and the French had enough forces available.'[10] The grounds for this assessment were similar to those of other officials. Nasser's action was seen as jeopardising the whole British position in the Middle East, a key strategic region in geopolitical terms. Only six weeks earlier Treasury, Foreign Office and Ministry of Defence officials had presented a paper entitled 'The Future of the United Kingdom in World Affairs' to a Cabinet Policy Review Committee.[11] This emphasised the dependence of both the United Kingdom and Western Europe on Middle East oil and suggested that 'we should recognise that the Middle East is now the most critical theatre politically'. Both politicians and officials drew on their common experiences of facing the fascist threat to British interests in the 1930s to develop an appropriate policy framework. The diplomatic lessons learned from those shared memories played a considerable role in influencing the behaviour of British policy makers during the Suez Crisis. There was little doubt in the Foreign Office that it would be necessary to confront Nasser successfully in order to protect Britain's world position. Furthermore, officials had little faith in the ability of international organisations to act decisively. Even Jebb, who had been closely involved with the establishment of the United Nations at the close of the Second World War, had little faith in the ability of that institution to respond to Egypt's action. His doubts were clearly demonstrated in a discussion he had with Norman Robertson, the Canadian High Commissioner in London, on 31 July 1956. After the

Canadian had voiced fears about the consequences of British military action and the failure to involve the UN, Jebb replied:

> I said that, old United Nations man though I was, I could not myself share his comparative optimism about the attitude which the Eastern States would be likely to take up in the General Assembly in the circumstances contemplated.[12]

In addition to accompanying Pineau during the discussions taking place in the immediate aftermath of Nasser's announcement, Jebb was charged with chairing a Foreign Office committee set up to discuss future collaboration with France in the Middle East. The result of the committee's deliberation was a memorandum entitled 'France and the Middle East', which outlined the main issues that needed to be raised with French politicians and officials. The starting point for any joint action by the two countries had to be an agreement on the general objectives of the proposed military operation against Nasser. The paper suggested that the goal of the assault on Egypt should be 'to produce another Egyptian Government which will be prepared to accept the new international settlement for the Suez Canal that will emerge as a result of the proposed international conference.'[13]

It is important to note that there was to be no return to the policy of occupation, which had been the main plank of British policy in the Middle East. Officials believed that maintaining British influence in the region was 'increasingly a political rather than a military question';[14] any long-term military deployment might give succour to Arab nationalism. Neither did senior officials foresee a return to the status-quo ante as far as management of the Suez Canal was concerned. However, military action was considered necessary to produce the downfall of the Nasser regime in Egypt and its replacement with an administration which would be more amenable to Franco-British persuasion.

This clear affirmation of the aggressive bent of British government thinking was followed by an evaluation of several policy questions, which might threaten effective Franco-British co-operation. Ironically, in view of what was to come, the first of these issues identified was the potential intervention of Israel during the proposed Suez operation. The paper suggested that:

> Anglo-French action in the Canal Zone will probably be misrepresented, to our damage in the Arab world, as part of an imperialist plot hatched with Israel. It is, therefore, important

that we and the French (and the Americans) should agree to use our influence to keep Israel right out of the dispute.

As part of the effort to prevent any such misinterpretation of Franco-British actions, officials stated that any attempt by the Israelis to exploit an attack on the Canal Zone to snatch territory from Egypt should be forcibly opposed. Indeed, Jebb's committee argued that the two allies might be presented with an opportunity to force the Israelis back beyond their 'existing boundaries'. The paper also considered the question of future arms supplies to Israel, proposing that if the French government could be persuaded to adopt the British policy of small-scale supply to Arab and Israeli alike, it would assist the attempt to present a public image of even-handedness to both the Arab and the wider world.

In connection with the impact on international perception of any Franco-British co-operation in the Middle East, the report drew attention to the continuing French colonial war in Algeria. As we have already seen, officials were very aware of the unpopularity any attack on Nasser would provoke in the Arab world, so they were concerned about the added opprobrium of collaborating with France, which they described as 'the most unpopular Western country in the Arab world'. Gladwyn Jebb, having observed the malignant effect of the Algerian conflict on French political life, had already urged a more pro-active British policy towards the war. On 17 July 1956, nine days before the Suez Crisis broke, the Ambassador had sent a long dispatch to Selwyn Lloyd on the problems in North Africa.[15] In it he argued that Western interests in the Maghreb would only be secured by the rapid adoption of a 'liberal' policy towards Algeria. The best way to ensure this would be through more active support for the French from their allies, a suggestion that was well received by other officials. In 'France and the Middle East' ministers were urged to emphasise their willingness to give public backing to a 'liberal settlement which would visibly provide for Algerian autonomy with adequate political opportunities for the Moslem majority'. Officials believed that clear signs of such a policy might at least attenuate Arab enmity towards France.

The final area of concern identified in the paper was the highly contentious issue of the future development of the Baghdad Pact. Given that Britain had no desire to re-establish its formal military presence in the Middle East, its influence would continue to be promoted through the commitment to the Baghdad Pact. Previous French criticism of the Pact had been based on two foundations: the destabilising effect that the new organisation had had on Middle Eastern affairs and, more specifically, the nature of Iraqi ambitions in Syria and the Lebanon, countries which France regarded as being in its sphere of influence in the region. Jebb's committee believed that successful action against Nasser would inevitably lead to increased Iraqi influence in the Levant. They thought it highly unlikely that the French could be persuaded to encourage the further expansion of the Baghdad Pact. However, they hoped to reassure the Quai d'Orsay that any increase in Iraqi power in the Middle East would not be inimical to French interests.

The importance of this memorandum in any analysis of Gladwyn Jebb's role during the Suez Crisis cannot be underestimated. In the first place it provides us with a snapshot of official thinking under his influence in the first week of August 1956. What is most noteworthy about the paper is the remarkable optimism demonstrated by this group of officials. While they recognised the threat nationalisation posed to Britain's position in the Middle East, it presented great opportunities to eliminate many of the problems that had eroded that position since the Second World War. The document is also significant because it formed the basis for much of Jebb's involvement during the rest of the crisis. The report's recommendation that Israeli participation in any future military operation should be minimised was reinforced by the Egypt Committee. During a meeting at 11 Downing Street held to discuss Jebb's paper, the Chancellor of the Exchequer Harold Macmillan had pointed out that Israeli intervention might enhance the chances of success in the Canal Zone. However, he was unable to convince the meeting which concluded that Israeli participation should 'stop short of active intervention'.[16] When Macmillan tried to revive his idea in discussion with Eden and Selwyn Lloyd, he was brusquely put in his place by the Prime Minister, who told him that 'it was none of his business anyway'.[17] There could be no clearer signal to officials that the Israelis should have been kept out of the Suez Affair.

Having completed his work on the committee, Jebb returned to Paris in order to negotiate an understanding with the Mollet government. His instructions, largely based on the memorandum already discussed, reinforce the perception that the British government saw the crisis as a chance to develop a common Franco-British policy on the Middle East. It was 'a golden opportunity of removing at least some of the misunderstandings which have clouded Anglo-French relations in the Mediterranean'.[18] The records of Jebb's meetings with Christian Pineau and Louis Joxe, the Secretary-General of the Quai d'Orsay, contain plenty of evidence that this was a misperception.[19] While the two delegations found it easy to agree on the objectives of a military operation against Egypt, there was very little progress in dispelling the differences on broader Middle East issues. Jebb and Pineau agreed that the Arab–Israeli dispute could only be resolved through frontier changes, but the French thought that Israel should make strategic gains whereas Britain favoured Arab claims. On the question of arms supplies the record is confused. Jebb's account suggests that there was agreement on the need to regulate arms sales to Israel. The French record shows that they thought that Britain was not hostile to further shipments so long as they were conducted secretly rather than through the Near East Arms Co-ordinating Committee. Finally, Jebb failed to make any progress on selling the Baghdad Pact to the French team. The discussions only served to demonstrate that Franco-British co-operation over Suez was a marriage of convenience rather than a long-term commitment to a joint policy in the Middle East. Britain wanted to topple Nasser to maintain its position in the region, while France believed that 'one successful battle in Egypt would be worth ten in North Africa'.[20] These differences in the basic motivations behind their support for military action had important implications for the way the crisis unfolded. French interests could only be properly defended by military action against Nasser, while Britain's aims might have been achieved through diplomacy alone.

Once these discussions had been concluded, Jebb returned with his French colleagues to London to participate in the Three Power meetings taking place on the fringes of the first London Conference. The work of Jebb as an ambassador in these situations was twofold: using his close contacts within the French delegation to facilitate communication; and using his knowledge of the day-to-day conduct of French government to provide insights into French positions.[21] On 24 August Selwyn Lloyd and Pineau held a bilateral meeting to discuss Algeria, the future of the employees of the Suez Canal Company and the imposition of economic sanctions against Egypt. Selwyn Lloyd's main concern at the meeting was to prepare a favourable international climate for any eventual military action in the Canal Zone. The two ministers talked about the timing of any approach to the United Nations, concluding that they should wait for the Egyptian response to the Menzies mission. At the close of this meeting the Foreign Secretary Selwyn Lloyd asked Jebb to follow up these discussions when he return to Paris. He was instructed to pay special attention to the United Nations issue and the possibility of any concessions to Israel.

However, the former question was preying on the mind of Lloyd, who decided to gather the opinions of his senior officials on going to the United Nations. Jebb was very wary about any United Nations involvement in the Suez question although he believed that a successful outcome was possible if the Americans gave their full support.[22] His caution was due to the problem of how to convince world opinion that Nasser was the villain of the piece. He noted that up to this point the Egyptians' conduct of the operation of the Canal had not been widely condemned as 'arbitrary'. If the two governments could not demonstrate that the passage of shipping through the Canal was actually endangered, the ambassador felt that 'a considerable section of public opinion will come to a conclusion that we are "riding for a fall"'. The problem of the international community, which had not really impinged on official thinking at the start of the crisis, was of growing significance in the minds of British officials and ministers. Jebb returned to this topic during a meeting between Pineau and Selwyn Lloyd on 5 September 1956.[23] The Foreign Secretary wondered what the two allies should regard as the trigger for launching their military operation. Jebb pointed out that Nasser might choose to spin out negotiations rather than flatly reject the Eighteen Power proposals. He added that 'unless there was some positive incident on which to peg our case, we should find things very different in the Security Council'. There was a clear possibility that an approach to the United Nations would severely limit the freedom of Britain and France to act militarily against Nasser.

Throughout the first three weeks of September Jebb continued to facilitate Franco-British collaboration, reporting to London on French apprehension over the fragile state of British public opinion and their doubts about the resolve of British politicians.[24] The Ambassador kept in regular contact with both ministers and Quai d'Orsay officials to discuss French views on the Suez Canal Users' Association proposals of the US Secretary of State, John Foster Dulles, and reference to the Security Council. In a brief meeting with Pineau on 17 September the

French perception of the stakes involved in the crisis was clearly stated. Jebb reported that Pineau believed that it might be possible to get rid of Nasser without deploying force if 80 per cent of user countries joined a Users' Association. Otherwise, the French Foreign Minister thought that reference to the United Nations was only 'window-dressing', as Britain and France would be 'completely finished' if they did not use force to crush Nasser.[25] It was shortly after this meeting that the French minister, demonstrably keen for greater action against Egypt, launched contacts with the Israelis about a possible joint operation to secure the Suez Canal.[26]

On 26 September Anthony Eden and Selwyn Lloyd flew to Paris for discussions with their French counterparts. The unwillingness of Dulles to provide the proposed Users' Association with any teeth had riled the French delegation, who returned from the Second London Conference even more determined to use military force. For over an hour the ministers met without their officials in what was described by Eden as a 'very difficult' meeting.[27] The main problem, according to the British Prime Minister, was the French demand that the crisis be resolved by the end of October. In his biography of Selwyn Lloyd, Thorpe has suggested that the exclusion of officials from this meeting marked the beginning of the secret diplomacy that eventually led to collusion with Israel.[28] However, there is little evidence that Gladwyn Jebb felt excluded from the policy making process at this time in the crisis. On the morning that the two ministers arrived in Paris, the ambassador met his American counterpart, Douglas Dillon, to discuss the London Conference and the prospects for the United Nations debate. Jebb expressed the opinion that the French Cabinet thought the reference to the UN would be unproductive and would expect the road to be cleared for military action from the middle of October onwards. Dillon reminded him of the 'great fears' that the Eisenhower administration had about any potential military action, especially if it occurred before the presidential election. Jebb's response was to suggest that, in that case, military action should be delayed until later in November or early December.[29] Yet the next day Jebb told Dillon that the use of force against Egypt was ruled out, unless the Canal was shut down or there was a serious deterioration in the Egyptian political situation.[30]

These conversations reflect the confused state of British thinking on the crisis by the end of September 1956. The Mollet government had not really shifted away from the position it had taken from the outset. They still wanted to launch a military attack on the Canal Zone and regarded all diplomatic initiatives as distractions. Although British ministers and officials were still ready to countenance the use of force, there is plenty of evidence to suggest that broader international concerns were at the forefront of their minds. Jebb recorded in his memoirs that 'as the crisis wore on; as the attitude of the Americans and others was revealed; and as we became involved in what was in effect a process of negotiation, I personally became persuaded that force was out'.[31] Eden's deep concern about the overt belligerence of his French colleagues is clearly demonstrated in his record of his meetings on 26 September.[32] The State Department concluded from Dillon's report on his conversations with Jebb that the British were 'restraining' the French.[33]

At the beginning of October a second Middle East crisis began to add to the pressure Eden was under. While Selwyn Lloyd and Pineau were in New York, negotiating with Mohammed Fawzi, Nasser's Foreign Minister, there was also increasing tension on the border between Israel and Jordan. As Jebb's discussions in August with the French had demonstrated, Franco-British co-operation was based on a common dislike of Nasser rather than shared convictions on the future of the Middle East. Britain was bound to offer military assistance if Jordan was attacked under the Anglo-Jordanian Treaty. It only had the forces to do this or attack Nasser, not both. The solution to this quandary proposed by the Foreign Office was to encourage Iraq to move some of its forces into Jordan. Neither of the possible actions was particularly palatable to the French. Military action by British forces against Israel would, according to Jebb, have 'pretty ticklish' consequences for Franco-British relations, given the level of support for Israel within the Mollet government.[34] On the other hand, the movement of Iraqi troops into Jordan would not only exasperate these pro-Israeli sentiments, but would also reawaken French concerns about British attempts to supplant their interests in the Levant. The confluence of the two developments would form the background to Eden's decision to accept the French plan for collusion with Israel.

While Selwyn Lloyd seemed to be making some progress in New York, Jebb was being bombarded by warnings from French sources about the volatility of the Israelis. On 12 October Albert Gazier, the minister supervising the Quai d'Orsay while Pineau was at the United

Nations, summoned the Ambassador to his office to discuss the Iraqi deployment. Gazier urged him to push London to seek further assurances from Nuri about the nature of his plans. The matter was considered so important that Jebb was treated to a similar performance the following day.[35] Officials in both London and Paris were unsure about the direction of French policy, although the groups shared a suspicion that France was encouraging the Israelis to occupy the West Bank. During the afternoon of 13 October Guy Mollet telephoned Eden to arrange a visit by Gazier. The minister would deliver a special personal message. Eden agreed to receive the French minister at Chequers the following day. When Jebb asked the Foreign Office if he could accompany the French party on the visit, the request was denied. Diplomats from both sides were to be excluded from the event.

Into this atmosphere of heightened tension and intrigue Jebb added a further element. He reported to both the Minister of State Anthony Nutting and the Permanent Under-Secretary at the Foreign Office, Sir Ivone Kirkpatrick, that evidence had become available that the French had recently delivered up to 95 Mystère IV aircraft to the Israelis, possibly accompanied by French aircrew.[36] These planes would give the Israelis air superiority in the region, increasing their ability to launch an offensive. Jebb suggested that Eden should use the opportunity of his meeting with Gazier to raise the general issue of Israel, 'impressing on him very strongly that it would be fatal to encourage the Israelis in any way at the moment over and above giving them such assurances as we legitimately can'. Nutting, in charge of the Foreign Office in Selwyn Lloyd's absence, brought the information to Eden's attention as soon as the Prime Minister returned from the Conservative Party Conference in Llandudno. Eden was immediately concerned that the French were encouraging the Israelis to attack Jordan, an assessment shared by the Foreign Office. However, Eden rejected Nutting's advice that Britain should now encourage the Iraqis to advance into Jordan to deter the Israelis. When Nutting continued to press his case, Eden responded truculently and concluded the conversation by shouting: 'I will not allow you to plunge this country into war merely to satisfy the anti-Jewish spleen of you people in the Foreign Office'.[37] Eden was minded to wait and see what the French had to say the following day rather than listen to the advice of his officials.[38]

By the time Eden and Selwyn Lloyd visited Paris on 16 October, the Prime Minister's mood had changed. Jebb had received no details of the Chequers meeting where Gazier and Challe had outlined the French plan to the Prime Minister. When he quizzed Maurice Bourgès-Maunoury, the French Defence Minister, about the meeting on 16 October, the Frenchman was vague and evasive, although he revealed that the French were expecting Nutting to arrive with a reply to Gazier's message.[39] The unexpected arrival of the Prime Minister and his Foreign Secretary, the latter having rushed back from New York, seemed to presage something urgent. Jebb took the opportunity of the drive from the airport to the embassy to ask Eden whether he had received his telegram about the delivery of the Mystères. Eden acknowledged receipt of the message and let the issue drop, never to be spoken of again. That evening the British ministers had two hours of talks with their French counterparts, the ambassador and other officials remaining outside. The feeling among the officials was that force was no longer an option, the effect of any action on sterling being a major consideration. Their ministers took a different attitude.

Following the departure of the two ministers, Jebb immediately put his complaints about his continued exclusion from Franco-British discussions on paper. He wrote in a letter to Selwyn Lloyd:

> I do not complain, but it is, I believe, a novel arrangement for diplomatic business of the highest importance to be conducted by the Principals without any official being present, even to take a note. I am sure that you feel that this is a good method of proceeding, and anyhow it is for you to say. But however great the advantages of the new system, it has one very considerable disadvantage so far as your representative on the spot is concerned. This is that, although he has to live with one of the principals and has to continue negotiations with him in his absence of his own Principal, he has no means, apart from a few remarks which the latter may let fall, of knowing what actually happened when the Principals met.[40]

Selwyn Lloyd, jet-lagged, ill and no doubt confused, was left by Eden to deal with the angry ambassador, who threatened to resign in a manuscript letter if he was not informed of what was going on. On 18 October Jebb met Sir Ivone Kirkpatrick, whom Jebb considered a 'personal friend of long standing'.[41] The Ambassador pressed his colleague for information about the secret talks, but Kirkpatrick needed clearance from Selwyn Lloyd before he could let Jebb into the picture. The Foreign Secretary asked Eden's advice about how to deal with these questions. Eden suggested that he should apologise to the ambassador and inform him that the position was unchanged. The Prime Minister justified Jebb's exclusion on the grounds that meetings without officials had been held regularly during the war.[42]

This proved to be an unsatisfactory position for both the Foreign Secretary and Ambassador. Jebb remained in London, unwilling to accept his exclusion and trying to find out what was going on. Selwyn Lloyd cancelled a meeting with Jebb on 23 October in order to take a secret flight to attend the Sèvres Conference, but he finally faced him in his room at the House of Commons on the following evening. The minister began the meeting by acknowledging the ambassador's anger at his treatment. He then proceeded to give a general account of the secret talks, which included the information that the meetings had involved the Israelis. The two men had a further conversation at Lloyd's flat at No. 1 Carlton Gardens on 28 October, where Selwyn Lloyd made it clear that an Israeli attack on Egypt was 'fixed up for tomorrow'. Jebb was surprised to discover that the Americans had not been brought into the picture and told the Foreign Secretary that he was concerned about the outcome of the proposed plan.[43]

Having been let into the secret at the final moment, Jebb returned to Paris and continued to liaise with his French contacts. Once the Anglo-French ultimatum to Israel and Egypt was announced on 30 October, it soon became apparent that the Americans were not going to support the intervention. Isolated in the United Nations, threatened by the United States and with sterling under severe pressure, Eden was forced to ask Mollet to agree to a cease-fire on 6 November. Nearly the entire Foreign Office was aghast at the series of events. Geoffrey McDermott, one of the few officials in the know, reported that 'the general reaction in the FO was that we did not know whether to laugh or cry at the idiotic stratagem of the ultimatum'.[44] Jebb's reaction to this treatment was similar to his colleagues'. He disliked the fact that he had not been considered trustworthy enough by Eden to have been involved from the beginning. Even after he had been put in the picture about the nature of Eden's secret diplomacy by Selwyn Lloyd, he continued to protest to both the Prime Minister and the Foreign Secretary about his exclusion from high-level meetings and the lack of information. The letter he sent to Eden on the eve of a visit by Gazier to London on 14 November amply demonstrates the anger the ambassador felt:

I suppose that it is understandable that the French Socialist Government should take such elaborate measures to prevent their own Ambassador from knowing what their real policy is, but I can hardly believe that Her Majesty's Government will adopt the same attitude towards myself! I am sure therefore that you will find it possible, by one means or another, to give me some account of what passes tomorrow. Needless to say, I would not, in such circumstances, reveal to anybody here that I was 'in the know'.[45]

Jebb also believed that things would have turned out more positively if normal policy making procedures had been followed. When Macmillan visited Paris on 16 November, the ambassador was ready to suggest that the reason for the recent failure had been the lack of consultation of experts. The minister concurred, but told Jebb that they had to 'make the best of it, and stick together'.[46]

The vast majority of officials were willing to accept the future Prime Minister's plea. After all, they did not share the public's moral distaste for the military intervention in the Canal Zone. There was also plenty of traditional diplomatic work to be completed. The immediate problems caused by the Suez fiasco had to be faced up to and officials also had to study the wider effects on future British foreign relations. Jebb played a part in the Foreign Office's reassessment of the future of British policy in the Middle East.[47] Sir Paul Gore-Booth was put in charge of the review, although he had been one of the loudest internal critics of Eden's actions. The resulting paper maintained that, while some retrenchment of British interest would be necessary, Britain would still have a major role to play in Arab affairs, particularly through the Baghdad Pact. Jebb, along with several other ambassadors, believed that the impact of Suez had been much more serious. In a letter to Kirkpatrick on 4 January 1957,[48] he suggested that over-reliance on Baghdad might have its dangers. The whole of British policy in the region would collapse if there was a change of regime in Iraq. In his opinion, the failure of the Suez operation offered an opportunity to reduce political commitments in the Middle East. Resolution of the Arab–Israeli conflict could now be left to the United Nations, while any other entanglements in the region were problems where 'we are more likely to burn our fingers…than to achieve our aims'.

More central to his own position as Ambassador in Paris, Jebb had to assess the impact of the failure of the Suez operation on Franco-British relations. The initial reaction in France was mixed: only a small section of French public opinion had blamed the United Kingdom for the failure; for the majority the United States was the 'villain of the piece'.[49] Indeed, the ambassador was able to report that, against all the odds, the Suez crisis seemed to have strengthened both the Mollet government and France itself.[50] However, there also seemed to be a resignation that Suez had proved that the United Kingdom and France were now no more than satellites of the United States. French officials concluded an analysis of Franco-British co-operation at Suez by stating: 'We have believed in a Franco-English magic formula. This setback has shown us that alone our two countries lack the weight sufficient to influence seriously the balance of power.'[51] It seemed clear that there would be a change of direction occurring in French foreign policy.

For Jebb, one coincidence seemed to characterise the nature of this change. Eden's phone call to Mollet on 6 November had interrupted a meeting between the French Prime Minister and Chancellor Adenauer on the Common Market negotiations. In his memoirs Jebb reflected on the German's presence at the Elysée that day, drawing the conclusion that it was obvious from that point on that the French would turn more towards the West Germans and away from the entente with Britain.[52] Suez seemed to have confirmed the views of many French people that their country's future lay in a new Europe. Jebb himself had for a long time been convinced that there needed to be closer links between Britain and Europe, but he advocated this line with much more force from November 1956 onwards. His analysis seemed to be echoed at the heart of government, in Eden's 'Thoughts on the general position after Suez'[53] and in Selwyn Lloyd's 'Grand Design', presented to the Cabinet on 5 January 1957. This document proposed that 'if Britain are to be a first-class power with full thermo-nuclear capacity, it can only be done in association with other countries'. These countries were to be the other six members of the Western European Union. The Foreign Secretary's paper was rebuffed by Salisbury, Lord Home and Anthony Head, who argued that British interests could be best protected by 'co-operation with the United States'.[54] This was the policy that Macmillan chose to adopt.

In the final analysis there was no doubt in Gladwyn Jebb's mind that the Suez operation had been a blunder. Indeed, he wrote in his

Memoirs that 'the chances of obtaining any worthwhile result were demonstrably less than those of humiliation'. He laid the blame squarely at the feet of the Prime Minister, who had let his obsession with 'not letting Nasser get away with it' cloud his judgement of the wider issues. However, it should not be forgotten that many officials, Jebb among them, had also been willing to advocate a military overthrow of Nasser at the outset of the crisis. As far as the place of Suez as a watershed in post-war British foreign policy is concerned, Jebb was less certain. In hindsight, he was not convinced that a peaceful resolution of the crisis would have prevented the subsequent erosion of Britain's world position. Nevertheless, he admitted that the crisis confirmed in his mind the need for a fundamental change in emphasis in Britain's external policy, moving away from the old imperial concerns of the Commonwealth and towards the nations of Western Europe. It was this shift that Macmillan, Selwyn Lloyd and much of the Foreign Office found hard to accept, even after the bitter lessons of November 1956.

NOTES

1. Jebb admits his ambition in his *Memoirs of Lord Gladwyn* (London: Weidenfeld & Nicolson, 1972) but it is also effectively demonstrated by his clear approval of Sir Roger Makins as Permanent Under-Secretary of the Treasury, recorded in P.M. Williams, (ed.), *The Diary of Hugh Gaitskell, 1945–1956* (London: Cape, 1983), p.562.
2. Lord Gladwyn, *Memoirs*, p.266.
3. See D. Healey, *The Time of My Life* (London: Penguin, 1990), p.107; N. Henderson, *Inside the Private Office* (Chicago, Academy, 1987), p.87; N. Nicolson (ed.), *Harold Nicolson: Diaries and Letters 1945–1962* (London: Collins, 1968), p.308; B. Pimlott (ed.), *The Political Diary of Hugh Dalton 1918–40, 1945–60* (London: Jonathan Cape, 1986), p.65.
4. See *The Independent*, 26 Oct. 1996; *The Guardian*, 26 Oct. 1996.
5. A. Seldon, *Churchill's Indian Summer: The Conservative Government 1951–1955* (London: Hodder & Stoughton, 1981), p.387. See also K. Young (ed.), *The Diaries of Sir Robert Bruce Lockhart, Vol.2, 1939–1965* (London: Macmillan, 1980), p.659.
6. PREM 11/1344, Makins to FO, tel.136, 19 Jan. 1956; Eden minute of memo from Evelyn Shuckburgh about high-level consultations with the French on the Middle East.
7. FO371/121327, Beith to Hadow, 15 Feb. 1956.
8. FO 371/124443, Harrison minute, 17 July 1956; draft agenda, note by Anderson, 23 July 1956; Reilly to Harrison, 24 July 1956.
9. FO 371/119081, record of conversation between Eden and Pineau at 1 Carlton Gardens, 29 July 1956; meeting at 10 Downing Street, 30 July 1956.

10. Lord Gladwyn, *Memoirs*, p.282.
11. CAB 134/1315, PR(56)3, 1 July 1956. Cabinet Policy Review Committee members included Eden, Salisbury, Macmillan, Selwyn Lloyd and Monckton.
12. FO 371/119088, Jebb minute, 31 July 1956.
13. PREM 11/1099, FO minute, 3 Aug. 1956.
14. CAB 134/1315, PR(56)3, 1 July 1956.
15. FO 371/124431, Jebb to Lloyd, 17 July 1956. For official reaction see FO371/124445, Anderson minute, 24 July 1956, and other minutes by Caccia and Lloyd.
16. PREM 11/1099, record of a meeting held at 11 Downing Street, 3 Aug. 1956.
17. See W.S. Lucas, *Divided We Stand* (London: Hodder & Stoughton, 1991), p.159.
18. PREM 11/1099, draft instructions to Jebb, 7 Aug. 1956.
19. PREM 11/1099, The Suez Canal Crisis: Anglo-French Discussions, undated; *Documents Diplomatiques Francais* 1956, Vol.2 (Paris: Imprimerie Nationale, 1989), pp.240–42.
20. FO 371/119081, record of conversation between Eden and Pineau at 29 July 1956.
21. PREM 11/1099, Lloyd and Dulles refer to Ambassadorial meetings with Joxe, where Joxe confirmed that Pineau would take the United States line at Lancaster House on 21 Aug. 1956.
22. FO 800/740, Jebb to Lloyd, 3 Sept. 1956.
23. FO 800/740, meeting in Pineau's office, Paris, 5 Sept. 1956.
24. PREM 11/1100, Jebb to FO, tels 281 and 282, 7 Sept. 1956.
25. PREM 11/1102, Jebb to FO, 17 Sept. 1956.
26. Lucas, *Divided We Stand*, p.209; K. Kyle, *Suez* (London: Weidenfeld & Nicolson, 1991), pp.209–10.
27. PREM 11/1102, Eden memo, 26 Sept. 1956.
28. D.R. Thorpe, *Selwyn Lloyd* (London: Jonathan Cape, 1989), p.226.
29. *Foreign Relations of the United States, 1955–1957 (FRUS)*, Vol.XVI, (Washington, DC: USGPO, 1988), Dillon to State Department, 26 Sept. 1956, pp.585–6.
30. *FRUS, 1955–1957*, Vol.XVI, memorandum from the Secretary of State's Special Assistant for Intelligence to the Secretary of State, 5 Dec. 1956, pp.1249–71.
31. Gladwyn, *Memoirs,* p.282.
32. PREM 11/1102, Eden memo, 26 Sept. 1956.
33. *FRUS*, 1955–1957, Vol.XVI, p.1261.
34. FO 371/121487, Jebb to Nutting, 3 Oct. 1956.
35. FO 371/121488, Jebb to FO, 12 and 13 Oct.; Kyle, *Suez*, pp.291–6.
36. FO 800/741, Jebb to Nutting, 13 Oct. 1956. The figure turned out to be rather exaggerated.
37. A. Nutting, *No End of a Lesson* (London: Constable, 1967), p.88.
38. V. Feske, 'The Road to Suez: The British Foreign Office and the Quai d'Orsay, 1951–1957' in W. Craig and F. Loewenheim (eds), *The Diplomats, 1939–1979* (Princeton: Princeton University Press, 1994), p.187, for further discussion.
39. Thorpe, *Selwyn Lloyd*, p.232.
40. PREM 11/1100, Jebb to Lloyd, 17 Oct. 1956.
41. Gladwyn, *Memoirs*, p.269.
42. PREM11/1100, Eden to Lloyd, 19 Oct. 1956.
43. Thorpe, *Selwyn Lloyd*, pp.243–6.
44. G. McDermott, *The Eden Legacy* (London: Leslie Frewin, 1969), p.151.
45. PREM 11/1100, Jebb to Eden, 13 Nov. 1956.

46. M. Jebb (ed.), *The Diaries of Cynthia Gladwyn* (London: Constable, 1995), p.192.
47. Kyle, *Suez*, pp.529–31.
48. FO 371/127747, Jebb to Kirkpatrick, 4 Jan. 1957.
49. FO 371/124431, Jebb to FO, 17 Nov. 1956.
50. FO 371/130625, Jebb to Lloyd, 21 Jan. 1957.
51. Kyle, *Suez,* p.495.
52. Gladwyn, *Memoirs*, p.285.
53. PREM 11/1138, Eden memo, 28 Dec. 1956.
54. CAB 129/84, CP(57)6, 5 Jan. 1957.

The Limits of Opposition: Admiral Earl Mountbatten of Burma, First Sea Lord and Chief of Naval Staff

ERIC GROVE and SALLY ROHAN

In the mid 1960s, after retiring as Chief of Defence Staff, Mountbatten collected together his papers on the Suez Crisis. In dictating a covering minute to this 'File on the Suez Affair of 1956' he set out clearly his strongly held views. 'I do not believe,' he claimed, 'I have ever been so embarrassed, distressed and put in such a painful position as I was during the 3 or 4 months that the Suez crisis lasted, from the 26th July until well into November 1956.'[1] Mountbatten's position as First Sea Lord during the Crisis gave him a particularly central role. However, Mountbatten was hardly a normal 'official'. As a member of the British Royal Family and with intimate connections with the British political elite he had already been a Supreme Allied Commander (SEAC) and Viceroy of India by the time of his promotion to the professional leadership of his service.

His special relationship with the British Prime Minister was particularly unique for a Chief of Staff. He noted in 1965, in typical style, that,

> The Prime Minister, Sir Anthony Eden, was one of my oldest and closest friends. For at least 20 years we had discussed all political questions freely and I think it is not too much to claim that I was able to influence him more than he influenced me, for I had a progressive outlook from the beginning and he started with a rather reactionary Tory outlook and gradually came round more to my point of view. The fact that he attached importance to my points of view is demonstrated by the fact that he came, after having resigned as Foreign Secretary, with his No. 2 from the Foreign Office...to see me at Broadlands to consult

me as to what line they should take in the coming crisis which finally blew up into the Munich Affair.[2]

Mountbatten was never one to underestimate his own importance and as with all statements about his historical role these claims have to be treated with some scepticism. However, there can be no doubt that Mountbatten was a personal friend of the Prime Minister and this gave him, as First Sea Lord, not only a position in terms of policy influence but one which was also constitutionally problematic. As a serving officer of the crown his duty was to obey orders from his legal superiors but Eden made it clear that he also valued Mountbatten's political input. On 31 July 1956 Eden stated in a call to Mountbatten that 'I can't tell you how happy I am to have you with me during this time of crisis and I hope that you agree with all that I am doing'.[3] Mountbatten was to recall that 'the sentiment expressed in the first part is exactly the sort of remark I would have expected from such an old friend'. In the case of Suez, however, Mountbatten fundamentally disagreed with the approach of the Prime Minister, from the beginning of the Crisis using 'every possible opportunity to try and indicate how much I disapproved of what he was doing and he soon realised my disapproval. Nothing, however, I could do could shake his policy nor apparently shake his friendship for me.'[4]

Mountbatten's opposition to government policy seems to have been consistent throughout the Crisis. Recounting his views for posterity in September 1956, as events were still developing, he recalled that, 'My own feelings about the Suez Canal crisis were strong from the beginning. I felt it would be inexcusable for us to start an aggressive war which could not fail to entail thousands of civilian casualties merely to bring about the downfall of Colonel Nasser and the reoccupation of the Canal zone.' Such an action, in Mountbatten's view, would be 'acting against the charter of the United Nations which we ourselves had done so much to build up', putting a great strain on Commonwealth relations and serving only to bind the Arab nations more closely to Nasser with all of the potential for a devastating oil embargo against Britain which might ensue.[5]

Rather confusingly, during his later years, Mountbatten claimed to have supported the idea of a military *coup de main* at the outset of the crisis using naval forces to seize Port Said and the first 25 miles of the canal.[6] However, more contemporary evidence clearly shows that whilst he did point out the potential of his naval and marine forces for such an operation he did not recommend that it be carried out. As his own dictated record demonstrates,

> I replied that the whole Mediterranean fleet was at that moment assembled in Malta in anticipation of my visiting them and that to the best of my knowledge they were all at some 4 to 6 hours notice for sea and that if an immediate signal were sent they could all sail by Friday morning. I pointed out that they could reach Port Said within a couple of days fast steaming, and I also presumed that the Royal Marine Commandos could be released from Cyprus within this time and could be picked up on the way.

On delivery of this opinion Mountbatten notes that:

> The Prime Minister was delighted – (almost too delighted) – with this information but I pointed out that the Fleet by itself could only carry out a bombardment but I did not see what good it would be repeating the history of the bombardment of Alexandria in 1878. [sic]...Furthermore I pointed out that the 1200 Royal Marines in the Commando brigade could very easily be put ashore in Port Said and seize the causeway but it would be extremely difficult to maintain them there in the face of Egyptian opposition.

Therefore he 'recommended that unilateral action by the Royal Navy and Royal Marines should not be taken'.[7]

As acting Chairman of the Chiefs of Staff Committee, Sir William Dickson being unwell, Mountbatten began to prepare plans for eventual military action to topple Nasser that the Prime Minister clearly desired. However, given Eden's interest in Mountbatten's views, and in the context of his earlier telephone conversation soliciting Mountbatten's support, the First Sea Lord sought, on the first of August, to put his political concerns on paper in a draft letter to the Prime Minister. In this letter Mountbatten stressed the importance of maintaining world support for the British position, something which would be forfeited if Britain was to launch an invasion of Egypt. Mountbatten's concerns that world opinion would not favour an 'imperialistic' offensive on the part of the British led him to promote the view that the concentration of force being created was purely precautionary. It seemed to Mountbatten 'that the surest way to enlist support for our cause is to offer terms to Nasser which it would be patently unreasonable and provocative for him to reject'. Mountbatten clearly considered Nasser to be an essentially reasonable man but also one who 'really needs to bring off increasingly bold "coups" to bolster up his regime's hold on the country'. Therefore, Mountbatten was to suggest that 'we should apply economic sanctions and pressure in the ways best calculated to goad him into further high-handed action, which would antagonise the world at large, and also British opinion'.[8] Whilst this may have been portrayed by Mountbatten as Britain's trump card, it is questionable whether he shared the Prime Minister's view of Nasser as a 'megalomaniac'. These early responses may have been less an expression on Mountbatten's part of the desirability of 'goading' Nasser and more an attempt at redirecting policy to the political and economic arena, a view supported by his later expression of concern with regard to the legal and moral right of the invasion and the ability of it to succeed in the long term.

The First Lord, Cilcennin, prevented this document going forward partly, as Mountbatten was to recognise later, for his 'own good' and 'partly on constitutional grounds'. Mountbatten 'fought him very bitterly trying to get him to withdraw his veto', but nevertheless was gratified to find that the First Lord seemed to agree with the First Sea Lord over his general attitude to the handling of the crisis. Undeterred, Mountbatten sought out Sir Walter Monckton, the Minister of Defence, to report his conversation with the First Lord and seek his support for sending his letter to the Prime Minister. Monckton sided with Cilcennin and reaffirmed the veto. Mountbatten was to note in his reminiscences some nine years later that 'this was a great pity and in fact a mistake, however unconstitutional my act would have been, because it might have been the means of pulling up the Prime Minister in his headlong rush to disaster at the very beginning'.[9]

However, Mountbatten went on to note that Monckton 'saw eye to eye with us both over the crisis. We all three felt that an armed amphibious assault against opposition in a built up area (since there are no practically no landing places in Egypt which are not built over) would cause the death of thousands of innocent women and children since we obviously had to bomb and bombard the coast defence gun positions without which the assault could not take place.'[10] This concern with the likelihood that the navy would inflict large-scale civilian casualties was to be a consistent element of Mountbatten's opposition to armed intervention.

The three men seem to have also discussed the Commonwealth dimension about which Mountbatten had strong feelings. Mountbatten informed Cilcennin that Lord Home, the Commonwealth Secretary, had told the Egypt Committee of the Cabinet that the Canadians foresaw the disintegration of the Commonwealth and the United Nations as a consequence of British armed intervention in Egypt. Mountbatten was naturally concerned, as former Viceroy, regarding India's attitude to British policy. He was 'convinced that India would almost certainly leave the Commonwealth if we started a war and I thought that Ceylon and Pakistan would follow suit.'[11] Mountbatten was in close contact with India's representative at the Eighteen Nation London Conference on the Canal crisis, Krishna Menon. He went so far as to suggest that Menon approach ministers who were favourable to India's and his own view of the crisis. 'I told him that of all the ministers whom I had heard discuss the Suez situation Sir Walter Monckton was the only one who appeared to share to the full my own views which were so largely sympathetic toward India's views...there would certainly be two or three cabinet ministers with a broad liberal approach.' However, Mountbatten was concerned that he had not yet heard anyone in the Egypt Committee 'speak out strongly against a plan to invade Egypt and reconquer the country by force of arms without reference to the United Nations'. Whilst Mountbatten recognised that 'it was out of the question my being able to take any active part in the political discussions', he was keen to provide Menon with 'important' advice, encouraging his active presentation of Commonwealth views to the British elite.[12]

On or about the 20 August Mountbatten drafted a resignation letter to the Prime Minister which he sent to the First Lord, who replied that the letter had been 'noted'. In this letter, Mountbatten expressed his grave doubts as to the legitimacy and operational viability of British policy. Not only would the United Kingdom's 'indefensible step' of military action against Egypt undermine the United Nations, but it would carry with the it the potential for a thermo-nuclear confrontation. Mountbatten was moved to write to the Prime Minister: 'Now the decision has been taken, however, to launch an aggressive war, I feel that I would be failing in honesty and integrity if I did not beg you to reconsider your action.'[13] Both Cilcennin and Monckton, who also saw the resignation draft, considered that it was unconstitutional for a military officer to resign 'on receiving orders for a military operation' and recommended that the letter not be sent.[14]

Whilst Mountbatten was expressing these private doubts he honoured Cilcennin's request that 'we three (First Lord, First Sea Lord and Minister of Defence) must be the only people who know how your mind is working'.[15] Indeed, such was Mountbatten's public commitment to planning the operation that the current Head of the Naval Historical Branch was moved to write in 1986 that 'the account of Mountbatten's opposition to Suez published in Philip Ziegler's biography does not square with those that I have heard from members of the Naval Staff at the period'.[16] There is evidence that some senior members of the Naval Staff were privy to Mountbatten's doubts and to some extent supported them. Vice Chief of the Naval Staff (VCNS), Admiral Sir William Davis was moved to offer a written statement of support of Mountbatten's position, noting that 'the anxiety you expressed at frequent intervals to the Chiefs of Staff about the consequential effects of action against Egypt – if they had not provoked us beyond endurance – was I believe fully shared by many people in the Admiralty. It was certainly shared by the late First Lord.'[17] While this may have been true, it has been Ziegler's contention, following interviews with contemporary naval officers, that most were 'given no inkling that Mountbatten had reservations about the wisdom of the enterprise... Still less did the junior officers and men suspect that there were doubts on high.'[18] As Mountbatten himself put it shortly after the event: 'I determined to do everything in my power to carry out these orders loyally and to the fullest extent possible as regards getting the Royal Navy and Royal Marines ready for Operation MUSKETEER. I do not believe that any of the three Service Chiefs of Staff worked harder or more loyally or achieved more to meet the wishes of the Prime Minister in getting the operation ready.'[19]

Mountbatten was careful to record that his long serving secretary, Rear Admiral Ronald Brockman, was in complete disagreement with the First Sea Lord for the first time in their working partnership. Mountbatten reports that Brockman 'was violently in favour of the Prime Minister's policy and during the active phase of the Operation used to pass messages of enthusiasm via Elizabeth Collins to my wife which needless to say upset her very much'.[20] Edwina, Countess Mountbatten, notorious in London society for her left wing views, was firmly opposed to Eden's enterprise and complained to her husband that despite his apprehensions he should be taking a stronger stand in opposition. He wrote to her on the 5 August 1956, 'I'm sorry that we seem so often to have got at cross purposes about Egypt. Basically we feel the same and I am doing all and more than I ought to do as a serving officer to try and work for a peaceful solution.'[21] Sending his wife and daughter on their prearranged Spanish holiday, Mountbatten remained in London, although the postponement of the operation enabled a four day break at the end of August at Balmoral, keeping in touch with the Admiralty through a scrambler telephone.

At Chiefs of Staff Committee meetings during August Mountbatten had concentrated on the long-term implications of Operation MUSKETEER. On the 14 August he raised the question of whether it might be possible to form a post Nasser government with any kind of popular support.[22] At the meeting one week later in a discussion focusing on the command structure of the operation, Mountbatten returned to his former theme stating that there was a very real danger that Operation MUSKETEER 'would cause serious and continuing disorder in the Middle East countries and necessitate the long-term retention of considerable forces in the area to maintain law and order'.[23] With a major defence review in process Mountbatten was worried that the requirement for major garrisons in the Middle East might lead to extra pressure for Royal Navy cuts.[24] On 23 August Mountbatten called for an examination of the long-term military commitment in the Middle East. 'He was concerned because on the one hand we were building our forces for operations against Egypt and on the other we were examining what measures we could take to reduce our forces.'[25]

Mountbatten's opposition to MUSKETEER went much deeper than this, however. His main opponent in the Chiefs of Staff was the Chief of the Imperial General Staff, (CIGS), Sir Gerald Templer. In the words of the latter's biographer Templer 'saw Nasser as a Communist tool, and as a menace to British interests in the Middle East and to Britain's allies and strategic position there. His own experience in Jordan had demonstrated vividly the extent of Nasser's influence, especially if allied with Saudi money. Jordan had been kept out of the Bagdad Pact; Iraq was an obvious next target. The Gulf and Britain's oil supplies might then be threatened directly.'[26] For Templer, Mountbatten's attitudes toward the planned operation were verging on cowardice and Mountbatten notes that he went so far as to call the First Sea Lord 'yellow' at a Chiefs of Staff meeting.[27]

For Mountbatten, however, the wider political and indeed moral aspects of the situation in the Middle East led him to question the validity and utility of taking military action. The government's proposed solution would fail to solve the problem of Britain's future position both in the Middle East and the wider world; indeed, the government would do much to undermine it. Mountbatten's close connections with the Indian Congress Party gave him a particular understanding of the novel dynamics of third world nationalism, something which Eden and many others in the British decision-making establishment failed to comprehend.

Mountbatten's understanding of the political aspects of the situation led him to question the utility of any policy which failed to recognise the political context of the Egyptian position. In a rebuff to Templer's call for 'resolute' military action, Mountbatten stated that,

> if we were fighting a visible enemy who was trying to dominate the Middle East by force of arms I should back you to the limit...but there is no such enemy...The Middle East conflict is about ideas, emotions, loyalties. You and I belong to a people which will not have ideas that we don't believe in thrust down our throats by bayonets or other force. Why should we assume that this process should work with other peoples? You cannot, I suggest, fight ideas with troops and weapons. The ideas and the problems they create are still there when you withdraw the troops. What effect...would it have on our troops? Can the British way of life, that you and I believe must be preserved at all costs, survive if we use our young men to repudiate one of its basic principles – the right to self-determination – as permanent occupation troops.[28]

Immediately on his return from Balmoral on 1 September, and with 'D-Day' two weeks away, Mountbatten attended a meeting with the First Lord and Minister of Defence in Cilcennin's bedroom, both politicians being ill. The three men 'had a free and frank off the record discussion lasting one and a half hours'[29] during which the two ministers advised Mountbatten that it might be illegal to resign his post, despite his argument that the Nuremberg trials had provided a precedent. Mountbatten argued that 'a serving officer could not escape the guilt of shooting down women and children merely because his government had told him to do so'. He feared that if he failed to resign he would be held at least partially responsible for the civilian deaths caused. Cilcennin and Monckton, whilst sympathetic, noted that if the actions were sanctioned by the UN or even the British parliament Mountbatten would be 'absolutely wrong' and failing in his duty if he did not stay in office. They concluded that only if the operation went forward in its current form – a major attack on Alexandria with heavy civilian casualties – resignation might be difficult but appropriate. Monckton, who had revealed that he had already threatened his own resignation in Cabinet, was reported by Mountbatten as saying, 'I had always thought my own decision was going to be the most difficult in my career but your decision will be ten times as difficult as that.'[30] Mountbatten, however, remained adamant. 'I solemnly assured them both that nothing would deter me from insisting on the Prime Minister accepting my resignation if he ordered MUSKETEER to go forward even though I realised that most of my friends in the Royal Navy and in the services generally might ostracise me for my conduct and that I should certainly lose my promotion to Admiral of the Fleet which I so much looked forward to on 22 October.' Monckton said that if Mountbatten really was adamant he should wait until he himself had resigned and then he should see Eden alone to tell him of his feelings without a resignation threat. If Monckton's resignation was accepted and if, on the day following, Mountbatten's protest was ignored, it would then be 'proper' for the First Sea Lord to hand in his letter of resignation bringing up to date the existing draft.[31] Only Cilcennin's imminent replacement as First Lord by the less sympathetic Lord Hailsham prevented him offering his resignation along with his colleagues.

When the new First Lord was briefed by the Naval Staff on MUSKETEER on 3 September, Hailsham, a previous supporter of the operation, according to Mountbatten, told the First Sea Lord that

> he had never been so horrified by anything in his life as to find that we were solemnly going ahead with an operation which started with the bombing and bombardment which could not fail to kill thousands of innocent women and children and would then involve us in a campaign which the CIGS himself had estimated could not take less than two or three months unless the Egyptians cracked completely. He himself had been an ardent advocate of the use of force as the ultimate sanction but he had never envisaged anything as horrible as this and he was in despair as to what to do.[32]

Mountbatten advised his political master to talk to Monckton. The following day there was a meeting of the Minister of Defence with the three service ministers. At this meeting only the Secretary of State for War, Anthony Head, expressed any support for MUSKETEER as it stood. Mountbatten and the other Chiefs of Staff were now pressing for a decision on MUSKETEER. Their professional judgement was that it could not be postponed for more than 21 days in all, of which 11 had already passed. Shortly before the 21 day deadline the Commander-in-Chief, Middle East Land Forces, General Sir Charles Keightley, the designated Commander-in-Chief of MUSKETEER, saw Mountbatten privately at the Admiralty 'to express his extreme disquiet with the present plan which he thought too horrible to contemplate'. Keightley shared Mountbatten's views of the long-term impact of the operation. Mountbatten reports him as saying that 'a war of this nature would make the whole of the Middle East almost untenable and would entirely defeat the objects he thought the government had in view'.[33]

He asked the First Sea Lord if the opinions of the Chiefs of Staff had been sought by Eden as to 'whether a war at all was the right solution', Mountbatten replying that the Chiefs had not been asked. Keightley then unveiled to Mountbatten a revised plan based on a 'more or less legitimate war' against the Egyptian airforce which he thought might bring about the collapse of Egypt without the need for an opposed landing. Mountbatten agreed to 'back this idea to the hilt' against the current 'horrible' plan. The Chiefs of Staff discussed Keightley's proposal but Templer opposed it on the grounds that he doubted the feasibility of an air offence alone working. Mountbatten 'spoke out very strongly' and made the case for providing greater governmental flexibility, continuing to advocate the new idea, lobbying both Monckton and Hailsham and eventually the Chiefs of Staff agreed to recommend the alternative 'as being more feasible, less brutal and giving the government greater flexibility'.[34]

The key meeting took place on Friday 7 September with the Prime Minister, Monckton, Keightley and the Chiefs of Staff present. Mountbatten asked Eden whether he would 'care to hear any political views from the Chiefs of Staff'. To Mountbatten's surprise Eden gave him full rein and he then 'held forth'. Mountbatten emphasised the extent of likely civilian casualties if the existing plan were to be put into effect, noting Eden's surprise at the extent of the problem. Mountbatten went on to paint a dramatic picture of two to three days bombing and heavy bombardment by six-inch gun cruisers and the 15-inch guns of the French battleship, *Jean Bart*. He made it clear that before the first marines or parachutists had arrived terrific casualties would have been inflicted. He 'presumed that we were sure to be taken before the United Nations by Egypt', as the 'full horror' would have been revealed by the photographs of war correspondents or Egyptian propaganda. Mountbatten estimated that the present plan involved the minimum of two and possibly three months before the Canal Zone would be taken. Eden seemed quite incredulous at this, but the aggressive Templer supported Mountbatten's pessimistic assessment. Eden said that he had been under the impression that British forces could be in Cairo within five days, but Mountbatten replied that would only be so 'if we could motor up the desert road without opposition'. He warned that if the Egyptian Army fought it would take 23 days to get to Cairo alone. The Prime Minister claimed that 'the Egyptians were yellow and would crumble immediately' but Mountbatten cited the example of the police barracks incident in 1952 when Egyptian police had held out against British Centurion tanks, although the Prime Minister said that this was an 'exceptional case'. Mountbatten then carried on in a style which was distinctively his:

> I then tried to point out that every Egyptian must now feel that they had got rid of the British occupation, that they were free and liberated and that their country was worth fighting for. In the case of the Egyptian army fighting badly against Israel, this I thought was because they had suddenly discovered that the contractors had been corrupt and so had their senior officers. They had neither the right munitions nor the right leadership and felt it was useless to carry on the fight.[35]

Keightley agreed with Mountbatten's assessment of the Egyptians' resolve and Eden was impressed by the unity of the military view he was receiving.

At the Cabinet meeting which was to follow that afternoon Operation MUSKETEER (REVISE) was conceived, Eden using many of the arguments that Mountbatten had so eloquently put forward.[36] The Egypt Committee had before them a memorandum by the Minister of Defence in which the implications of postponing Operation MUSKETEER and a plan for a possible alternative operation were presented.[37] Before the meeting Mountbatten had briefed Hailsham on what he had done and the First Lord had congratulated him on his courage and for saving him 'from a very embarrassing situation'. After the Cabinet decision Hailsham wrote a note of thanks to Mountbatten and in a 'scrambled' telephone conversation Mountbatten records that 'he could not thank me enough for what had been achieved'.[38]

The 7 September meeting was probably Mountbatten's finest hour in the entire Suez affair. Without his strong personal commitment to abandoning the operation in its original form it is possible that Eden's enthusiasm would have carried the Chiefs of Staff along the path of a major attack on Alexandria with all of its potentially disastrous consequences.

As the Chiefs of Staff discussed the new plan and its implications Mountbatten returned to his theme of the need for a long-term policy. At meetings on the 18 and 25 September, Mountbatten pressed for a thorough examination of the long-term commitment of British forces in Egypt in the event of Nasser's capitulation.[39] Writing directly to the Chairman of the Chiefs of Staff on 27 September, Mountbatten suggested that 'I did not think you intended to exclude the investigation on the actual military commitment in Egypt and the Middle East generally after capitulation... I hope you will be able to remove the limitations on the JPS paper implied in the present minute.'[40] When the Joint Planning Staff presented their report on 9 October on 'Problems of Military Occupation and International Control of the Suez Canal Area', Mountbatten stressed that it 'was essential to put clearly before ministers the consequences of undertaking Operation MUSKETEER REVISE. This might involve the occupation of Egypt or at least of the Canal Zone for a considerable period. Any new government in Egypt could probably remain in power only so long as some form of occupation continued.'[41]

The joint planners were sent back to work to produce a report on the military implications of mounting Operation MUSKETEER REVISE which they presented on 24 October.[42] This spelled out the dire consequences for British forces of the proposed action which would require a land force of three to four divisions and Naval and Air Force units, with civilian and administrative support. These commitments would result in 'our consequent inability to meet other possible commitments involving land forces except at the expense of our contribution to NATO' and would also require the retention of national service at its current level in the British army, the prolonged retention of reservists and the indefinite withdrawal of at least one infantry division from Germany. When this was discussed by the

Chiefs of Staff the following day Ziegler claims that it was 'at Mountbatten's insistence' that the Chiefs included the statement that 'we should endeavour to gain Egyptian co-operation by avoiding occupation or by restricting it to the minimum'.[43] This document was presented to the Egypt Committee the following day, but was angrily rejected by Eden who directed that it should be withdrawn as it was inappropriately political.[44]

Mountbatten did not let his deep opposition to the concept of Suez interfere with his professional judgement. The best example of this was when Eden instructed that there was to be no naval bombardment of Port Said. Admiral Sir Guy Grantham, Naval Commander in Chief Mediterranean, was horrified by this and flew to London to consult Mountbatten. The First Sea Lord took Grantham before the Chiefs of Staff who decided that he should see Eden personally. Grantham persuaded the Prime Minister that some bombardment was essential and that 'the operation could not be jeopardised by any absolute bans against the use of whatever force might be required.[45] Given Mountbatten's earlier campaign against bombardment of civilian areas it is particularly noteworthy that he should have supported the Admiral in this matter. His naval officer instincts rebelled against the prospect of the heavy landing-force casualties that might be inflicted by beach defences untroubled by covering fire. Grantham had mentioned the precedent of the Dieppe raid in 1942, one that had particular salience for Mountbatten himself. His association with this costly failure as Chief of Combined Operations had been one of the longstanding blemishes on his career.

The First Sea Lord also used this opportunity to test out one of his pet projects. He had introduced to the Naval Staff the idea of converting some light fleet carriers to carry commandos to be landed by helicopter. This had been opposed by the Staff on the grounds that it would be a misuse of the ships. When he pointed out that there were insufficient aircraft for the available carriers the Staff argued that it was preferable to use their ships companies to man gun-armed cruisers. The Suez Crisis allowed Mountbatten to raise this concept again and HMS *Ocean* and HMS *Theseus* were rapidly converted for the helicopter landing role. Mountbatten 'managed to scrounge' the helicopters of the Joint Experimental Helicopter Unit (JEHU) together with the Fleet Air Arm's first anti-submarine warfare helicopters to provide the necessary air groups.[46]

The final crisis for Mountbatten occurred in early November as the operation was about to begin. The First Sea Lord had taken refuge in the belief that MUSKETEER REVISE, which provided for preliminary bombing of Egyptian military defences, might prevent the necessity for a landing against serious opposition. Eden, however, was insisting that landings take place at the earliest opportunity. The Egyptians were dug in ready to resist. On 2 November the UN General Assembly called for a cease-fire, making the negative political impact of the landings, still three to four days away, only too clear. Mountbatten now wrote to Eden without asking for permission from his immediate superiors. The hand-written note is worth quoting in full:

> My dear Prime Minister, I know that you have been fully aware over these past few weeks of my great unhappiness at the prospect of our launching military operations against Egypt; and, indeed, as recently as Thursday of last week, after your dinner to the Gruenthers, you told Edwina and me that you realised how much I hated making the preparations which had been ordered.
>
> It is not the business of a serving officer to question the political decisions of his government; and although I did not believe that a just and lasting settlement of any dispute could be worked out under a threat of military action, I did everything in my power to carry out your orders, as in duty bound, loyally and to the full, in working out the necessary naval preparations for building a position in which we could have negotiated from strength. Now, however the decisive step of armed intervention by the British has been taken; bombing has started and the assault convoy is on its way from Malta.
>
> I am writing to appeal to you to accept the resolution of the overwhelming majority of the United Nations to cease military operations, and to beg you to turn back the assault convoy before it is too late, as I feel that the actual landing of troops can only spread the war with untold misery and world-wide repercussions. You can imagine how hard it is for me to break all service custom and write direct to you in this way, but I feel so desperate about what is happening that my conscience would not allow me to do otherwise. Yours Ever, Dickie[47]

Eden replied on the scrambler telephone and according to Mountbatten 'he thanked me profusely for being such a good friend as to write and tell him freely what I really thought. When I begged him to act on my suggestion and allow me to turn back the assault convoy before it was too late he replied he could not possibly do that and hung up the telephone.'[48]

Early on 3 November a signal arrived from Keightley informing the Chiefs of Staff that he was expecting considerable resistance from newly discovered defences. He laid out three alternative courses of action, continuing with the Port Said operation with an adjusted support fire plan; continuing with the bombing for the full 14 days or moving the landings to Gaza. Mountbatten pressed for the Gaza option and suggested a possible additional alternative landing site at Haifa. He was, however, overruled and Port Said it was to be.[49] Mountbatten continued to be concerned about the prospect of civilian casualties and on 4 November wrote to Hailsham, reporting the contents of the letter he had written to Eden four days before:

> He (Eden) spoke to me on the telephone to thank me for my letter; he said he fully understood my feelings but was not prepared to turn back the assault convoy. He pointed out that operations had been directed only against military targets and that no civilians had been killed. The situation is now, however, worse in that General Keightley has telegraphed that any chances of easy entry into Port Said are removed. Though I realise as a result of this telegram that everything is being done, within the limits of the current plan, to lessen civilian casualties, I must make it clear that in my view such casualties cannot be avoided and it must in the main fall to the navy to inflict them.
>
> However repugnant the task the Navy will carry out its orders. Nevertheless as its professional head I must register the strongest possible protest at this use of my service; and would ask you as the responsible minister to convey that protest to the Prime Minister. I recognise that a serving officer cannot back his protest by resignation at a time like this, so I must ask you to handle this whole matter on behalf of the Navy. Bearing in mind all the implications, I must ask you after consulting the Prime Minister to give me the order to stay or to go.[50]

Whether Mountbatten expected the acceptance of his resignation is doubtful. He states in his record of events written in the 1960s: 'I fully expected to be released from my job with such a tough letter.'[51]

However, on reflection it would seem unlikely that any government would accept the resignation of such a prominent senior officer at a time when the armed forces of the Crown were about to go into battle. Hailsham wrote to the First Sea Lord on 5 November thanking him for his letter and the information about his correspondence with Eden. He reassured Mountbatten that:

> I think you are well entitled to entrust your doubts, difficulties and protests to me, as the responsible minister. It seems to me that the position is quite plain. If anything happens to impair the honour of the Navy I must resign. In the meantime you are entitled to be protected by a direct order from me. It is that you remain at your post until further orders. I will do my best to comply to your request that the Prime Minister is acquainted with your views as soon as possible.[52]

Hailsham's letter, accompanied by a hand-written covering note, was sent to the Prime Minister asking him to confirm his action, with the significant conclusion that 'I think it would be disastrous to relieve him now which is the only other possible course'.[53] Eden replied that he had not shown Hailsham Mountbatten's letter because it seemed to be 'an entirely personal one'. He enclosed a copy and supported the First Lord's actions. 'I think you were right to reply to him as you did and I certainly confirm your action.'[54] Although this document has the appearance of a personal note it is significant that it appears in the Prime Minister's file alongside a top secret minute noting that 'the paper about the First Sea Lord' had been shown to the Cabinet Secretary, Sir Norman Brook, who felt that it would 'serve very well'.[55] Mountbatten was soon to be relieved from the dilemmas of the Suez campaign. Given significant international pressure[56] the British government was forced to accept the conclusions of the Joint Planners that British interests could not be served other than by remaining 'in our present position until we can hand over to a UNO force'.[57]

Mountbatten's opposition to British policy over Suez was motivated by moral and political considerations as much as by Service and strategic interests. He took very seriously his position with regard to the Royal Family, the political elite and as a serving officer and in light of this it seems true to suggest that Mountbatten pushed his opposition to MUSKETEER as far as he reasonably could. It is probable that in his heart of hearts he did not want to step down as First Sea

113

Lord. He had been deeply affected as a boy by his own father's resignation from that post, and a man so concerned with status and rank as Mountbatten clearly must have been highly motivated to achieve and retain the status of First Sea Lord, the pinnacle of his profession and a post to which he had strong emotional ties.

Given this motivation, however, it is equally clear that Mountbatten was strongly moved by his political understanding of the Suez situation, an understanding formed by his close relationship with British and Indian political elites, and by a personal and professional moral code which, in his unique position, he was able to give expression to in both the political and military arena. That Mountbatten retained his post as First Sea Lord was of great significance to the future of the Navy, particularly in view of the Duncan Sandys Defence Review of 1957–58. It is probable that only a man with Mountbatten's political skills and privileged position could have mounted such an effective defence of the Royal Navy's interests during that difficult period.[58]

NOTES

1. Broadlands Archive (BA), Mountbatten Papers, N106(3), 'File on the Suez Affair of 1956', 1965, p.1.
2. Ibid.
3. Ibid.
4. Mountbatten Papers, 'File on the Suez Affair of 1956', p.1.
5. Mountbatten Papers, N106(3), 'First Sea Lord's Part in the Suez Crisis', Paper A, 1956, p.7.
6. P. Ziegler, *Mountbatten* (London: Collins, 1985), p.537.
7. Mountbatten Papers, 'First Sea Lord's Part…', pp.1–2.
8. Mountbatten Papers, N106(5), 'Draft letter to the Prime Minister,' Annex 1, 1 Aug. 1956.
9. Mountbatten Papers, 'File on the Suez Affair of 1956', p.2.
10. Mountbatten Papers, 'First Sea Lord's Part…', pp.5–6
11. Ibid.
12. Ibid., p.6.
13. Mountbatten Papers, N106(39), copy of Mountbatten's original letter of resignation, 20 Aug. 1956.
14. Mountbatten Papers, 'File on the Suez Affair of 1956', p.2
15. Mountbatten Papers, N106(40), note from First Lord of the Admiralty, Viscount Cilcennin.
16. J.D. Brown, 'Mountbatten as First Sea Lord', *RUSI Journal*, June 1986, p.64.

17. Mountbatten Papers, N106(9),Vice Chief of Naval Staff to First Sea Lord, 20 Nov. 1956.
18. Ziegler, *Mountbatten*, p.542.
19. Mountbatten Papers, 'First Sea Lord's Part…', p.8.
20. Mountbatten Papers, 'File on the Suez Affair of 1956', p.2.
21. Mountbatten Papers, SS149, Letter to Countess Mountbatten, 5 Aug. 1956.
22. DEFE 4/89, COS (56) 80th mtg, 14 Aug. 1956.
23. DEFE 4/89, COS (56) 82nd mtg, 21 Aug. 1956; DEFE 4/89, COS (56) 83rd mtg, 23 Aug. 1956.
24. E.J. Grove, 'Mountbatten as Chief of Naval Staff', in Aspects of British Defence and Naval Policy in the Mountbatten Era (Unpublished), University of Southampton, 1992, p.23.
25. DEFE 4/89, COS (56) 83rd mtg, 23 Aug. 1956.
26. J. Cloake, *Templer: Tiger of Malaya* (London: Harrap, 1985), pp.347–8.
27. Mountbatten Papers, 'File on the Suez Affair of 1956', p.3.
28. Ziegler, *Mountbatten*, p.539.
29. Mountbatten Papers, 'First Sea Lord's Part…', p.8.
30. Mountbatten Papers, 'First Sea Lord's Part…', p.10.
31. Mountbatten Papers, 'First Sea Lord's Part…', pp.10–11.
32. K. Kyle, *Suez* (London: Weidenfeld & Nicolson, 1991), p.235, argues that Hailsham's personal fears about bombardment stemmed from his contact with Monitors (specialised coastal bombardment vessels) during the Second World War: 'The destruction they could cause was massive and its description had been so vivid that it had remained with him.' Hailsham is reported as having told William Clark: 'There is one thing in this that I simply cannot stomach and that is the bombardment from the sea by the British fleet of the open city of Alexandria.'
33. Mountbatten Papers, 'First Sea Lord's Part…', p.12.
34. Mountbatten Papers, 'First Sea Lord's Part…', p.13.
35. Mountbatten Papers, 'First Sea Lord's Part…', pp.14–15.
36. PREM 11/1104, EC (56) 25th mtg, 7 Sept. 1956.
37. PREM 11/1104, EC (56) 43, 7 Sept. 1956.
38. Mountbatten Papers, 'First Sea Lord's Part…', p.15.
39. DEFE 4/90, COS (56) 94th, 18 Sept. 1956; and COS (56) 95th mtg, 25 Sept. 1956; Mountbatten Papers, N106(10–7).
40. Mountbatten Papers, N106 (10–8) 'Letter from First Sea Lord to Chairman', COS Committee, 27 Sept. 1956.
41. DEFE 4/91, COS (56) 97th mtg, 9 Oct. 1956.
42. DEFE 6/37, JP (56) 160 Final, 24 Oct. 1956.
43. Ziegler, *Mountbatten*, p.543; DEFE 4/91, COS(56) 105th mtg, 25 Oct. 1956. The amended paper changed the original introductory remark: 'A prolonged British occupation of Egypt is likely to require the following forces' and replaced it with the words: 'We should endeavour to gain Egyptian co-operation by avoiding occupation or by restricting it to the minimum. Should a prolonged occupation be necessary, it is likely to require the following forces.' See Mountbatten Papers, N106 (10–11).
44. PREM 11/1104, EC (56) 63, 26th Oct. 1956.
45. Kyle, *Suez*, p.375.
46. E.J. Grove, *Vanguard to Trident* (London: Bodley Head, 1987), pp.189–90.
47. PREM 11/90, Mountbatten to Eden, 2 Nov. 1956.

48. Mountbatten Papers, 'File on the Suez Affair of 1956', p.3.

49. Mountbatten Papers, 'Naval Responsibility for Inflicting Civilian Casualties'.

50. PREM 11/1090, copy of letter from First Sea Lord to First Lord, 4 Nov. 1956.

51. Mountbatten Papers, 'File on the Suez Affair', p.3.

52. PREM 11/1090, First Lord to First Sea Lord, 5 Nov. 1956.

53. PREM 11/1090, First Lord to Eden, 5 Nov. 1956.

54. PREM 11/1090, Eden to First Lord, 5 Nov. 1956.

55. PREM 11/1090, undated minute.

56. Mountbatten was to raise the issue of the presence of the 6th Fleet in the area of operations on a number of occasions. This demonstrated not only a significant military problem, but also the strength of opposition of Britain's most important ally. See DEFE 4/91, COS(56) 108th mtg, 1 Nov. 1956; 109th mtg, 2 Nov. 1956; and 111th mtg, 5 Nov. 1956. It was recorded at the 111th Meeting that Mountbatten said: 'The presence of the 6th Fleet in its present position was a continual nuisance to our naval and air operations. The United States Commander had been asked if he could move but had replied that he had taken up his position on direct orders from his Government.'

57. 'The expressed British aim for the current operation has been to separate Egyptian and Israeli forces and to ensure the security of the Suez Canal. Tacit aims have been to impose a satisfactory settlement of the Suez canal dispute with Egypt and to effect the downfall of Nasser... It is clear that we can no longer achieve our tacit aims...except by renewing fighting and thus flouting the United Nations resolutions with the added danger of bringing about Russian intervention.' DEFE 6/37, JP(56) 175 (F), 7 Nov. 1956.

58. Grove, 'Mountbatten as Chief of Naval Staff' (1992).

The Missing Link?
Patrick Dean, Chairman of the
Joint Intelligence Committee

W. SCOTT LUCAS

In his long diplomatic career, Patrick Dean was a Foreign Office adviser at the Nuremberg trials, head of the German Political Department, Permanent Representative to the United Nations and finally ambassador to the United States. Yet he will forever be remembered for a brief moment in the Suez Crisis. It was Dean who accompanied Donald Logan, the Private Secretary to Foreign Secretary Selwyn Lloyd, to the second Sèvres meeting with French and Israeli officials on 24 October 1956. At that secret encounter, Britain, France and Israel agreed to the collusion that launched the Suez War with Egypt.

This memory of Dean is misleading, not because of his later exploits in Washington, but because it distracts us from his real significance during Suez. His role was not that of an emergency envoy but of an essential liaison. Sometimes he fulfilled his nominal duties as Superintending Under-Secretary of the Permanent Under-Secretary's Department and Chairman of the Joint Intelligence Committee to link the Foreign Office, the military and MI6; sometimes official channels were bypassed as Dean passed *ad hoc* communications between Prime Minister Anthony Eden and the intelligence services. Patrick Dean's story is the core of a much broader and much more significant tale of a British system which was so chaotic and disjointed that it produced not one but several contradictory foreign policies.

Until mid-1956, Patrick Dean had enjoyed a steady but unspectacular rise up the Foreign Office ladder, with the reward of an appointment as Assistant Under-Secretary in 1953. The importance of the promotion lay not just in the title but in Dean's duties, for he would oversee the work of the Permanent Under-Secretary's Department. The PUSD, created in 1948 as part of a dramatic reorganisation of British machinery for foreign policy, has received little attention from historians, primarily because of the government's success in withholding most of its files from declassification. Its anonymity has concealed its vital role. The PUSD was the 'home' for the Permanent Under-Secretary's Committee, loosely modelled on the State Department's Policy Planning Staff, which carried out medium- and long-term planning. It also sheltered the Joint Intelligence Committee, the interdepartmental body reviewing developments and British operations.

As the supervising official of the PUSD and the effective link between the Foreign Office and MI6, Dean had a position of unique importance in covert activities. It was he who accompanied MI6 officials to Washington in February 1953 to discuss how to overthrow the Mossadeq government in Iran, the opening of months of negotiations and operations that would result in a coup in August.[1] Dean also was able to maintain his position while others in the covert network lost theirs. In spring 1956, a failure in communication meant that the PUSD's liaison with MI6 did not inform his superiors of a plan to spy on the ship, the *Ordzhonikidze*, carrying Soviet leaders Georgi Bulganin and Nikita Khrushchev to Britain. The plan went awry with the decapitation of the frogman Buster Crabb and a formal Soviet complaint to the British government. In the aftermath, not only the PUSD liaison but also the head of MI6 was replaced.

Nasser's nationalisation of the Suez Canal Company in July offered the PUSD the opportunity for redemption. Four months earlier, the Eden Cabinet had authorised the 'isolation' of the Nasser regime through Project OMEGA with political and economic measures, propaganda and support for rival Middle Eastern governments. At the same time, MI6 was pursuing more radical projects not only to assassinate or overthrow Nasser but also to topple the Syrian and Saudi governments.[2]

Thus, in the weeks after the nationalisation, a new structure, ranging from the working-level Egypt (Official) Committee and the Defence Transition Committee to the Ministerial 'War Cabinet' – the Egypt Committee – was superimposed on the existing network.[3] At the centre was Dean. Not only did his chairmanship of the Joint Intelligence Committee ensure that he knew much of the information passed to both old and new committees, but as the 'line manager' for the liaison between the PUSD and MI6, he was nominally aware of operational developments.

The problem for Dean was that the system worked in theory rather than practice. There was no assurance that a member agency would provide the Joint Intelligence Committee with relevant information, nor could one assume that the Foreign Office was notified of pertinent MI6 operations. In the case of Egypt, the outcome was chaos. MI6, believing that the Foreign Office was 'soft' on Nasser, was diligently pursuing its own agenda. They widely disseminated information from an agent, codenamed LUCKY BREAK, who was allegedly within Nasser's inner circle. According to the source, Nasser, supported by the Soviet Union, was bent on establishing personal hegemony over the Middle East. William Clark, Eden's Press Secretary, recorded LUCKY BREAK's impact: 'It is clear that Nasser has gone further than I'd ever supposed towards a tie-up with the Communists.'[4] On one occasion, Eden transmitted information to US President Dwight Eisenhower, based on LUCKY BREAK's 'intelligence', that Nasser intended to overthrow the monarchies of Iraq, Jordan and Libya, remove King Saud from power in Saudi Arabia, and establish 'purely Arab republics' in Tunisia, Algeria and Morocco.[5] There is no evidence, however, that LUCKY BREAK existed outside the creative imaginations of MI6 officers who wanted more aggressive operations against Egypt.

MI6's impact was even more dramatic when they told CIA representatives, in London to negotiate OMEGA, of their wishes to overthrow several Middle Eastern regimes, working with Israel if necessary. US Secretary of State John Foster Dulles complained to colleagues, 'The British are making more drastic plans than we are.' The CIA's station chief in Cairo was so disturbed that he allegedly told Egyptian contacts about British intentions.[6]

On this occasion the Foreign Office, conveying to Ministers the priority for Anglo-American co-operation, was able to restrain MI6 and return to OMEGA. They faced another obstacle, however, in the quick temper of Eden. The Prime Minister once rang Minister of State Anthony Nutting at the Savoy on an open telephone line and demanded, 'I want Nasser murdered, don't you understand?'[7] Uttered to the Foreign Office, such statements could be dismissed as hysterics; uttered to MI6 contacts, they fed the intelligence service's propensity for assassination plans.[8]

What then was Dean's place in this tangled bureaucracy? Dean himself was scrupulously faithful to the Official Secrets Act, giving away little about his role. In an interview in 1989, he claimed 'no special knowledge about what turned out to be the events' in Suez.[9] A memorandum prepared for other enquirers was devoted to Sèvres, ignoring Dean's far more significant work before and after that meeting. Dean offered the inaccurate dismissal:

> In the months following the seizure of the Suez Canal by Nasser I was generally aware that a great deal of detailed planning of various sorts for the recovery of the Suez Canal was going forward within the Ministry of Defence and that the Eastern Department and the P.U.S. Department were concerned. I cannot now remember very much about the details, with which I was never closely concerned, although I do remember hearing about possible plans for the use of Cyprus as a staging point.[10]

On the rare occasion when a historian tried to publish an account of Dean's work with the PUSD, the former Ambassador was especially reticent.[11] Thus there was no accurate portrayal: Dean's version is correct only to the extent that he was not a visible presence in British policymaking and operations. Only three officials in the Foreign Office were to be informed of all intelligence and planning: Permanent Under-Secretary Sir Ivone Kirkpatrick, Dean and Dean's deputy, Geoffrey McDermott.[12]

In the aftermath of Nasser's nationalisation of the Suez Canal Company, Dean's first task was to arrange the terms of co-operation with the French. British ministers and civil servants had long been fearful about 'lapses' in French security, a fear compounded by tension between London and Paris over France's policies in North Africa and aspirations for a greater presence in the Middle East. Thus, Dean was despatched to Paris to receive assurances about French reliability from Prime Minister Guy Mollet and Foreign Minister Christian Pineau.[13]

As the government focused upon a military response, Dean then allegedly went on vacation. By the time of his return to Whitehall in September, the situation had changed radically. Protracted negotiations over the future of the Canal and problems with military preparations had provoked elements in London to return to covert planning to overthrow Nasser. MI6 officials and Julian Amery, a Conservative MP and the son-in-law of Chancellor of the Exchequer

Harold Macmillan, met a 'shadow' Egyptian government of dissident military officers and politicians. Their agreement to create a suitable pretext for an uprising led to the significant change in British military plans from a large-scale ground assault to a campaign of bombing and propaganda.[14]

Dean, meanwhile, had been given an unexpected, if welcome, double promotion from Assistant Under-Secretary to Deputy Under-Secretary. The meteoric rise owed less to Dean's merits than it did to his sensitive position between the Prime Minister, the Foreign Office and MI6. It would be rather unseemly for a Grade 4 Assistant Under-Secretary to handle 'need to know' information about the schemes to remove Nasser from power.

Dean may not have been the channel for transmission of MI6 plans to other agencies. In the most notable case, the MI6 programme for aerial and psychological action to destabilise Nasser was 'converted' into a military scheme and its provenance obscured, probably by Brigadier Bernard Fergusson, in charge of the military's psychological warfare. Dean's importance seems to have been as an *ad hoc* liaison between MI6 and Eden. As Archibald Ross, Assistant Secretary of State during Suez, noted:

> As things began to hot up, [Eden] did take Dean over as his Foreign Office man... As the crisis developed and decisions became more and more crucial, it was not so much the Foreign Office submitting advice as Eden using a member of the Foreign Office to do what he thought had to be done.[15]

Dean's presence gave the Prime Minister the opportunity to bypass a Foreign Office he found troublesome. With Eden treating the channel as one of informal communication, Dean did not necessarily inform his superior, Kirkpatrick. The result was that Kirkpatrick, one of the most 'hawkish' officials for action against Nasser, did not know how far covert plans had progressed. Similarly, Foreign Secretary Lloyd, who increasingly turned towards a negotiated solution for the crisis, did not realise that he was being undercut by the unofficial links.

Dean's importance was underlined by a top-secret mission he undertook in Washington. Anglo-American planning over OMEGA had continued into the autumn, with US officials hoping that London would eschew military action in favour of covert operations to undermine Nasser. In early October, Dean led a British delegation, which also included MI6's George Young and psychological warfare specialist Ralph Murray, into talks with the CIA and the State Department. Top priority was final approval of a plan to overthrow the Syrian government.[16] (Asked about the mission 35 years later, Dean nonchalantly denied all knowledge. Asked about the plan for Syria, he replied, 'That's news to me.'[17])

The ultimate irony was that Dean, having bypassed his superiors, would find his own position sabotaged by the collusion with Israel. Apparently the official who had risen through his access to and channelling of secret information never knew of the French approach to Eden on 14 October proposing a tripartite assault upon Egypt. According to Dean's memorandum, 'I never heard of any plans which involved joint plans or discussions with either the French or the Israelis and I have no reason to believe that there were any,' an assertion seconded by the other envoy to Sèvres, Donald Logan.[18]

Like other officials such as Kirkpatrick who had favoured Nasser's downfall, Dean was distressed by the decision to work with the Israelis to accomplish the task. In particular, he was concerned about the effect on Anglo-American co-operation. Dean was among the few in Whitehall who knew of the agreement with the US to sponsor a coup in Syria, and he recognised, unlike Eden and his Ministers, that the Americans would believe that collusion with Israel would undermine rather than enhance Middle Eastern operations.

Dean's involvement immediately led to diplomatic farce, with the official torn between loyalty to the Prime Minister and disquiet with the arrangements. On the evening of 24 October, Dean was to host a dinner for Frank Wisner, the CIA's head of covert operations. At the last minute, Wisner was informed that Dean would be unavailable. Of course Wisner, whose agency was unaware of any contact between Britain, France and Israel, had no idea that the cancellation was due to Dean's sudden trip to Sèvres.[19] Four days later, the CIA liaison in London, Chester Cooper, picnicked with Dean: 'Dean just had apparently difficult session with Lloyd. Very tense. Pressed him for reason – Hungary? Middle East? Dean replied, "You and I are in for much trouble, and it isn't because of Hungary."'[20]

Ironically, though, the catastrophe of Suez turned into a personal triumph for Dean. Many in Whitehall lost political careers or influence, some such as Anthony Nutting for objecting to the collusion, others like MI6's George Young for being too aggressive in trying to eliminate Nasser. Dean, however, was rewarded for his loyalty and discretion. When Dean joined the British delegation to the Bermuda summit in March 1957, a US intelligence assessment noted:

> Perhaps the most interesting personality of [officials in the Foreign Office] is Dean, whose rise in the Foreign Service has been meteoric... In his present position he is the principal adviser to the Foreign Minister on intelligence developments (particularly concerning defence and military matters and atomic energy), and he is also a major operating head of an important part of British information-collecting activities and operations.[21]

From his domain over PUSD, Dean was instrumental in the post-Suez reorganisation of the Foreign Office. Increased emphasis was placed on the 'new' threats in the Middle East rather than the menace of Soviet Communism. For example, the Information Research Department, the co-ordinating organisation in the Foreign Office for covert propaganda, was split into two sections with one solely responsible for the Middle East. (Dean never would confirm that he supervised the work of the Information Research Department, offering only 'Maybe' to enquiries.[22]) The payoff for Dean was his despatch to New York as Permanent Representative to the United Nations and then to Washington as Ambassador. One prize eluded him, however, possibly because of the Suez legacy. He never ascended to the peak of career service in the Foreign Office, the post of Permanent Under-Secretary.

In the end, frustratingly little can be said about Patrick Dean. He wrote no memoirs, gave few interviews and, to my knowledge, left no private papers for others to consult. Because he did not have the temperamental personality of an Ivone Kirkpatrick, he did not provoke many recollections from former colleagues. Unlike other Ambassadors to the US, such as Oliver Franks, he never moved beyond the Foreign Office to head royal commissions that would gain public prominence. So Dean's story remains a tale of post-war British policymaking. He was an 'organisation man' in an organisation which had gone awry. All bureaucracies are riddled with intrigue and mishap but, resting on informal connections and impromptu communications, the British system was especially susceptible to confusion and 'maverick' activity. Not only was there more than one policy during Suez, but MI6's persistence, if not its judgement, finally gave it a fatal influence leading to the debacle of November 1956.

Without men like Patrick Dean, the British system would have collapsed. Whatever his misgivings about the chaotic conditions that made policy in the Eden government – the Prime Minister's temper, Harold Macmillan's deviousness, MI6's outrageous schemes – he never shirked his role as formal or informal liaison. Although he was uneasy about collusion, he did not consider resignation or even protest to other officials. In fact, he later claimed that he perceived no 'sense of betrayal' by Foreign Office staff despite the near-revolt by junior officials after the Anglo-French invasion of Egypt.[23]

Irrespective of the merits of loyalty, Dean's attitude was counter-productive in the long run. By propping up the shaky structure for policymaking, he contributed to the muddle that allowed MI6 to operate outside 'official' policy. It is not significant whether or not Dean knew of collusion before he was despatched to Sèvres; his complicity lies not in his knowledge of Anglo-Israeli co-operation but in his knowledge of the Whitehall intrigues that sabotaged British operations before and after the Sèvres agreement. Unseen and unknown, he, as much as an Anthony Eden or a Harold Macmillan, contributed to the failure of Suez.

NOTES

1. C. Woodhouse, *Something Ventured* (London: Granada, 1982), p.123; K. Roosevelt, *Countercoup* (New York: McGraw Hill, 1979), p.120.
2. See W.S. Lucas, *Divided We Stand: Britain, the US, and the Suez Crisis* (London: Hodder & Stoughton, 1991), pp.93–103.
3. Both the Egypt Committee and the Egypt Official Committee minutes can be found in the CAB 134 series.
4. Lucas, *Divided We Stand*, pp.116–17.
5. PREM 11/1177, Eden to Eisenhower, 15 March 1956.
6. W. Eveland, *Ropes of Sand* (London: W.W. Norton, 1980), pp.168 and 171; D. Neff, *Warriors at Suez* (Vermont: Amana, 1981), p.217.
7. A. Nutting, *No End of a Lesson* (London: Constable, 1967), p.34; Anthony Nutting interview, Channel 4 Television, *End of Empire: Egypt*, 1985.
8. See P. Wright, *Spycatcher* (London: Viking, 1987), p.160. On another occasion, Eden asked a former CIA officer, Miles Copeland, to kill Nasser by shooting him or putting poison in his coffee. *The Times*, 19 June 1975; author's interview with Miles Copeland.
9. Liddell Hart Centre for Military Archives, King's College London, Suez Oral History Collection (LHCMA), Patrick Dean interview.
10. Memorandum by Patrick Dean, 1988, copy in author's possession.
11. Passages on Dean in W.S. Lucas's *Divided We Stand* had to be altered. In particular,

Dean demanded that the author record his denial of ever being a channel between Eden and MI6. Dean letter to author, 26 April 1991.

12. G. McDermott, *The Eden Legacy* (London: Leslie Frewin, 1969), p.133.
13. PREM 11/1126, Jebb to Eden, 11 and 14 Aug. 1956.
14. LHCMA, Julian Amery interview.
15. LHCMA, Archibald Ross interview.
16. US National Archives, Department of State, Lot 59 D 518, Box 35, US–UK Working Group Meeting, Washington, 1–3 Oct. 1956; Rockwell to Wilkins, 28 Sept. 1956.
17. LHCMA, Patrick Dean interview.
18. LHCMA, Patrick Dean and Donald Logan interviews; memorandum by Patrick Dean, 1988, copy in author's possession; Donald Logan interview with author.
19. E. Thomas, *The Very Best Men: Four Who Dared. The Early Years of the CIA* (New York: 1995), p.143.
20. C. Cooper, *The Lion's Last Roar* (London: Harper and Row, 1978), p.159.
21. US National Archives, Department of State, Central Decimal File, 741.13/2–757, London to State Department, Despatch 1912, 7 Feb. 1957.
22. LHCMA, Patrick Dean interview.
23. LHCMA, Patrick Dean interview.

Cadogan's Last Fling:
Sir Alexander Cadogan, Chairman of the
Board of Governors of the BBC

TONY SHAW

Sir Alexander Cadogan's role during Suez highlights what many historians have noted as the curiously idiosyncratic nature of the crisis, with 'oddities of the moment' impacting onto events almost as much as underlying forces.[1] Having entered the Diplomatic Service in 1908, Cadogan had risen to become one of the most distinguished civil servants of his generation, culminating in his appointment as Permanent Under-Secretary at the Foreign Office in 1938, followed by that as Britain's first resident representative at the United Nations in 1946. His 'remarkable powers of judgement and lucid discretion' attracted the confidence of a succession of foreign secretaries and prime ministers. During the Second World War his administrative duties and performances at inter-allied conferences gave him what many saw as a unique knowledge of world affairs. 'No one else,' writes David Dilks, 'occupied a position in British government comparable with Cadogan's in the years 1938–1950.'[2] His retirement from the Foreign Office in that year would, nevertheless, appear to have ruled out the possibility of Cadogan playing a meaningful part in any future national crisis.

Yet coincidence, combined with the closed nature of the British establishment, came to place Cadogan in a uniquely wide-ranging position when the Suez Crisis erupted in the summer of 1956. During the dispute he operated in three different spheres. These were apparently autonomous, but would ultimately prove antagonistic. First, as Chairman since January 1956 of the Commonwealth–American Current Affairs Unit (an offshoot of the English-Speaking Union), Cadogan automatically had a role in the promotion of British interests to Commonwealth and, principally, American audiences during the crisis. Second, as a government director of the Suez Canal Company since 1951, he was privy to policy-making and diplomatic exchanges at the highest levels. Finally, his chairmanship since 1952 of the British Broadcasting Corporation's Board of Governors allowed Cadogan direct access to, and potential influence on, the mass media's coverage of the dispute.

Further complications arose from Cadogan's relationship with Eden. Since Eden's appointment of Cadogan as Deputy Under-Secretary at the Foreign Office in 1936, the two of them had developed strong bonds of mutual respect and friendship. Like Eden, Cadogan was scarred for life by the memories of Britain's inter-war appeasement policy; thereafter, he almost instinctively viewed international relations from the perspective of the 1930s and trusted Eden's judgement in foreign affairs implicitly. Significantly, the crisis in 1951 caused by Egypt's abrogation of the 1936 Anglo-Egyptian Treaty was seen by him as 'the manifestation of a very great and menacing...nationalist movement throughout Asia and Africa'.[3]

By 1956, Nasser had become the self-proclaimed leader of this movement. Consequently, when in July he acted according to many observers in a manner uncannily reminiscent of Hitler to threaten the world's most important international waterway, Cadogan's framework of reference was crystal clear. Eden's policy – including the use of force – should be supported and Nasser's expansionist ambitions checked, with Britain acting alone if necessary. Certainly, Cadogan felt that little assistance of any value could be expected from the United Nations, a conclusion he had reached following frustrating years working at the League of Nations and in New York. This was borne out by Cadogan's private reaction to Eden's announcement on 30 July 1956 that his government could not accept any solution to the dispute which left the Suez canal in the control of a single power: 'That is a good formula, and I only hope we are decided to take all measures necessary to assure it!'[4]

This contribution examines in turn each of Cadogan's roles during the Suez Crisis and explores the inherent conflict of interest between them. It is shown that Cadogan's overall impact on Suez lay more in the sphere of the presentation of government policy than in its actual formulation. While this by itself might not have shaped the course of events, it helps to shed light on the public dimensions of the crisis. It also raises wider questions relating to the scope for influence offered to those officials who were relative outsiders during the dispute, that is, without direct policy-making responsibility. Cadogan was at times more of a spectator than an active participant, illustrated most markedly by his fortnight's holiday in France at the end of August 1956 and his ignorance of many of the crisis's subtle aspects. The freedom to roam arguably offered its compensations, however, both for Cadogan personally and the British government.

The English-Speaking Union (ESU) had been founded by Sir Evelyn Wrench in 1918 to preserve the wartime understanding forged between Britain and the United States via inter-country cultural, literary and educational activities. Extended to the Commonwealth in the 1920s, 30 years later the privately-funded organisation had over 53,000 members worldwide promoting the cause of friendship via speaking exchanges, dinners and other non-sectarian, strictly non-propagandistic functions. In 1953, the Commonwealth–American Current Affairs Unit was established by the ESU to specialise in the dissemination (at home and overseas) of publications. It was also designed to complement the steadfastly long-term approach of its parent body by addressing those issues which from time to time affected relations between the countries concerned in a more pressing – even divisive – fashion.[5]

By appointing Cadogan as Chairman in January 1956, the unit hoped to raise its profile more generally and further enhance its connections in diplomatic and business circles. The ex-mandarin quickly showed his worth. Within a few months, he had written personally to the Foreign Secretary, Selwyn Lloyd, requesting the Prime Minister's help in sponsoring the financially weak unit. The positive response he received demonstrated both Cadogan's political weight and the importance which Whitehall ascribed to cultural diplomacy on the eve of Suez. While Lloyd praised the unit's 'excellent work in increasing a wider understanding of British foreign policy in the United States and vice-versa', Eden spoke of the 'value [that] HMG attach to this work, which helps to influence those who mould public opinion and to interest them in the affairs of our English-speaking partners.'[6]

Throughout the Suez Crisis the senior members of the Current Affairs Unit – Sir William Ridsdale, former head of the Foreign Office News Department, among them – met monthly as normal. Cadogan himself appears to have rated the unit as the least important of his three spheres of interest during the crisis, probably because it was furthest from the centre of events. Despite his relative inactivity, however, Cadogan and the unit proved to be of some assistance to the government as a discreet instrument of Commonwealth–American elite cultivation. By using its established channels to explain the thinking behind Eden's Middle Eastern policy to leading opinion-formers, the unit also contributed not insignificantly to the government's own propaganda campaign. This was particularly important as regards the United States, owing to its pivotal role during Suez, and the perceived influence of 'leading opinion' in the foreign policy-making process there.

Cadogan seems personally to have cared little for the Eisenhower administration's 'wobbly' policy in the summer of 1956 and shared Eden's view that Nasser's defeat was ultimately worth a temporary split with the United States. During the Second World War he had formed the impression of John Foster Dulles as 'the woolliest type of useless pontificating American', and no evidence suggests he had altered his opinion since. The output of the Current Affairs Unit, however, struck a more constructive line, emphasising the mutuality of Anglo-American interests and the need to act in unison. In August, it produced a revised background brief on Middle East problems and included a supplement giving the basic facts and figures on Suez 'which enable one to have a clearer understanding of the issues at stake'. The unit also worked in tandem with the ESU's magazine, *The English-Speaking World*, to publish in the United States articles, speeches and letters by non-political heavyweights setting out Britain's case for the defence. When a damage-limitation exercise was required in the aftermath of Operation MUSKETEER (REVISE), it disseminated material from luminaries who were trumpeting the notion of a more open and flexible Anglo-American alliance. Among these was the highly-respected former British Ambassador to Washington, Sir Oliver Franks.[7]

Given the direct link which Whitehall for years had drawn between American public opinion and the fulfillment of British interests, moves by the Foreign Office to influence the ESU's activities during Suez were inevitable. With Cadogan at the heart of the organisation, liaison was simply made that much easier. Cadogan (and Ridsdale) met Foreign Office information officials on several occasions to swap suggestions about publicity tactics. This enabled the Current

Affairs Unit to target particular groups of Americans – journalists, businessmen, the Jewish lobby and so on – with material similar in its anti-Nasser nature to that disseminated officially by the Foreign Office's American-based propaganda agency, British Information Services. This did not necessarily mean that the unit was reduced to a government adjunct. For instance, having been briefed in mid-August by Douglas Dodds-Parker, Parliamentary Under-Secretary at the Foreign Office and chief propaganda strategist during Suez, Cadogan departed more disaffected than enlightened. Dodds-Parker's techniques of persuasion appeared too clumsy to someone schooled for so long in the Foreign Office's traditionally passive, low-key approach.[8]

As for the overall effects of the ESU's efforts, these would appear to be minimal. The Current Affairs Unit was doubtless useful as an amplifier of British interests in the United States but, owing to its predominantly anglophile audience, this was largely a case of preaching to the converted. The ESU might have contributed to the relatively swift healing of Anglo-American relations in the wake of the crisis. However, given the debilitating public ructions which surfaced within the ESU itself over Eden's bungled operation, even this is open to debate. At one ESU meeting in early December, Cadogan himself rowed angrily with a speaker who was extolling the virtues of the UN. To him, that organisation's performance during Suez had been at best muddled, at worst scandalous.[9]

Cadogan had been one of the three government directors of the Suez Canal Company for five years when the Suez Crisis erupted. The others were ex-Indian civil servant Sir Francis Wylie and Lord Hankey, former cabinet secretary and a leading supporter of the politically-influential 'Suez Group', formed in 1952 mainly by Conservative backbenchers with the aim of preventing a policy of 'scuttle' from the Suez Canal Zone. The directors liaised regularly with the company's Management Committee and kept the London government informed of events through the head of the Foreign Office, to whom they were subordinate. It was this position which potentially offered Cadogan the opportunity to lend his vast diplomatic experience most directly to the central policy-making process during the Suez Crisis. This was illustrated within hours of Nasser's nationalisation when Eden's Private Secretary, Guy Millard, telephoned Cadogan to ask the whereabouts of Jacques Georges-Picot, the company's General Manager. Although Cadogan's offer to come to Downing Street himself instead was declined, he was informed of – and able to profer advice on – the meeting of ministers, officials and service chiefs being hastily arranged there.[10]

As has been well-documented[11] the Suez Canal Company itself played a relatively uninfluential role in the crisis as a whole despite its obvious centrality to events. Both the British and French governments decided almost immediately that Nasser's coup had utterly transformed the future operation of the Canal. The company's concession was due to expire in 1968 anyway, when everything was to revert to the Egyptians. Fighting to restore the company was therefore pointless; it made greater sense – politically and diplomatically – to promote, instead, management by a new international commission made up of the principal maritime powers, on which Egypt would be given 'suitable representation'. The result was that the company's officials were largely locked out of the key diplomatic exchanges from the very start of the crisis, much to the chagrin of Georges-Picot. The Eden government was particularly aware of the company's imperialist image overseas and therefore sought to distance itself publicly from the statements constantly emanating from the Rue d'Astorg.[12]

At the same time it was imperative for Eden that the usurped company should not rock the boat by contradicting government objectives or by precipitating crises which disrupted the Egypt Committee's delicate diplomatic–military schedule. Con-sequently, there were discreet meetings throughout the summer of 1956 between ministers, officials and company management. The British government directors complemented this direct contact by effectively acting as mediators between ministers and management, and working to present a united front publicly. Either working individually or collectively, the three appear to have played a prominent role in the handling of two particularly thorny issues: whether – and if so, when – the company's pilots should be withdrawn from the Canal, and how the nationalisation could be proven illegal.[13]

On hearing the nationalisation news on the night of 26 July, Eden's instinct led him to favour the mass resignation of the Suez Canal Company's non-Egyptian pilots. This was also the reaction of the company's senior management, the thinking being that Nasser would be confronted with an immediate and major crisis caused by his inability to operate the Canal safely. Ministers soon realised, however, that closing the Canal would disrupt oil supplies, which in turn jeopardised the military preparations. It was better therefore to wait until these were complete before forcing Nasser's hand. Having been briefed along these lines, Cadogan and Wylie were given the task of persuading the company's Board of Directors – many of whom were on the 'war path' – to accept Eden's case and instruct their employees to stay on for the time being at their posts. With help from the British commercial directors, they succeeded in doing this in early August.[14]

However, by the time the Cabinet took the decision in mid-September to sanction the withdrawal of the pilots, one of its last remaining disruptive tools, Cadogan's confidence in the government's tactics had clearly diminished. He still believed that force would eventually have to be used against Egypt, 'but we must be careful to keep ourselves, if possible, on the right side of the line, and it is well that our hotheads should not be given a free reign'. With the then failure to turn the pilots' evacuation into a *casus belli* via Operation PILEUP, which bundled shipping together at either end of the Canal in the (forlorn) hope of creating chaos, Cadogan's faith in the government's policy and his own role as company director ebbed further. During the second London conference in late September, he was 'quite bewildered as to what anybody's intentions might be'.[15]

While the Canal pilots were a source of anxiety and frustration for British ministers and officials during Suez, the legal debate surrounding the actual expropriation of the Suez Canal Company caused fundamental difficulties. Eden had initially regarded Nasser's act as a blatant breach of international law, only to be disabused of this by the Foreign Office's legal advisers who outlined the contractual complexities involved. If the British government were to use military force, however, it was essential that Nasser be branded a criminal, both in the technical and political sense. The upshot was a publicity campaign conducted by the Foreign Office aimed at establishing categorically the illegality of the Egyptian president's action. The Suez Canal Company played a significant part in this, encouraged by the British government directors and Selwyn Lloyd. Cadogan and his partners were well-positioned to ensure that the company's arguments dovetailed with the Foreign Office's, and to act as publicists themselves. Emotive charges, accompanied by detailed legal memoranda, were issued against Nasser for 'robbery', 'conscription of the foreign personnel' and even reviving 'the idea of living space'. These were combined with the publication of the company's plans for future development, drawn up so as to show that the Canal, so far from being capital-producing, was a capital-demanding asset. Nasser's plan to exploit the Canal's riches for the Aswan High Dam project was, in other words, a dangerous chimera.[16]

How persuasive these arguments were is debatable. Coming from the chief injured party in the dispute, it was inevitable that many people detected bias. Moreover, the Foreign Office itself, despite strenuous efforts, failed to produce what it viewed as an absolutely watertight case for illegality. The justification for any use of force suffered correspondingly.[17] In a more general sense, Cadogan reflected these misgivings and disquiet the longer the diplomatic phase of the crisis progressed. At the start of the dispute he had relished the chance to step back into his Foreign Office shoes via the company directorship and participate in negotiations at the highest levels. Remarks in his diary testify to the acute sense of duty he felt towards the government; 'in these times,' he wrote in mid-August, 'if one is asked to help in any way, one cannot refuse.' In his role as a company director, Cadogan in fact proved to be a useful source of information for ministers on the stance adopted by the potentially troublesome senior management. More importantly, perhaps, he helped to transmit to the management the need for patience and deference. As Georges-Picot put it, the three directors' interventions in the autumn of 1956 'showed they wanted to support their government's policy of discretion and thus keep the company from openly taking any position that was too sharply defined'.[18]

Cadogan's brief did not extend into the actual sphere of policy-making, however; nor did it afford him full inside knowledge of the Egypt Committee's secret objectives. As the crisis deteriorated, therefore, Cadogan grew increasingly pessimistic, with his partial access to information leading him to believe that the government might try something reckless. He was not close enough to the inner Cabinet, though, to be able to issue any warnings or advice. The result by mid-October 1956 was the similar feelings of impotence and confusion experienced by many of those officials who were involved far more centrally but found themselves increasingly, and ominously, circumvented. In Cadogan's opinion, Eden by this point faced the onerous choice between a UN-based compromise ('leading nowhere …except perhaps the abyss') and a military operation which failed to carry the majority of opinion. The likely outcome in both cases was 'a ghastly fiasco'.[19]

Had it been confined to the two areas already discussed, Cadogan's contribution to the Suez Crisis, while interesting, would not have been particularly noteworthy. Adding his third role to the equation, however, puts a different perspective on matters. As Chairman of the Commonwealth–American Current Affairs Unit and a director of the Suez Canal Company, Cadogan effectively had been free to follow his own diplomatic instincts during the Suez Crisis and act as a loyal supporter of Eden's cause. As Chairman of the BBC's Board of Governors, on the other hand, Cadogan was the head of an organisation obliged to approach such disputes as Suez, and current affairs generally, from a strictly impartial and objective viewpoint. This not only made his overall role more complex but also established a potential conflict of interests. It is not altogether clear whether Cadogan himself thought he was compromised. What is apparent is that it was his position at the BBC, outside Whitehall, which paradoxically brought him into closest contact with ministers during Suez and which was the role he took most seriously during the crisis.

Cadogan's appointment as BBC Chairman by Churchill in July 1952 had struck many observers as distinctly curious. As the first ex-civil servant to be chosen for the post, he aroused fears in some circles of the BBC becoming too 'official' – especially when that summer also saw the arrival of a new Director-General, Sir Ian Jacob, a former Assistant Military Secretary of the Cabinet. Moreover, Cadogan admitted to knowing nothing of broadcasting (he had never even seen a BBC television programme), and took a dim view of the journalistic profession. He had himself privately expressed doubts to Churchill about his lack of qualifications for the job. 'All you have to do is be fair,' the Prime Minister replied. 'And sensible, I suppose,' Cadogan added, with Churchill nodding assent. This combination of ignorance and a sense of propriety has given Cadogan the reputation as being a hands-off chairman, as one who deferred to those in the BBC who knew their area of speciality better. 'He had only rare contacts with those who produced the programmes, partly because he did not wish to undermine the position of the Director-General, partly on account of his horror at wasting others' time and his own,' writes David Dilks. 'He felt he did not know enough to offer useful advice'.[20] But the archival record – Cadogan's unpublished diary and BBC files – tells a rather different story. Cadogan in fact held strong views about the role of broadcasting, particularly in its coverage of politics, and the

Chairman's own powers within the BBC's hierarchy – both of which would have an impact on the Suez Crisis.

The chief function of the nine-strong Board of Governors, according to the BBC's constitution, was to act as the trustees of the public interest. This meant maintaining a healthy distance from the day-to-day process of decision- and programme- making, which was held to be the preserve of the Board of Management (headed by the Director-General). Being also on the board of the Corporation itself, however, gave the governors the final responsibility for the management of the BBC. While this 'organic' form of organisation had its advantages, it also confused matters by allowing the governors – if they wished – to interfere with the editorial independence of the broadcasters. From an early stage at Broadcasting House, Cadogan showed himself to be a firm and energetic supervisory chairman, cancelling talks, insisting on advance scrutiny of selected scripts and prescribing modifications. He was especially sensitive to issues relating to politics and national security, stifling debate and causing resentment among BBC staff as a result. The strong links which the BBC already had with Whitehall were also considerably reinforced.[21]

The doubts concerning the BBC's organisational and policy-making structure, which Cadogan had heightened since his arrival, were bound to grow more acute during a period of national crisis. Yet this was all the more so with the Suez dispute given the importance which the Eden government attached to propaganda. The Egypt Committee's strategy was predicated on Nasser's downfall via military force. This could not be publicised openly, however, for fear of alienating a large proportion of domestic and international opinion. Nor could it be put into effect immediately, owing to the services' unpreparedness. In order to build up and maintain over weeks the level of public support required for war, therefore, the main public-opinion formers needed to do the ministers' bidding (wittingly or unwittingly), demonising Nasser and presenting the use of force as necessary. The result was arguably the most demanding and intensive propaganda campaign conducted by a British government since the Second World War. This placed the mass media in a critical position, calling for vigilance and leadership of the highest qualities.[22]

During the first two weeks of the crisis Cadogan appears to have played no explicit part either in the relationship between the government and BBC, or in influencing the Corporation's output. A regular fortnightly meeting of the Board of Governors produced nothing of any consequence. On 10 August, however, the same day on which Cadogan had met Selwyn Lloyd with the Suez Canal Company directors, he received a telephone call from Eden. The Prime Minister had called to complain about the BBC's refusal to allow Robert Menzies, his Australian counterpart who was visiting Britain, to appear on television to talk about the Crisis two days before the London Conference was due to open on 16 August. The Foreign Secretary was already booked to make a radio appearance on 14 August, and the BBC's temporary liaison with the political parties, John Green, had therefore informed Downing Street that two pro-government broadcasts in close succession would call the corporation's objectivity into question. To break programmes to allow a Commonwealth premier to make a quasi-ministerial broadcast would, moreover, be 'both a precedent and an act of emphasis'. Cadogan thought this 'really nonsense', and immediately telephoned Ian Jacob to say that Menzies must be allowed to speak, 'no matter what our traditions and inhibitions might be'. Menzies consequently appeared on *Highlight* on 13 August, criticising those 'beset with intellectual doubts' about the government's right to use force and making a compelling case for the illegality and immorality of Nasser's coup.[23]

To argue that Cadogan's actions in this instance were determined by his support for military action would be inaccurate. It was perhaps more the case of an ex-mandarin's deferential tendencies heightened during an international crisis affecting British interests. However, for Cadogan to dictate programming arrangements according to Eden's wishes was contrary to the rules governing political broadcasting and, given the threats which Number Ten had issued the BBC during the episode, merely encouraged further interference. Harman Grisewood, the BBC's Director of Spoken Word, was deeply dissatisfied with the apparent installation of a private line between Broadcasting House and Downing Street. If Eden insisted on communicating directly with anyone at the BBC it should have been with the Director-General or his assistant. 'What worried me about this…was not so much the contact itself, as the danger that the Chairman would misunderstand his role and the Prime Minister would encourage him to assume more of an executive responsibility than was practical or constitutionally proper.' Grisewood knew how 'devoted' Cadogan was to Eden.[24]

Even before this incident, senior officials at the BBC had in fact already expressed private concern with the Corporation's failure to report the conflicting views about Eden's policy that existed in Britain – a charge which, when levelled publicly, Cadogan refuted. On 15 August, therefore, the BBC re-arranged its nightly schedule to present a range of opinions on Suez, including that of Nasser's former Minister of National Guidance, Salah Salem. Having been dissuaded from trying to ban the programme outright, after the broadcast Eden again contacted Cadogan, this time to accuse the BBC of misrepresenting the state of British opinion and to remind the Chairman of the governors' burden of 'responsibility'. In order to press home the issue, he then raised with Jacob the possibility of appointing a senior minister as general overseer of broadcasting. Cadogan once more misread the situation. Rather than asserting the BBC's independence from government, he promised Eden that the corporation would stick to 'straight news' during the London Conference. Cadogan was a firm believer in the dangers of media intrusion upsetting the diplomatic process. Added to this, he incorrectly attributed the Prime Minister's outbursts to anti-BBC zealots in Whitehall whom Eden would control once given the chance. The effect of his actions was to undermine further BBC morale and strengthen the government's propaganda campaign.[25]

The longer the crisis lasted, the closer the relationship between the BBC and politicians grew. In the wake of the abortive Menzies mission in mid-September, Hugh Gaitskell asked the BBC's permission to make his first Suez-related broadcast. Instead of simply granting the Leader of the Opposition's request for a slot on a conventional question-and-answer programme, however, Cadogan and Jacob arranged a special meeting with Gaitskell and R.A. Butler, the Lord Privy Seal, to discuss the whole issue of ministerial broadcasts. A new – though ultimately flawed – agreement was reached about the parties' future access to the airwaves, and the Labour leader subsequently appeared on television on 21 September, balanced by Selwyn Lloyd's *Panorama* interview a few days later.[26]

Cadogan was not the only BBC official who felt obliged to consult Westminster in light of what Jacob termed the 'unusual situation' produced by the dramatic internal arguments about British policy in the Middle East. But there seems little doubt that his influence was instrumental in determining the organisation's cautious approach towards reporting the crisis during this period. Cadogan personally deplored the parliamentary division over Suez that arose during the emergency debate in mid-September, believing it was against the national interest. It is not altogether surprising therefore to find the Board of Governors' minutes for 13 September state 'that the BBC should do nothing to underline the existence of party division and disunity at a time of crisis'.[27] Drawing a direct link between such guiding principles and output is not easy; the BBC was after all a large bureaucracy on which it was difficult for the governors to impose their distinctive will. Nevertheless, programmes continued, as at the start of the crisis, to fall far below the corporation's usual standards of comprehensiveness and objectivity. Thus, despite (or, perhaps, because of) Eden's criticisms of the BBC's anti-government bias, the Corporation was to a considerable extent playing his tune.[28]

Cadogan springs to prominence in many conventional accounts of the Crisis once operation MUSKETEER (REVISE) is launched owing to the infamous row between Downing Street and the BBC over Hugh Gaitskell's right to broadcast on the eve of the Anglo-French landings. To focus entirely on this episode, however, runs the risk of simplifying the BBC's role at the height of the crisis and Cadogan's ambiguous part therein. The first news that Cadogan heard of the government's decision finally to go ahead with the use of force was when Eden issued his ultimatums to Israel and Egypt in the Commons on 30 October. He was completely ignorant of the tripartite conspiracy, believing Israel's invasion of the Sinai to have been a huge stroke of 'luck' for the Prime Minister. That Eden had plans to turn the broadcasting medium into an arm of war was, nevertheless, already apparent. On 26 October, Cadogan and Jacob had held an emergency meeting with R. A. Butler to protest at the government's threat to cut the funding of the BBC's External Services by £1 million (one fifth of the total). They managed via delaying tactics to resist this attempt to 'shock' the corporation into a timely collective obedience, though Bush House was forced to agree to Butler's other measure – the installation of a Foreign Office liaison officer 'to advise the BBC on the content and direction of their overseas programmes'. More ominously, Harman Grisewood was told by Eden's Press Secretary, William Clark, in the final week of October that the government was preparing an 'instrument' to take over the BBC altogether. This would eventually prove to be false, but the fact that Grisewood chose not to pass on the 'burdensome information' to

Cadogan indicated his lack of complete trust in the Chairman's judgement at a crucial stage of events.[29]

The divisions within BBC circles which had developed during the Suez Crisis came to a head at a critical meeting of the Board of Governors on 1 November. According to Grisewood, who was, together with Norman Bottomley, Deputy Director-General, effectively running the BBC's day-to-day affairs following Ian Jacob's departure for Australia on 26 October, the Corporation was at this point on the verge of a potentially fatal split over its coverage of the emerging hostilities. Eden, it appears, had lost no time in raising with Cadogan the sensitive question of broadcasting criticism of the military operation which the troops would be able to pick up on the eve of battle. The Chairman subsequently told the acting Director-General that this would be demoralising and dangerous. Bottomley and Grisewood disagreed, however, arguing with Cadogan before the board meeting that it would be neither proper nor practical to suppress news in one service and allow it another. These and other issues relating to the BBC's objectivity formed the basis of heated discussion during the governors' meeting itself. The result was that Cadogan's viewpoint was defeated, with the board taking the decision to 'continue to apply the policy...it had followed hitherto both at home and in the External Services'. Thus, the External Services' press reviews, which had already contained material castigating Eden's actions, continued as normal.[30]

If a revolt within the BBC had been averted, this was far from the case within the country at large. Eden had told the Cabinet on 24 October that the attack against Egypt had to be 'quick and successful' for it to be accepted by political and public opinion; significantly, Cadogan swiftly reached the same conclusion. 'The nation is split in two, from top to bottom,' he noted in his diary on 1 November. 'If we could have a complete *and rapid* success, we might get away with it. Otherwise, I don't like the prospect.' The thousand-mile distance between Port Said and Malta, where the task force was based, meant of course that presenting the world with a military *fait accompli* turned out to be a logistical impossibility. Desperate to answer his critics and re-establish the propaganda initiative during the three day phoney war between the bombings and the landings, on 3 November Eden accordingly broadcast to the nation for the second time during the Suez Crisis. His cool and impressive performance depicted the 'police action' as essential to 'put out the forest fire' of conflict in the Middle East.[31]

Cadogan's role in the notorious dispute that followed Gaitskell's request for a right to reply to the Prime Minister was, contrary to many accounts,[32] quite predictable. There are certain interesting aspects, however. Given his personal loyalty to Eden and support for the military operation, Cadogan would doubtless have preferred to censor the Labour leader. He was fully aware of the delicate balance of parliamentary and public opinion at this point and thought that it would have been justifiable in the national interest. Nevertheless, considering his recent arguments with fellow governors, plus the afore-mentioned agreement reached in mid-September which many believed had sanctioned the Opposition's automatic right to reply to a ministerial broadcast even if it was not controversial, Cadogan effectively had no choice but to authorise Gaitskell's television appearance on 4 November. Eden's confession that his own broadcast had been 'as controversial as possible' was anyway, as Cadogan himself wrote, 'tantamount to admitting it *was* controversial'. In the event, Gaitskell's time on the air probably did him more harm than good. His appeal to Tory waverers backfired and implicit condemnation of the British forces only hours away from battle struck many people as treacherous. The broadcast's counter-productive effects were recognised by no less an authority than Cadogan himself. The speech was in his view, 'disgraceful… But I don't mind, we have given him enough rope!'[33]

News of the successful landing by the Anglo-French forces on 5-6 November was greeted with relief by Cadogan, who believed this would lift the pressure considerably on Eden and the BBC. It proved to be a false hope on both counts. In the weeks after the 7 November ceasefire, the BBC suffered unprecedented criticism from Conservative backbenchers for its alleged systematic bias against the government during the recent crisis. Earlier threats to the External Services' funding also re-surfaced, though now of a yet more 'forbidding' nature. Cadogan's instinct in these testing circumstances was to instruct the BBC to keep its head down and wait for the recriminations to dissipate. Consequently, when the press began to substantiate rumours of 'collusion' in mid-November, Cadogan disbelieved the theory personally and urged Bottomley and Grisewood to handle the potentially explosive subject with 'a degree of caution'. The

Corporation subsequently suppressed the story, and in the process relinquished arguably its last chance of having a decisive impact on what was left of the Suez Crisis.[34]

Documentary analysis, supported by a review of output, shows that the BBC as a whole interpreted its own ideals of impartiality and objectivity in a dubious fashion during the Suez dispute. To lay the responsibility for this entirely at Cadogan's feet would clearly be inaccurate – his resistance to government cuts to the External Services alone makes a mockery of one Labour MP's assertion that he acted as a 'Foreign Office deadbeat' during the dispute. The more realistic judgement is that the institutionalised nature of the BBC rendered it instinctively deferential to authority, especially during a period of national crisis. When, on top of this, the government devised 'innumerable schemes to discipline' the Corporation, its inherent weaknesses were laid bare. Sir Ian Jacob called Suez 'a bad dream', reflecting the difficult – and in many ways, unique – dilemmas faced by those in the higher echelons of the BBC.[35] Cadogan himself seems to have been unaware of the BBC's direct involvement in a joint Foreign Office/MI6 covert propaganda operation aimed at the Arab world, and designed specifically 'to get rid of Nasser'.[36] Nevertheless, he served as an important channel of communication between the BBC and Whitehall on several occasions during the Crisis, and in so doing played a not insignificant part in determining how the public viewed the dispute.

Despite his apparent ubiquity, Sir Alexander Cadogan was by no means wholly and intimately engaged with the twists and turns of the Suez Crisis. His diary consistently reveals the pent-up frustration of a former Foreign Office official of the highest rank forced to spend his weekends gardening and relying on the newspapers for the latest information about the most serious crisis to have hit Britain since 1945. He was not only entirely ignorant about the tripartite negotiations, but even lacked a full understanding of what objectives lay behind Eden's actions and pronouncements. He therefore qualifies as a relative outsider during the Suez crisis, with no policy-forming functions whatsoever.

However, his very distance from Suez's nerve centre paradoxically afforded him potentially greater influence than many other officials. Cadogan was able to view the crisis from three specific angles. He himself appears to have seen no inherent clash of interest between the three positions and consequently was able to turn the links between them to his (and the government's) advantage. His first-hand knowledge of the government's preparations for the first London Conference via the Suez Canal Company directorship, for example, led Cadogan to impose a ban on any BBC broadcasts that might harm the smooth diplomatic process. Being alert to the weakness of the government's legal case against nationalisation, again via the directorship, encouraged him to conduct the ESU's publicity campaign from a more politico-economic perspective. His chairmanship of the ESU unit brought him into closer contact with the Foreign Office, which in turn made him more sympathetic to its policy of marginalising the Suez Canal Company and Whitehall's desire to see the BBC's External Services represent British overseas interests as strongly as possible. Finally, Cadogan's personal relationship with the Prime Minister allowed him to intuit Eden's needs across the broad range of activities, augmented by direct contact when necessary.

But, as the dispute progressed, Cadogan found his very versatility something of a liability. He was not able to determine the course of events to the extent he wished in any of his three fields of activity; here, the contrast with the respect and influence accorded him in the later stages of his career at the Foreign Office, when his powers could be more concentrated, was stark. The ESU's efforts were discreetly effective but ultimately too tangential to affect US policy or Anglo-American relations in any decisive way. As a Suez Canal Company director he was in an important intermediary role, but was often by-passed because the management of the company itself sought direct access with the Foreign Office and ministers. While the looseness of the BBC's constitutional conventions allowed Cadogan to push the Chairman's rights to the limits, the assistance he rendered Eden's policy, though considerable, was restricted by bureaucratic complexities and a lively tradition of independence from government.

In this way, Cadogan resembled many of the other officials who were closer to events at the political, diplomatic and military centre of Suez. The difference between him and a high proportion of these officials, however, was that Cadogan remained loyal to Eden and the policy of force (inside the UN if possible, outside if necessary) throughout. Like many of his generation – particularly Sir Ivone Kirkpatrick – Cadogan saw Suez as essentially a re-run of the Rhineland Crisis. To an extent, he felt that he personally had been responsible for the failures and expediency of British policy then; he was not about to repeat the mistake 20 years later. Thus, as Cadogan told Kirkpatrick in an intriguing conversation between a former and current Foreign Office head towards the end of November 1956, he was critical of the inept way in which the government had intervened with force at the start of the month rather than the use of the military option itself. The problems which quickly arose due to opposition within Britain, the United States, UN and Commonwealth all should have been foreseen. The implication was that he would have anticipated them had he been at the Foreign Office's helm.[37] Be that as it may, by the end of 1957, Cadogan had taken the decision to retire completely from public life and devote more time to his beloved painting. The Suez Crisis therefore represented, if not Britain's, then certainly Cadogan's last fling.

NOTES

1. D. Reynolds, *Britannia Overruled: British Policy and World Power in the Twentieth Century* (London: Longman, 1991), p.205.
2. Sir Llewellyn Woodward, *British Foreign Policy in the Second World War, Vol.1* (London: HMSO, 1970), p.xxx; D. Dilks (ed.), *The Diaries of Sir Alexander Cadogan, 1938–1945* (London: Cassell, 1971), p.16.
3. Dilks (ed.), *Cadogan*, pp.791, 795.
4. Sir Alexander Cadogan Papers, Churchill College, Cambridge, ACAD 1/27, 1956 Diary, entry for 30 July 1956; Dilks (ed.), *Cadogan*, p.796: 'It is perhaps best to say at this point [early in the crisis] that Cadogan shared Eden's view of Nasser as an unscrupulous demagogue of paranoic tendencies.'
5. *The English-Speaking Union: A Decade of Progress, 1945–1955* (London: Riverside Press, 1955); Commonwealth–American Current Affairs Unit, 'UK Dependencies in Brief', May 1954, Pamphlet No.3 (London: HMSO, 1954).
6. FO 800/731, Lloyd to Eden, 11 May 1956; Cadogan Papers, ACAD 4/9, Jan. 1956.
7. Cadogan Papers, ACAD 1/27, 1956 Diary, entry for 7 Aug. 1956; D. Neff, *Warriors at Suez* (New York, Linden Press, 1981) p.143; *English-Speaking World*, Sept. 1956, Vol.XXXVIII, No.5, p.16; Nov. 1956, Vol.XXXVIII, No.6, p.50; Jan. 1957, Vol.XXXIX, No.1, pp.12–27.
8. FO 953/1688/PG11639/15, Stewart (IPD head) to Beeley, 7 Aug. 1956; CAB 130/121, GEN 561, Peck memo., 8 March 1957; FO 953/1689/PG11639/3, Stewart to Horn, 1 Aug. 1956; FO 953/1610/P10118/109, Peck memo. to IPD, 20 Nov. 1956; Cadogan Papers, ACAD 1/27, 1956 Diary, entry for 14 Aug.1956.
9. Cadogan Papers, ACAD 1/27, 1956 Diary, entries for 12 Nov. and 4 Dec. 1956; FO 953/1714P1011/3, minute by Dodds-Parker, 31 Dec. 1956 and FO 953/1715/P1011/32(A), Grey to Harvey, 28 March 1957.
10. Cadogan Papers, ACAD 1/27, 1956 diary, entry for 26 July 1956.

11. See, for example, Jacques Georges-Picot, *The Real Suez Crisis* (New York: Harcourt Brace Jovanovich, 1975) and K. Kyle, *Suez* (London: Weidenfeld & Nicolson, 1991).

12. PREM 11/1098, CM (56) 54, Confidential Annex, 27 July 1956; Georges-Picot, *Real Suez Crisis*, pp.68, 74–76.

13. Georges-Picot, *Real Suez Crisis*, pp.79, 92, 94, 111.

14. FO 371/119080, Wylie to Watson, 30 July 1956; Georges-Picot, *Real Suez Crisis*, pp.78–79; *Foreign Relations of the United States, 1955–57, Vol.XV* (Washington D.C., USGPO, 1988), doc. 2, pp.3–5; Cadogan Papers, ACAD 1/27, 1956 Diary, entries for 2–3 Aug. 1956; FO 371/119099/JE 14211/604, Wylie to Watson, 7 Aug. 1956.

15. Cadogan Papers, ACAD 1/27, 1956 Diary, entries for 10 and 19 Sept. 1956; CAB 128/30 Pt. II, Watkinson memo., 10 Sept. 1956; FO 371/119140/JE 14211/1757, Giles to Logan, 18 Sept. 1956.

16. CAB 128/30, CM (56) 54, 27 July 1956; CAB 134/1216, EC(56) 24th mtg., 4 Sept. 1956; CAB 134/1302, meeting between Lloyd and Suez Canal Sub-Committee, 10 Aug. 1956; FO 371/119116/JE14211/1074, Hankey to FO, 22 Aug. 1956; CAB 134/1302, ME (O) (SC) (56) 14, 14 Aug. 1956; CAB 134/1302, ME (O) (SC) (56) 15, 15 Aug. 1956.

17. FO 800/747 file, Fitzmaurice to Rae, 17 Aug. 1956, and Fitzmaurice to Coldstream, 6 Sept. 1956; FO 371/119114/JE 14211/1006, Dodds-Parker to J. Phillips, 17 Aug. 1956; FO 371/119159/JE14211, Fitzmaurice to Dodds-Parker, 19 Oct. 1956.

18. Cadogan Papers, ACAD 1/27, 1956 Diary, entry for 9 Aug. 1956; Georges-Picot, *Real Suez Crisis*, pp.111.

19. Cadogan Papers, ACAD 1/27, 1956 Diary, entries for 2 and 12 Oct. 1956.

20. A. Briggs, *The History of Broadcasting in the UK, Vol.4, Sound and Vision* (Oxford: Oxford University Press, 1979), pp.449–451; C. Richardson, *From Churchill's Secret Circle to the BBC* (London: Brassey's, 1991), pp.234–235; Dilks (ed.), *Cadogan*, p.792.

21. *BBC Handbook 1957* (London: BBC, 1957), pp.8–11; Cadogan Papers, ACAD 1/24, 1953 Diary, entry for 8 Jan. 1953; ACAD 1/26, 1955 Diary, entries for 7 Jan., 11 Jan. and 4 April 1955; ACAD 1/27, 1956 Diary, entry for 19 Jan. 1956.

22. The Eden government's propaganda strategy during the Suez Crisis is outlined in T. Shaw, *Eden, Suez and the Mass Media: Propaganda and Persuasion during the Suez Crisis* (London: I. B. Tauris, 1996), pp.1–12.

23. Cadogan Papers, ACAD 1/27, 1956 Diary, entry for 10 Aug. 1956; BBC Written Archives, Caversham, Barkshire, R34/1508/1, Conversation between Green, Lindsay Wellington, Director of Sound Broadcasting, and Norman Bottomley, Director of Administration and acting Director-General, 10 Aug. 1956; R34/1508/3, 'A Study of Successful Resistance to Government Pressure', pp.2–3; FO 371/119110 file, 13 Aug. 1956; University of Birmingham, Avon Papers, AP 14/4/61, Eden to Menzies, 13 Aug. 1956.

24. G. Wyndham-Goldie, *Facing the Nation: Television and Politics, 1936–1976* (London: Bodley Head, 1977), pp.178–9; H. Grisewood, *One Thing at a Time* (London: Hutchinson, 1968), p.196.

25. BBC WAC R34/1508/1, Conversation between Green, Wellington and Bottomley, 10 Aug. 1956; R34/1508/1, Board of Management Minutes, BMM 391, 13 Aug. 1956; R43/1508/1, Cadogan to Sorenson, Chairman of the National Peace Council, 14 Aug. 1956; Bodleian Library, William Clark Papers, 7, p.114, 15 Aug. 1956; R34/1508/1, transcript of *Special Survey of the Suez Crisis*, 15 Aug. 1956; PREM 11/1089A file, Eden-Cadogan exchange of letters, 16 and 17 Aug. 1956; PREM 11/1089A file, Clark to Eden, 17 Aug. 1956; Cadogan Papers, ACAD 1/27, 1956 Diary, entry for 17 Aug. 1956.

26. BBC WAC R1/1/24, Board of Governors Minutes, 13 Sept. 1956; R34/1508/1, Account of Meeting between Jacob, Cadogan, Gaitskell and Butler, 14 Sept. 1956. Ministerial broadcasts, as laid down in the 1947 BBC *aide mémoire* governing political broadcasting, were obliged to be strictly non-controversial. It was agreed at this meeting, however, that the government and opposition could, 'in times of crisis', make ministerial broadcasts of a 'politically controversial nature'. This blurred the distinction between a ministerial and party political type of broadcast, and still left unresolved the definition of what constituted 'controversial' material. This helped cause the heated dispute over political broadcasts when Suez reached its climax in early November, 1956. R34/1508/1, Report on Ministerial Broadcasts by Harman Grisewood, sent to Norman Bottomley, 22 Nov. 1956, p.1; R1/1/24, Board of Governors minutes, 27 Sept. 1956.

27. BBC WAC R34/1508/1, Account of Meeting between Jacob, Cadogan, Gaitskell and Butler, 14 Sept. 1956; Cadogan Papers, ACAD 1/27, 1956 Diary, entry for 14 Sept. 1956; R1/1/24, Board of Governors Minutes, 13 Sept. 1956.

28. See, for example, such BBC commentaries as *At Home and Abroad*, 28 Aug. and 18 Sept.; *From Our Own Correspondent*, 15 Sept., 7 and 14 Oct.; and *The World This Week*, 15 Sept. 1956. Transcripts in BBC WAC.

29. Cadogan Papers, ACAD 1/27, 1956 Diary, entries for 25, 26 and 30 Oct. 1956; FO 953/1644/PB1011/60/G, Nutting to Jacob, 25 Oct. 1956; BBC WAC R34/1508/3, 'A Study of Successful Resistance', pp.11–12; R34/1508/1, Dodds-Parker to Jacob, 26 Oct. 1956; Grisewood, *One Thing at a Time*, pp.199–200; R34/1508/3, Grisewood's 'Reminiscences', dated 9 April 1969.

30. Grisewood, *One Thing at a Time*, pp.200–1; BBC WAC R34/1508/3, 'A Study of Successful Resistance', pp.16–18; PRO FO 953/1755/PB1011/32, Clark to Harvey, 3 April 1957.

31. CAB 128/30, CM (56) 73, 24 Oct. 1956; Cadogan Papers, ACAD 1/27 1956 Diary, entry for 1 Nov. 1956; William Clark Papers, 7, p.148, 2 Nov. 1956; *The Listener,* 8 Nov., pp.736–7.

32. See, for example, A. Briggs, *The History of British Broadcasting in the UK, Vol.5, Competition* (Oxford: Oxford University Press, 1995), pp.96–100; Grisewood, *One Thing at a Time*, pp.201–4.

33. Cadogan Papers, ACAD 1/27, 1956 Diary, entries for 2–4 Nov.; BBC WAC R34/1508/3, 'A Study of Successful Resistance', p.7; R34/1508/1, Grisewood to Bottomley, 1 Nov. and account of events, 3–4 Nov., 1956; Benn Archives, political diaries and papers of Tony Benn, pp.22–26, 3–4 Nov., 1956; P. Williams (ed.), *The Diary of Hugh Gaitskell, 1945–1956* (London: Jonathan Cape, 1983) p.435.

34. Cadogan Papers, ACAD 1/27, 1956 Diary, entries for 5, 20 and 21 Nov. 1956; BBC WAC R34/1508/3, 'A Study of Successful Resistance', pp.22–29; *Hansard,* Vol.560, cols. 1023–1102, 14 Nov. 1956; R34/1508/2, Grisewood to Bottomley, 20 Nov. 1956; R34/1508/2, Grisewood to Beadle, 20 Nov. 1956.

35. *Hansard,* Vol.560, cols. 1051ff, 14 Nov. 1956, comments by George Wigg, Labour MP for Dudley, who also accused Jacob of being 'a Tory stooge'; Briggs, *Governing the BBC*, p.213; Richardson, *Secret Circle to the BBC*, p.249.

36. BBC WAC R34/1508/1, Dodds-Parker's agenda for the next day's Foreign Office/MI6 Advisory Committee meeting, 11 Oct. 1956, and subsequent memoranda sent to the Egypt Committee, dated 19 Oct. 1956; Richard Norton-Taylor, 'BBC connived with MI6 to oust Nasser', *Guardian*, 16 Sept. 1994, p.8.

37. Cadogan Papers, ACAD 1/27, 1956 Diary, entry for 29 Nov. 1956.

In the Company of Policy Makers:
Sir Donald Logan, Assistant Private Secretary
to the Secretary of State for Foreign Affairs

CHRIS BRADY

On 2 January 1987 the Public Records Office opened its files on the Suez Crisis and among the usual important State papers was what amounted to the appointments diary of Selwyn Lloyd, the Secretary of State for Foreign Affairs. On the page for 22 October 1956 the planned engagements had been ruled through and above them, in the hand of Donald Logan, the following words were written: 'A day marked, among other things, by a nearly fatal car accident – for which my driving was not responsible.'[1]

When this snippet of history was first unearthed Peter Hennessy awarded it the title of the 'most masterly understatement penned by a public servant in recent times'.[2] Although this made good copy the use of the term *under*statement suggests that the reverse, hyperbole, was possible. The truth is, however, that hyperbole was simply not Logan's style. He was, and remains, even in retirement, the consummate Private Secretary, the archetypal civil servant. The reality behind Logan's diary entry makes this very point. The near-miss car accident to which he referred was actually no more than two cars passing too close for comfort at an unmarked cross-roads on the journey from Villacoublay airport to the secret meeting at Sèvres. Logan's only reason for mentioning it in the diary was so that it could act as a cryptic reminder 'of our clandestine visit to Sèvres. I had no idea that this scrap of paper would get into the public archives. I ought not to have been so flippant.'[3]

Although Logan became the complete civil servant he was not the archetypal entrant to the Service. He was born in London in 1917, during a Zeppelin raid according to his mother. Shortly thereafter his father, a Port of London Authority representative moved to the

146

Midlands where Logan eventually attended Solihull Grammar School. Just before his Higher Certificate examinations he was withdrawn from school at his father's insistence in order to avoid the impending disaster of abject failure which was considered inevitable. Logan admitted that he had done little work and his father was undoubtedly correct in his judgement. After a couple of unhappy weeks working as an office boy at ICI in Aston a friend of Logan's father obtained a position for Logan the younger in an insurance company. He stayed there for five years during which time he qualified as a fellow of the Chartered Insurance Institute.

At the outbreak of war he was offered a commission on the strength of his cadetship at Solihull Grammar. He accepted the commission and joined the Royal Artillery being posted almost immediately to Shrivenham dealing with the searchlight aspects of the anti-aircraft unit. Shortly after the United States entered the war Logan went to America as part of an advisory team on anti-aircraft operational routines which the British had learned during the Battle of Britain. It was in America that the Foreign Office first entered Logan's mind as an option for post-war employment. A friend mentioned the new 'Eden Proposals for the Reform of the Foreign Service' in which entrants did not *have* to be university graduates but could enter the service providing they were able to satisfy the examiners that had they gone to university they would have gained at least a second class honours degree. Logan sent off for an application form and kept it with him until the end of the war when he became one of the first 20 or so applicants under the new scheme. He survived the selection procedures, including the famous 'country house weekend', and joined the North American Department of the Foreign Office in January 1946 where his first job was dealing with the problem of GI brides. Despite being out of the ordinary in his entrance to the service his career was fairly traditional. From 1947–51 he was Commercial Secretary at the embassy in Tehran. He then spent two years on the Middle East desk in London before returning to the Middle East as the Assistant Political Agent in Kuwait. It was from there that he joined the Secretary of State's personal staff.

Logan had completed a seamless transition from Army Major to civil servant and understatement of the type mentioned above became his stock-in-trade. Thus when the editors of this volume asked that contributions should focus upon the officials and their contributions to the *policy-making process* during the Suez crisis, Logan presented an immediate problem – the problem being that his role in the Suez crisis was not as a policy maker but, as he himself has said, 'a bag carrier to a Minister'.[4] In this description he was not being unduly modest. Logan's job was, again in his own words, 'simply running around with Selwyn Lloyd...my master'.[5] Why then, should a figure of such self-confessed insignificance be of any interest? The answer is, of course, the proximity to power and the consequent viewpoint on the exercise and process of power that such individuals enjoy. In fact, the very choice of Logan as a subject for this volume, rather than any of the three other Private Secretaries to the Foreign Secretary (Denis Laskey, John Graham, Dick Langridge), is explained by such propinquity. What makes Logan interesting is his presence, largely accidental, just prior to and during the secret negotiations of the collusion episode in late October 1956. In his usual understated tone Logan described himself as a 'somewhat occasional spectator of the Suez affair, except for a sudden involvement during the week beginning October 22, 1956'.[6] It is upon that week that this contribution primarily concentrates.

Ironically, even the 'sudden involvement' Logan mentioned was due almost entirely to chance since everything in Lloyd's office was dealt with on an availability basis by any of the Private Secretaries who were physically located in the same room. The structure of the office was such that there was no specific division of duties. As a consequence there was no significance in the fact that it was Logan who accompanied Lloyd one weekend to his constituency in the Wirral where he had a speaking engagement. It was Lloyd's habit to take a Private Secretary with him on such occasions in order to deal with official papers and telephone calls. He usually tried to take a bachelor in to order avoid unduly upsetting the lives of the married men and, therefore, the then unmarried Logan was an obvious choice.

During the course of the weekend the Prime Minister, Anthony Eden, summoned Lloyd to London and instructed him to go to Paris the next day. Logan, as the Private Secretary to hand was, in turn, instructed by Lloyd to accompany him, as Logan put it, 'by pure chance'.[7] Perhaps pure chance is not entirely accurate since Logan was one of the Private Secretaries who accompanied Lloyd to New York in early October for negotiations with Fawzi, the Egyptian Foreign Minister, and Pineau, the French Foreign Minister, and was therefore already up to speed with the issue.[8] Additionally, Logan had a strong Middle Eastern background having previously been stationed in Tehran and Kuwait as well as serving on the Iranian desk in London for a while. Interestingly, Logan records that in New York it was Christian Pineau who was the stumbling block to progress at New York and not Fawzi. Pineau's co-operation was half-hearted, to say the least, and this led Logan to retrospectively conclude that the collusion plan was probably already on the French agenda at that stage.

Among officials Logan was uniquely placed at the centre of the action throughout the collusion period, as he was the only Briton to be present at *both* Sèvres meetings. Early on the morning of 22 October he accompanied Lloyd to Hendon airport and from there by special military plane to Paris.[9] En route to Hendon he was briefed on the details of the Chequers meeting of 14 October and the subsequent Paris meeting of 16 October. When later asked whether he was aware of the Chequers meeting of 14 October Logan admitted that he did 'have an inkling, but no more than that', that something was in the air.[10] He did know that Eden and Lloyd had met the French Prime Minister, Guy Mollet, and Pineau in Paris on 16 October with only the Ministers present, but had no direct knowledge of their discussion. On arrival at Sèvres, on 22 October, Lloyd and Logan were met by Pineau and taken directly into the conference room in which Mollet (French Prime Minister), Bourgès-Maunoury (French Minister of Defence), Ben-Gurion (the Israeli Prime Minister), Moshe Dayan (Israel's Chief of Defence Staff) and Shimon Peres (Director General of the Israeli Ministry of Defence) were already ensconced.

Lloyd had no papers with him. He presented the British case alone, drawing on what he understood to be Eden's intentions, but apparently showing no real enthusiasm for his task. At no stage during the meeting, which continued with an interruption for dinner from about 4pm until midnight, did Lloyd seek Logan's advice. Logan mused that Lloyd had 'no one to turn to except me, which he didn't'.[11] In the break for dinner, however, Logan *was* asked, by Lloyd, for his opinion on the likely reactions of the Arabs to the plan for the Israelis to attack the Egyptians. Logan opined that they 'would be astonished...but they might come to accept it provided we got it over quickly'.[12] Naturally the effect of his comment cannot be gauged and was no doubt negligible; it was, however, perceptive.

According to Logan, at the end of the meeting Lloyd was pressured by the Israelis to bring forward the response time of the RAF after the initial Israeli attack. The Israelis would naturally have been concerned that the Egyptian airforce should be disabled by the RAF before it could retaliate against Tel Aviv. British planning had assumed that a reasonable period to accomplish this would have been 48 or even 72 hours while the Israelis were pressing for a maximum of 36 hours. This was clearly a matter on which Lloyd was not in a position to make a decision himself and one which, therefore, needed to be taken back to London. Consequently around midnight Lloyd and Logan flew back to Hendon to seek advice on the Israeli request to advance the RAF attack.

The next morning, 23 October, it had become clear that a speedy decision was unlikely since it was an issue in which the Cabinet needed to be involved. Despite analyses that depict Suez as an example of Prime Ministerial autocracy, Eden invariably attempted to be constitutionally correct and referral to the Cabinet on a matter with such military significance would have been considered essential. As a result Logan was despatched back to Paris, again by special aircraft, to convey the information to the French and Israelis that the Cabinet was considering the problem but they needed more time. On arrival Logan encountered Pineau preparing to make the trip in the opposite direction because he was anxious that no more time should be wasted in obtaining what was, to the French at least, an urgent, and apparently straightforward, decision.

Logan handed him a letter from Lloyd which emphasised that Britain was not asking the Israelis to commit themselves in any way to a British request but were merely explaining what would be the British reactions to certain events. In his book, Pineau says that he refrained from showing it to Ben-Gurion believing that the obvious transparency of such a smokescreen would only infuriate him.[13] Ben-Gurion's anticipated reaction is just another indication of the irritation, on *all* sides, with the ludicrous lengths to which Eden was prepared to go to maintain the appearance of propriety. Given that Pineau had already decided to go to London for direct discussions with Eden he suggested that Logan may as well accompany him on the trip. On arrival in London, Logan was obliged to hide in the background in order to avoid any awkward questions as to his presence on the same plane as the French Foreign Minister. Pineau went directly to meet with Lloyd and from there on to see Eden.

The next morning, 24 October, Patrick Dean, an Assistant Under-Secretary at the Foreign Office, was woken in the small hours by Sir Norman Brook, the Cabinet Secretary and Dean's close friend. He was told that he had to report to No.10 as soon as possible because he 'was required to proceed to Paris later in the morning'.[14] He was also informed that he had 'to be very careful not to let anyone else know and keep very quiet about it'.[15] Dean took this admonition seriously, to the extent of booking a commercial flight to Paris himself, without going through the Foreign Office, only to find later that Eden had again arranged a military flight which could fly out and back on the same day, such was *his* perception of the urgency of the situation. Dean met Eden at 8.30 in the morning and was instructed to go to Paris to continue the discussions. Eden was still in bed and the meeting lasted no more than 15 minutes. Eden's brief to Dean was to

> make absolutely sure before final decisions were taken that the Israelis and French had no doubt whatever in their minds that British Forces would not move unless the Israelis had advanced beyond their frontiers against Egypt and a threat to the Canal had clearly emerged.[16]

Apparently Dean was astonished to have been brought into a scenario, of which he had only the haziest notion, in such an arbitrary fashion. He returned to the Foreign Office and asked the Permanent Secretary, Sir Ivone Kirkpatrick, for advice. Kirkpatrick showed no enthusiasm, or indeed surprise, at the turn of events and told Dean that since 'the Prime Minister had charged [him] with the mission [he] must carry it out'.[17] Dean went on to see Lloyd for a final briefing at about 10am where Lloyd added nothing other than to tell him that he would be accompanied by Logan. This pleased Dean because not only did he welcome continuity and support in his mission but also Logan's French was better than his. That Dean should have had no knowledge of the scheme, though a senior official in the Foreign Office, and that he should actually have queried the Prime Minister's instructions, indicates the level of mistrust that had developed between the Foreign Office and Eden. According to Logan, Eden was convinced that he 'knew what the view of the Foreign Office would be and he chose not to seek it'.[18] The Foreign Office, in their turn, were aware of this and felt they were deliberately excluded from the policy-making process and were naturally aggrieved by the situation.

151

Dean and Logan left almost immediately for Paris where they were met by General Challe and taken to a meeting with the same Israeli and French teams – except for the absent Mollet – as had been present at the previous meeting. Dean's task was to ensure that the Israelis fully understood that only a clear threat to the Canal would trigger British involvement. After some effort he judged that he had received from Dayan a commitment to initiate some significant military action around the Mitla Pass area which would satisfy Eden. Logan believed that it had been *extracted* with difficulty from the Israelis who were reluctant to give it.[19] If such a concession had not been forthcoming the British negotiators would have been in serious difficulty because they were given no flexibility at all in their brief.[20]

At the end of the meeting the French produced a record of the week's discussions which Dean was invited to sign – this was the now notorious Sèvres protocol. Dean sought Logan's opinion as to whether to sign the document and Logan could see no reason not to do so since it was an accurate account of the meeting. It was also assumed an agreed record might be useful since the positions had been reached only after delicate negotiations. Dean therefore signed the document *ad referendum*, i.e. to be further considered, which seemed to both men as completely without prejudice. The British team then returned to London and at about 10.30pm Dean reported to Eden and handed to him the British copy of the document. Also present at the time were 'Rab' Butler, the Lord Privy Seal, Harold Macmillan, the Chancellor of the Exchequer, Lord Home, the Secretary of State for Commonwealth Affairs, Anthony Head, the Minister of Defence, and Mountbatten, the First Sea Lord. Eden was clearly surprised and irritated at the existence of the document. As a consequence, the next day Dean and Logan found themselves ordered once more by military aircraft to Paris with instructions to seek the destruction of all copies of the document. They failed to achieve their objective primarily because the French saw no need to comply with the request, and also because the Israelis had already left with their copy. Four days later, 29 October, the Israelis launched their attack.

On his return from Paris, Logan 'reverted to his original role of dealing with papers in the Private Office'.[21] One of the first developments in this period was an instruction from Eden to the Foreign Office to send him all copies or translations of the documents which had been made. Clearly, he (Eden) was still concerned to maintain the utmost secrecy. In deference to that concern, the text of the protocol was kept secret, chiefly by the Israelis, for the next 40 years, until October 1996 when the three governments finally agreed to its release.

When asked whether his role as a Private Secretary was in any way different during the Suez crisis, Logan answered that during the months between the nationalisation in July and the beginning of the collusion in the middle of October there was no difference. As described by Logan the role of Private Secretary has no great mystique; it is quite simply to be the secretary to an individual. As a member of a team a Private Secretary facilitates the minister in his work and his handling of papers and advice. The fact that the individual served was a senior Secretary of State gave the post of Private Secretary status but in functional terms there was nothing out of the ordinary about the job description. As with all Private Secretaries, however, there is a high level of intimacy with a senior figure which adds kudos to the post. As stated elsewhere Lloyd had four such staff in his team who were, in addition to their responsibilities to Lloyd, also accountable to the Permanent Secretary at the Foreign Office, Sir Ivone Kirkpatrick. While the personal staff would, of necessity, have developed a degree of loyalty to the Secretary of State their own career prospects would have been more directly affected by the Permanent Secretary. This caused some difficulties during Suez because Kirkpatrick was closer to Eden's more hawkish views than he was to Lloyd's preference for a negotiated settlement. Logan thought that Kirkpatrick had a particularly difficult time with Lloyd over Suez because while 'he was a dutiful civil servant, who did what he was told, [he] also had no time for the developing world and he was perfectly prepared to see them given a bloody nose'.[22]

Despite the fact that Logan thought the general routine of the office basically remained unchanged during the majority of the crisis, he did admit that when he found himself drawn into the Sèvres negotiations in such an extraordinary way, it was as if he 'had left the Private Office for Wonderland'.[23] No doubt he would agree that there *is* a frisson in being a first-hand observer of history. However that may be, being so close to the centre of the action also carries with it certain responsibilities and in similar circumstances today a very real case for Logan's resignation might be made. Logan knew that Eden's statement to the House on 20 December, denying any foreknowledge,[24] was untrue and yet he remained silent. Should he have spoken up at that moment, or indeed immediately after Sèvres, or if unwilling to speak should he have resigned? Logan's answer is clear, it was neither his place to speak nor to resign. He has since said that 'it never occurred to [him] at the time that [he] ought to have resigned during those four days in Paris'.[25] The Prime Minister had decided on a plan to achieve a recognised national objective. According to Logan his resignation would only have resulted in putting the attainment of that objective in jeopardy. Secret military staff talks prior to allied hostilities are the norm in crises – why should Suez have been any different?

The issue of Eden's deception in the House clearly illustrates the contemporaneous attitudes of the civil service in general and Logan in particular. As early as 31 October, the leader of the opposition, Hugh Gaitskell, had been pressing Eden to come clean over the collusion affair. He made a blistering attack on the Prime Minister during a debate on the Middle East situation.[26] In that attack he argued that

> There can be no doubt at all about what the view of the world as a whole is on this decision of the British Government. They look upon it as a transparent excuse to seize the Canal to carry out the policy of force from which the government were deterred by public opinion here and in the world in August and September.[27]

He went on to say that there was 'an even worse story going round… It is the story that the whole business was a matter of collusion between the British and French Governments and the Government of Israel'.[28] Eden neither confirmed nor denied the allegations merely allowing Lloyd and other colleagues to deflect the criticisms in the course of the debate, with Viscount Hinchingbrooke producing one of his typically jingoistic smokescreens. However, in the debate of 20 December, Eden could not avoid confronting a slightly differently worded attack. Now his interlocutors asked had there been any 'foreknowledge of the Israeli attack'.[29] To this charge Eden replied that 'to say that Her Majesty's Government were engaged in some dishonourable conspiracy is completely untrue, and I most emphatically deny it.' He went on to assert that 'there was no agreement arrived at until I informed the House'.[30]

Logan was adamant in his response to any suggestion that he should have blown the whistle. He said that 'the idea that a civil servant should get up and say "the Minister is not telling you the truth" is a recipe for chaos and certainly disloyalty'.[31] It is Logan's contention that ministers are entitled to expect the highest degree of loyalty from civil servants, particularly those such as Private Secretaries who work so intimately with them. Only if he had found himself examined under oath would Logan have reconsidered his position. In fact, Civil Service instructions have consistently confirmed that responsibility to decide what information should be made available, and how and when it should be released, lies with ministers and not with civil servants. It is not for civil servants to frustrate the policies or decisions of ministers, although naturally, some choose to do so.

Logan's attitude should come as no surprise since it is pragmatic, realistic, and epitomises the image of British civil servants of the period. There is an anecdote of the time, probably apocryphal, which confirms Logan's views and one with which he would be unlikely to dissent. It is said that a potentially dissident group of Foreign Office officials consulted Attlee, in his capacity as a Privy Councillor, about their duty in the circumstances. Attlee is said to have told them: 'You're civil servants. Go away and do as you're told.'[32] Presumably they are expected to do so still.

Logan's role in *policy making* during the Suez Crisis was negligible but his role in the history of the Crisis has become considerable. Here is a man of genuine integrity and consistency who was present at a central, if bizarre, moment in modern British history and is content to tell the story without any trappings of self-aggrandisement; for that fact alone he is worthy of inclusion in this book. After Suez Logan slipped back into the familiar Foreign Office career pattern becoming, among other things, an Ambassador in both Guinea and Bulgaria, an Information Counsellor in the Embassy in Paris and the Permanent Leader of the UK Delegation to the United Nations Conference on the Law of the Sea. Reminiscing recently on a Radio 4 programme on the Suez Crisis Logan admitted to feeling 'totally outclassed' in the first meeting at Sèvres. He remembers that he turned to Lloyd and said 'Shouldn't I wait outside?' Lloyd replied, 'No, no, keep me company.'[33] Perhaps that is the clearest explanation of Logan's role in the Suez Crisis, and of all Private Secretaries – they keep the policy makers company.

ACKNOWLEDGEMENTS

I am indebted to Sir Donald Logan for providing information and advice in interviews and other communications during the period May–August 1997.

NOTES

1. FO 800/716, Lloyd appointments diary, entry for 22 Oct. 1956.
2. P. Hennessy and M. Laity, 'Suez – What the Papers Say', *Contemporary Record*, Vol.1 No.1, Spring (1987), p.7.
3. Liddell Hart Centre for Military Archives, Suez Oral History Project. Interview with Sir Donald Logan (LHCMA).
4. LHCMA interview with Sir Donald Logan.
5. Interview with author.
6. Interview with author.
7. Interview with author.
8. Denis Laskey was also present in New York.
9. Hendon was a military airport and the pair landed at Villacoublay, another military airport, in Paris. Although this was relatively normal practice it also had the advantage of making secrecy easier.
10. Interview with author.
11. Interview with author.
12. Interview with author.
13. C. Pineau, *1956 Suez* (Paris: Robert Laffont, 1975), p.157.
14. Memo drafted in 1987 by Patrick Dean about the Suez crisis: copy in the author's possession.
15. Ibid.
16. Ibid.
17. Ibid.
18. Interview with author.
19. LHCMA interview with Sir Donald Logan.
20. Interview with author.
21. LHCMA interview with Sir Donald Logan.
22. Interview with author.
23. Interview with author.
24. *Hansard*, 20 December 1956, cols. 1457–8.
25. LHCMA interview with Sir Donald Logan.
26. *Hansard*, 31 October 1956, cols.1445–64.
27. Ibid, col.1459.
28. Ibid.
29. Ibid., col.1457.
30. Ibid., col.1457–8.
31. *New Statesman*, February 1987.
32. P. Hennessy, *New Statesman*, February 1987.
33. BBC Radio 4, 24 July 1996.

Transatlantic Diplomat: Sir Roger Makins, Ambassador to Washington and Joint Permanent Secretary to the Treasury

SAUL KELLY

When the Suez Crisis broke in July 1956, Sir Roger Makins had been British Ambassador in Washington for three and a half years. He was due to return to London in the autumn to become Joint Permanent Secretary of the Treasury. He took up this post at the critical moment in mid-October when the Prime Minister, Anthony Eden, and his 'inner circle' of ministers secretly decided to join with France and Israel in attacking Egypt with the aim of bringing about the fall of President Gamal Abdul Nasser. He then had to deal with the economic consequences of the Suez War. He was in the unique position for a British official of being involved in the initial stages of the crisis while in Washington, and its later stages when in London. The transatlantic role he played in the Suez Crisis, therefore, is of particular interest to historians.

His main duties as ambassador before and during the Suez Crisis were to keep on good terms with the Eisenhower administration, conveying British policy to them, and to explain US policy to London without losing the confidence of the Eden government. He also had to promote the cause of good Anglo-American relations through speeches to select audiences of American opinion-makers. Makins found himself sometimes in the influential position of having to negotiate between the two governments. It helped, therefore, that he had close personal relationships with the key figures on both sides of the Atlantic.

Makins had first met Eisenhower during the Second World War, when he had been the deputy political adviser (under Harold Macmillan) to Eisenhower as Allied Commander, North Africa and Supreme Allied Commander, Mediterranean from 1942–43. They had worked well together and, after Makins became Ambassador in

Washington, he was a regular visitor to the White House not only on official business but on private social occasions.[1] Several historians have concluded, however, that Makins's relationship with the US Secretary of State, John Foster Dulles, was only a formal one.[2] But newly-available evidence shows that Makins established a close working and personal relationship with Dulles. He was also under no illusion as to the nature of the relationship between the President and his Secretary of State when it came to determining foreign policy. Makins wrote in his unpublished memoirs that:

> I found him [Dulles] accessible and easy to work with, he thought for himself and expressed his thought at some length. He also developed it over time, and this gave him a reputation for inconsistency with some of my colleagues who did not see him as often as I did... Out of office, he was friendly and genial and a good companion who took his bourbon with the best of them... One thing I quickly learned was that Dulles never took an important step or replied to representations on major issues without first consulting the President.[3]

Makins had been greatly helped in establishing close contacts with the Eisenhower administration by the fact that until October 1954 the Under-Secretary of State was Walter Bedell Smith. He had been Eisenhower's wartime Chief of Staff in the Mediterranean, and Makins had worked closely with him in Algiers. Makins and Bedell Smith, who knew Winston Churchill and Anthony Eden well from the war, were almost always able to clear up the frequent mis-understandings which arose between Dulles and Eden. Makins had many old friends in the State Department, as a result of his previous postings to Washington 1931–34 and 1945–47, and was a regular and welcome visitor. He never had any trouble communicating with them, with the exception of the stubborn, anti-British and hard of hearing Herbert Hoover, Jr., who succeeded Bedell Smith as Under-Secretary of State in October 1954. Makins's inability to establish a rapport with Hoover was to have serious consequences over the Middle East, in that it closed down that vital channel of communication which had existed with Bedell Smith for dealing with the disagreements and tensions between Eden and Dulles.[4]

Makins's close personal and working relationships with Eisenhower, Dulles, and other members of the Republican administration were to allow him as Ambassador in the run-up to the Suez Crisis and during its early stages to present and discuss in a cordial spirit what were often regarded by the Americans as unacceptable British policies. As will be shown in this contribution, Makins's aims were to reduce the tension in these Anglo-American exchanges, to secure a degree of American co-operation with British policy, and to keep Britain and the United States in step. Makins was a confirmed Atlanticist, who was convinced of the need for close co-operation between Britain and the United States in order to protect British interests and guarantee world peace. As Ambassador he was to work tenaciously to prevent any disruption to the Anglo-American partnership.

Donald Cameron Watt has pointed out that, on the British side, much of the misfortune which was to strike Anglo-American relations in 1956 can be blamed on Eden's tenure of the Foreign Office and No.10 Downing Street. His 'ability to understand the Americans was as limited as his ability to convince himself of American respect was unbounded'. In part Watt attributed Eden's shortcomings to 'the very considerable and largely unsung success Sir Roger Makins enjoyed in establishing relations of confidence with the State Department and Dulles'.[5] Watt's conclusions are confirmed by evidence from Makins's memoirs.

Makins regarded the failure of both Eden and the Permanent Under-Secretary at the Foreign Office, Sir Ivone Kirkpatrick, to understand the American perspective as the direct result of their never having served in any capacity in the United States. There was also the clash of personalities and intellects between Eden and Dulles. Makins observed that 'Eden was an intuitive man, who quickly became bored with Dulles's long expositions and stopped listening. After Dulles had finished talking, Eden was in the habit of passing some remark to state his position but Dulles would not take it in.'[6] Moreover, there was a widespread illusion in the British government, which was shared by the Chancellor of the Exchequer, Harold Macmillan, that President Eisenhower would override US national interests for the sake of the Anglo-American 'alliance', as he had done as a subordinate Allied commander during the Second World War. These failings were to distort British policy in the run-up to the Suez Crisis and during the crisis itself. Makins was to have no qualms about giving his opinion about the practicability of British policy in view of the limits imposed by the American position. He was able to do this because of the mutual respect and friendship which he had had since League of Nations days with Eden and Kirkpatrick, and Macmillan since the war in the Mediterranean. Makins's barely concealed dislike and contempt for Selwyn Lloyd also, paradoxically, led him to address the Foreign Secretary in forthright terms.[7]

As Ambassador in Washington, Makins had demonstrated his ability to help prevent a break-down in Anglo-American relations as a result of the crises in Europe, the Far East and the Middle East that occurred during the first Eisenhower administration.[8] This ability was to be tested to the limit during the Suez Crisis. Looking back on the crisis after 40 years he concluded 'that there was never really any identity of view between the British and U.S. governments on the Middle East.'[9] But at the time he was more sanguine about the prospects of Anglo-American co-operation in the region.

In a submission that went to the British Cabinet in February 1954, Makins denied that the Americans were trying, as some feared in London, to oust Britain from the Middle East. He pointed out that any desire to dominate in the State Department was kept in check by the US military and the Congress, who were against assuming major commitments in the region. He thought that whether Britain stayed in the Middle East would be dependent largely on its own efforts and how the British government adjusted to the American presence as a new factor in Middle Eastern politics. He believed, rather optimistically as it transpired, that as long as a proper understanding existed between London and Washington disruptive US diplomats in Cairo could be restrained. He was correct in thinking, however, that Britain's conclusion of agreements with Egypt and Iran in October 1954 (for which he had pressed) would, at least temporarily, increase British freedom of action in the Middle East. It also led to greater American respect for the British position in the region, though this was limited by Britain's failure to reach an agreement with Saudi Arabia over the Buraimi Oasis. Certainly, it encouraged the Americans to enlist British support in trying to solve the Arab–Israeli dispute.

Makins was aware of the potential which policy differences over the Middle East had to disrupt Anglo-American relations. He realised that Britain would always have to contend with certain innate American feelings and prejudices about the British position in the Middle East, which stemmed from their anti-colonialism and economic rivalry. He believed, however, that with a little luck and perseverance 'we had a good chance of building up American confidence in us and their desire to cooperate with us'.[10]

Makins's efforts in 1955–56, on instructions from London, to persuade the United States to join the Baghdad Pact came to nought. In a revealing aside in March 1956 to Herbert Hoover, Jr., he said that London did not seem to be getting his message that there was considerable Congressional opposition, inspired by the Jewish lobby, to the US joining a defence pact with the Arab states without a compensatory security guarantee for Israel. Although the Americans refused to join the Baghdad Pact, they were prepared at Makins's urging to become members of its economic and subversion committees and the military liaison group.

Although Britain and the United States disagreed over the Baghdad Pact, they were prepared to co-operate together in Plan ALPHA, the secret Anglo-American initiative to secure a peace settlement between Egypt and Israel. But it was a fragile co-operation, as was shown in late August 1955 by Eden's objections to a general speech by Dulles on ALPHA and a supporting statement by the then Foreign Secretary, Harold Macmillan. Makins later commented to the author Richard Lamb that this 'was a good example of the petulance to the point of unreason to which he [Eden] was always prone and which became intensified after his illness and when he became Prime Minister.' As he pointed out in his memoirs 'It was this sort of petulant intervention which had the potential to disrupt Anglo-American relations.'[11]

Eden's lack of understanding of the American position was again demonstrated over the negotiations in late 1955 on the financing of the Aswan High Dam. It took much effort by Makins to convince Eden that if the British government wanted 'to get into the poker game it had to put up the ante'.[12] In other words, the British government had to agree to contribute 20 per cent ($15 million) of the first stage grant of $70 million to help cover the foreign exchange costs, as well as conceding competitive bidding, in order to secure American participation in the dam project. Makins also had to work hard to persuade Hoover and the US Treasury Secretary, George Humphrey, to change their minds and back US funding of the dam. Hoover and Makins then put the deal to the Egyptians in Washington. This was followed by the offer from the International Bank for Reconstruction and Development (IBRD), which the Egyptians then considered. This was a good example of Makins's ability to overcome entrenched attitudes and differences of approach in London and Washington in order to secure an agreement on a particular issue. But it could only succeed if the principal players had common and overriding objectives, in this case their mutual desire to prevent the Soviets following up their arms deal with Egypt by financing the Aswan High Dam.[13]

Makins had to deal with the criticism by Dulles of the British government's attempt to force Jordan into the Baghdad Pact in contravention of its assurance that it would not expand the pact, a move with which Makins had no sympathy. He had also to contend with Eden's refusal to help the Americans to split the Saudis from the Egyptians by making concessions (which were favoured by Makins) in the dispute with Saudi Arabia over the Buraimi Oasis. There were also Anglo-American differences, with which Makins had to deal, over Britain's support for the Iraqi Prime Minister, Nuri Said, and over Cyprus, where Britain's head-on clash with the Greek Cypriots and the mainland Greeks over Enosis threatened NATO.[14]

Moreover, what Scott Lucas has called the 'unprecedented Anglo-American concord on Middle Eastern policy',[15] namely the OMEGA Plan (the long-term programme to cut Nasser down to size) was soon threatened by Eden's desire for a 'quick-fix' solution to Britain's problems in the Middle East and his impatience with the American reluctance to be seen to be co-operating with the British in the region, which he claimed undermined Western influence. Makins had been involved in the drawing up of the OMEGA Plan and had been careful to relay to London the American preference for a political and economic, rather than a military response to the Egyptian problem. This provides the key to his subsequent approach to the Suez Crisis.[16]

The opening gambit in Operation OMEGA was the decision to let the Aswan High Dam project 'wither on the vine'. This was facilitated by the stalemating of the loan negotiations due to Egyptian objections to the conditions attached by the British, the Americans and the World Bank. Egyptian recognition in May 1956 of Communist China also hardened Congressional opposition to the United States helping to finance the dam. In order to prevent the Soviets putting forward a bid, however, the US and British governments signalled their apparent willingness to continue the negotiations. But Makins warned Hoover in mid-June that this tactic had failed since the Egyptians were negotiating with the Soviets over the dam.[17]

Anxious to avoid becoming too dependent on the Soviet Union, Nasser rejected the Soviet offer of an interest-free loan and sent his Ambassador to the United States, Ahmed Hussein, back to Washington to inform Dulles that Egypt would drop its objection to the Western loan conditions. However, after seeing the President on his farm at Gettysburg (where he was recuperating from a severe bout of ileitis), Dulles informed Makins on 13 July that 'his opinion was hard against proceeding' with the US funding offer. He had been swayed by Congressional opposition and American concern that it would lead to rampant inflation in Egypt, as well as Egyptian objections to reducing arms purchases and to imposing austerity measures. Dulles told Makins that if the US government 'decided to take this course, it might be better to tell the Egyptians what the situation was, while holding out [the] hope that they would recover economic aid in some other form'.[18]

The need for proper co-ordination of the new Anglo-American approach to the Aswan Dam project, and further moves in Operation OMEGA, put a premium on clear and trusted channels of communication. Yet on 17 July 1956 Dulles learnt that Makins was to return to London and would be replaced by Sir Harold Caccia. Makins commented in a letter to his father that:

> Its typical of our present rulers that having dithered for months and finally taken a decision they want to announce it immediately at the most inconvenient time for me. He [Dulles] took it all very much amiss, which was of course a compliment to me though hardly HMG! He first of all said 'Its crazy' and then observed that it would effect Anglo-American relations as they all had such confidence in me and felt that they could treat me with absolute frankness etc., etc.[19]

The explicit confidence that Dulles had in Makins was demonstrated when the British government was made privy to the deliberations within the Eisenhower administration that led up to the withdrawal on 19 July of the offer to finance the dam. Diane Kunz, Keith Kyle, Scott Lucas and Robert Rhodes-James have shown in their various accounts of the Suez Crisis, that Makins gave London adequate warning of US intentions, despite the statements of Eden and Lloyd in their respective memoirs.[20] Makins in his own unpublished memoirs adds that 'Dulles's hand had been forced by the Congress which threatened, if the Secretary of State did not kill the project, to do so itself, thereby usurping the Executive's power to make foreign policy.'[21] When the Eden government on 20 July announced that it agreed with the US decision and was also withdrawing its grant, the IBRD loan offer automatically collapsed. Makins recalled that the French Ambassador to the United States, Couve de Murville, was the only one in Washington to predict accurately how the Egyptians would react: 'They will do something about Suez. That is the only way that they can touch the western countries.'[22]

During the crisis that followed Nasser's nationalisation of the Suez Canal Company on 26 July, Makins drew heavily not only on his own formidable reserves of strength but on his personal friendships with the principal actors on both sides of the Atlantic. He sought to reduce the tension in the Anglo-American exchanges on how to proceed against Nasser and to secure a degree of co-operation on the imposition of financial sanctions against Egypt and on contingency planning on oil supplies. The Eden government had immediately introduced full financial sanctions against Egypt and wanted the Eisenhower administration to follow suit. Makins and the British Embassy's Economic Minister, Lord Harcourt, saw Hoover on 28 July to discuss the protection of the Suez Canal Company's assets, the blocking of Egyptian balances in the United States, the halting of the payment of Canal dues and plans to meet the possible closure of the Canal (including rationing and alternative oil supplies). Makins reported to London that the objections which Hoover and his advisers raised gave him the impression that they:

> were weak and irresolute in the face of this crisis, and are tepid
> about taking any vigorous action… The State Department do not
> feel themselves directly involved as principals in the dispute with
> Egypt and are acutely aware of the domestic repercussions which
> strong action (eg. involving the prospect of the rationing of oil)
> might have.[23]

Makins impressed on the Foreign Office the need, if it wanted to take firm action with US support, to make a strong impression on the American envoy to London, Robert Murphy, Jr.[24]

After considerable internal debate, the Eisenhower adminstration agreed to joint planning on oil supplies (in which Makins was involved) and froze Egyptian government and Suez Canal Company assets in the United States. Unlike the British and French governments, however, it excluded private Egyptian funds and future accruals and continued to pay Canal dues to Egypt. The Eisenhower administration was alarmed at the report from Murphy in London that Eden and Lloyd were intent on using force against Nasser. Dulles stated to Makins on 30 July that:

> the US Government would not be in sympathy with any attempt to make the Egyptian Government rescind their nationalisation decrees, or to regard them as inoperative, under the threat of force. As long as there was no interference with the navigation of the Canal, and no threat to foreign nationals in Egypt, there is no basis for military action and therefore no case could be made to Congress or would gain public support for US military intervention.[25]

Makins learnt that Murphy had been instructed by Dulles, with Eisenhower's approval, to insist on the avoidance of the use of force and to propose an international conference under the Constantinople Convention of 1888 on the Suez Canal. He reported to London that Dulles's attitude confirmed:

> the pessimistic impression that I derived from my conversation with Mr Hoover... In prevailing conditions we can look for little help from Washington... No better moment could have been chosen by Nasser for his move as far as the United States is concerned. Having been provoked by the threat of Congressional action into a precipitate rejection of the Egyptian approach over the Aswan Dam, the United States Administration is now helpless, in the face of Congressional inaction and possible recalcitrance during an election campaign, to take strong action – even if they are disposed to do so, which at present they are not.[26]

Makins made it very clear to London on several occasions during the summer and early autumn of 1956 that the Eisenhower administration was opposed to the use of force against Egypt in the run-up to the US presidential election on 6 November. In urging the Foreign Office to support Dulles's proposal for the establishment of the Suez Canal Users' Association (SCUA) and long-term economic sanctions against Egypt, he warned on 9 September about the dire strategic, financial, economic and political consequences for Britain and France of taking military action without US support:

I do not myself see how we and the French can achieve our objective unless we have American resources committed to our side. For example since the Canal and probably the [oil] pipeline would be interrupted we should be completely dependent on American co-operation for oil supplies to Western Europe…It is a matter of comment here, both private and public, that British opinion is sharply divided, especially on the use of force. As in the case of Cyprus, this is a serious impediment to support for our policy in the United States.

I have said nothing about Anglo-American relations. A go-it-alone policy of military intervention would obviously deal them a body-blow. There are times perhaps, (they are surely very rare), when we must take our own line because our national interest transcends even the need to uphold the Atlantic Alliance. But this, I think, is true only when there is an issue of profound substance dividing us. Here it is a case of our wanting to perform an operation one way and the Americans another, but if we keep their immense power working in our favour, is it not preferable to try theirs?[27]

In its anxiety to secure US support against Nasser, the Eden government was prepared to back the SCUA plan. Makins was involved in the ensuing discussions with Dulles and the State Department. He impressed upon Lloyd that it was 'vitally important' for continued Anglo-American co-operation that Eden's planned statement to Parliament on SCUA should take into account the US government's aversion to the use of force.[28] He confided in a letter to his father that he had been 'working continously and, I hope, with some small success, to keep things together; the Americans have played up very well on the whole, especially in view of the plunging and paroxysms of HMG.'[29] In the event Makins's advice was ignored. Eden made a belligerent speech in the House of Commons and Dulles retorted on 13 September that 'the United States did not intend to shoot its way through the Suez Canal'.[30] Disillusioned with SCUA, which was soon rejected by Nasser, the Eden government returned to the idea of an appeal to the UN Security Council as a pretext for military action against Egypt. Six weeks of Anglo-American negotiations, which Makins had helped to encourage, had been wrecked by Eden's desire to punish Egypt and his lack of understanding of the American position.

Makins later reflected that Eden, Lloyd, Kirkpatrick and Macmillan 'never really understood...that SCUA was really a device by Dulles to try and gain time until the US Presidential election was over'.[31] As his warnings to London demonstrated, Makins had an acute understanding of the US position and had sought continued Anglo-American co-operation on the basis of Dulles's proposal for political and economic, rather than military, action against Egypt (that is, a return to the OMEGA Plan). It is possible that Eden and Kirkpatrick thought Makins was too pro-American in his analysis. But they could hardly have failed to be aware of the strong American aversion to the use of force. In anticipating that the Eisenhower administration would not or could not intervene against any military action before the US presidential election (an impression which was misleadingly conveyed by Macmillan to Eden after his talk with President Eisenhower in Washington in late September), they totally misread the situation. This was due to their limited understanding of the American political system and the constitutional position and difficulties of the President. As Makins pointed out in his memoirs, 'Eisenhower, despite being an old wartime friend of Eden and Macmillan, was not going to let that friendship interfere with the protection of US interests'.[32]

Makins was present at Macmillan's separate meetings with Eisenhower and Dulles on 25 September and with Murphy on 29 September and has written 'that there was no basis at all for Macmillan's subsequent optimistic message to Eden'.[33] Eisenhower made only passing references to the Suez Crisis to Macmillan. Makins reflected that this may have been deliberate since Eisenhower had made his opposition to the use of force clear in his letters to Eden and he was not about to confuse the matter by opening up another line of communication with the British government through his old friend Macmillan, the Chancellor of the Exchequer, who was in Washington for the meetings of the IBRD and the International Monetary Fund (IMF). Macmillan 'misinterpreted Eisenhower's cautious remarks on the subject to mean that he would not stand in the way if the British and the French decided to use force against Nasser'.[34] Moreover, he ignored the explicit warnings from Dulles and Murphy that the Eisenhower administration would not condone any Anglo–French military action against Egypt before the presidential election on 6 November, after which time it intended to implement the OMEGA Plan in order to bring about Nasser's 'downfall within a few months'.[35] It should be noted that though Makins and Macmillan both knew Murphy and Eisenhower well, from their war service together in North Africa and the Mediterranean in 1942–43, Makins did not make the same mistake as Macmillan in taking American peacetime co-operation for granted – due, no doubt to Makins's greater knowledge and experience of the American political scene.

In his last fortnight as British Ambassador in Washington Makins was not closely concerned with the Suez Crisis since the scene of diplomatic action had moved to the United Nations in New York. But on 5 October he paid a farewell visit to the White House where President Eisenhower revealed his latest thoughts on the crisis. It was clear, as Makins reported to Eden, that Eisenhower and Dulles were alarmed at the strained state of Anglo-American relations:

> It was always a source of great unhappiness to them when they did not quite see eye-to-eye with the PM and his colleagues. But there was no doubt whatever that public opinion in the United States was firmly opposed to [the] use of force before every possibility of finding a peaceful solution had been exhausted. The effect in the country of such action at the present time could be most serious. Moreover, he himself could not see how the affair would end if force were attempted. In his opinion it could scarcely fail to lead to a chaotic situation in the Middle East, which would encourage further Soviet penetration.[36]

Following Eisenhower's lead, Makins sought in a series of farewell speeches to bolster the Anglo-American 'alliance' by putting the Suez Crisis into a Cold War perspective. In his 'Window on the World' broadcast on 8 October, and his speeches to the Overseas Writers Association on 9 October and the Pilgrims Society on 11 October, Makins suggested that the Suez Crisis was an attempt by the Soviet Union to split the Anglo-American partnership.[37] He warned that this was intended to weaken the Western alliance and lead to an increase of Soviet influence in the Middle East. Drawing on his nearly 30 years experience of Anglo-American relations, he thought it impossible for Britain and the United States to agree on every problem. But he regarded their disagreements (such as on the Suez Crisis) as being over timing and tactics rather than the substance of policies. Unfortunately these differences had been exaggerated by prejudiced and ignorant commentators on both sides of the Atlantic. He identified a need for both Britons and Americans to look at issues from each other's perspective instead of indulging in an ill-informed transatlantic slanging-match. As he told the Pilgrims on 11 October, the day of his departure from the United States, he had made the Anglo-American partnership his 'business'. Although he was leaving the British Embassy in Washington to take up his new post at the Treasury in London, he consoled himself

> with the reflection that politics and economics are merely different sides of the same coin, that I am not leaving the field of Anglo-American relations, but merely moving to a different part of the same field and, finally, that the impact of the Treasury on external policies, if less obvious, may be more incisive than the impact of an Embassy.[38]

These words were to prove uncannily prophetic.

When Makins left the United States, he had grounds for optimism in believing that the Suez Crisis was nearly over, since Britain and Egypt were about to reach agreement in New York on the 'Six Principles' for the operation of the Suez Canal. He had helped to bring this about. His warnings against the use of force, coupled with those from Eisenhower and Dulles, were part of that pressure exerted from Washington which delayed matters long enough in London for other factors to exert an influence and nearly bring about an end to the Suez Crisis, namely the caution of the Foreign Office which led it to push for a diplomatic solution in New York and the need to revise the military timetable because of the onset of winter. If he had been so inclined, Makins could have taken some credit for the fact that the Anglo-American 'alliance', though severely strained by the Suez Crisis, was still intact.

Makins took up his new job as Joint Permanent Secretary at the Treasury on 15 October, the day after Eden decided to collude with France and Israel to attack Egypt. Surprised that no minister, not even his old friend Harold Macmillan, the Chancellor of the Exchequer, wanted to see him to discuss the American position on the Suez Crisis, and sensing that something was up, he made it his business as an old 'Whitehall warrior' to find out what was going on. When he found out from Kirkpatrick the following day, he was taken aback. It had never occurred to him that the British government would act without US support.[39] In his memoirs Makins admits that had he been in

Washington when he learnt of 'the extent of the deception being practised on the Americans, I would have taken the first plane to London to make the situation clear to Eden and the Egypt Committee. If they had then ignored my advice, I would have been forced to reconsider my position'.[40] As it was, Britain was without an ambassador in Washington at a critical moment. Both Makins and his successor, Sir Harold Caccia, thought that this was deliberate since 'the ambassadors were to be kept out of the picture'.[41]

Makins predicted that the policy of collusion would end in disaster and he began to prepare himself mentally for it. But he could not take any direct action, since it had nothing to do with the Joint Permanent Secretary of the Treasury. His job was to run the Treasury and advise the Chancellor on financial matters. It was not until Sunday, 28 October, when Macmillan called him to Birch Grove and told him what he already knew, that Makins felt able to act. He made it clear to Macmillan that the use of force against Egypt would have a profoundly negative effect on Anglo-American relations and asked what was being done to liaise with the Americans. Macmillan had already called for the maintenance of informal links with the Americans, when he warned the Cabinet a few days earlier about the precarious state of Britain's gold and dollar reserves as a result of the crisis.

Both the Treasury and the Bank of England were agreed that US support was vital for the success of any subsequent approach by Britain to the IMF to bolster the reserves, though they differed over the timing of the approach. But the sudden awareness of the likely American reaction seemed to galvanise Macmillan into action and he and Makins immediately drafted some telegrams to Washington. It was to take the momentous events of the next nine days, when the condition of the pound became critical, to persuade Macmillan to abandon his support for the policy of military intervention and to convince the Cabinet of the need to accept a cease-fire in order to try and secure US assistance for an IMF loan and other economic measures (including access to Western Hemisphere oil). But he had begun, on Makins's advice, to take practical steps to secure that assistance as early as 28 October.[42]

The reason why Macmillan took Makins's advice then, having ignored similar advice from the former Permanent Under-Secretary to the Treasury, Sir Edward Bridges, can be put down to Macmillan's increasing worry about the steadily deteriorating economic, domestic and international situation and his implicit trust of Makins, which stemmed from their wartime experiences of working together in North Africa and Italy. After that, whenever Macmillan was in office, he wanted Makins as his adviser. When he became Chancellor of the Exchequer, he requested that Makins become Joint Permanent Secretary at the Treasury on Sir Edward Bridges's retirement (the other Joint Permanent Secretary was Sir Norman Brook who was put in charge of the Civil Service, while remaining Cabinet Secretary). When Makins left the Treasury in 1960, Macmillan offered him the choice of becoming Permanent Under-Secretary at the Foreign Office or the Chairman of the UK Atomic Energy Authority. Makins chose the latter post because he was uniquely qualified for it, having being involved with the British atomic energy programme since its inception.[43]

Macmillan has been accused by Diane Kunz of deliberately inflating the reserve losses figures – he stated that £100 million ($280 million) had been lost in a week, when the Treasury on 7 November indicated that the figure was about £30.4 million ($85 million) in order to persuade the Cabinet on 6 November to agree to a cease-fire.[44] But Makins later denied that this was a deliberate error by Macmillan 'as this was not his style at all.[45] He did not know the reason why the Chancellor got the figures wrong but surmised that it might have been due to a simple miscalculation. It should be pointed out that Macmillan did not receive the actual figures from the Treasury until the day *after* the crucial Cabinet meeting.

The main thrust of Makins's advice to Macmillan throughout the rest of the Suez Crisis was the need to secure US support for an IMF loan for Britain and other economic measures. These included arranging a waiver on the US Loan, selling UK dollar securities in New York, fixing an US Export–Import Bank (EXIM) Loan to buy oil, and ensuring adequate oil supplies from the US. Without US support any British approach to the IMF was bound to fail and the Governor of the Bank of England, Kim Cobbold, wanted this guarantee before he would agree to any such approach.[46]

Once official communications at the top between Eden and Eisenhower were cut off, following Anglo–French military intervention in Egypt, it was clear that it would be no easy task to obtain US support. In the absence of Dulles, who was out of action in hospital, the anti-British Hoover was acting Secretary of State. He successfully prevented a high-level Anglo-American meeting on the grounds that it might drive the Arabs into the arms of the Soviet Union. He also prevented the appointment of the pro-British Bedell Smith as a special presidential adviser. But Makins's knowledge of the Washington scene and his extensive transatlantic contacts offered a way around this, an opportunity of informal contacts or, as Makins put it, for neighbours 'to talk over the garden fence'.[47] Both Makins and his friend, Lord Harcourt, the Economic Minister at the British Embassy in Washington were personal friends of the US Treasury Secretary, George Humphrey. The latter, along with Hoover, was the most vehement opponent of co-operation with Britain and, following Dulles's hospitalisation, the most influential of Eisenhower's advisers. He was a personal friend of the President and, on the question of financial support for Britain, he had obviously a greater say than Hoover.[48]

At Makins's suggestion, Harcourt was instructed to prepare the ground for a subsequent British approach to the Eisenhower administration by speaking to Humphrey about this and the likely American response. On Makins's advice, Macmillan sent a message to Humphrey on 21 November (which Makins helped to draft) dealing with the broader political background and consequences. In addition, and on his own initiative, Macmillan stressed the seriousness of Britain's economic position to the US Ambassador in London, Winthrop Aldrich, and indicated that he and the Lord Privy Seal, R.A. Butler, not Eden, now had political control. This was conveyed to Washington. The cumulative effect of all this was to persuade the Americans to reopen communications with the British through Macmillan and Butler (which gave Makins a position of influence). Moreover, it allowed Eisenhower to overcome the opposition of those in his administration who opposed reconciliation with Britain.[49]

As a result of these contacts, Harcourt and the new British Ambassador in Washington, Sir Harold Caccia, reported in late November that Humphrey and the Eisenhower administration shared the British government's concern at the desperate plight of sterling and said that if Britain and France withdrew from Egypt, the US would not only supply loans and oil but even press the Egyptians to accept an international authority for the Suez Canal. It was Macmillan and Butler who eventually convinced the Cabinet, which was unaware of the secret contacts with the Americans, of the need, given the serious depletion of Britain's reserves since September, for withdrawal by a definite date, in order to secure American support. But it was Makins who kept them supplied with the necessary information (especially on the reserve figures) and defeated any attempts to adopt a new policy. When the Minister of Education, Sir David Eccles, suggested to Macmillan that Britain should turn its back on the United States and establish its leadership of Western Europe by incorporating it in the Sterling Area, Makins (who had attended Winchester College, as had Eccles) commented that he was not 'at any time in favour of what is known on the Continent as a "renversement des alliances", which I had always thought was a Gallic rather than a Wykehamical conception.'[50]

Makins did not exaggerate the dangers of the financial crisis. He did not believe that it was a repeat of the 1949 devaluation crisis. He noted that 'European and other allies currencies were then unbalanced – not the case today (with 1 or 2 exceptions)'.[51] But he drew on the experience that he had gained in the 1949 devaluation talks with the Americans. He was acutely aware that this was an Anglo-American problem, with implications that went far beyond the exchange rate of sterling and Britain's dollar reserves. It involved the functioning of the Anglo-American partnership, which he regarded as the keystone of the Western alliance. Consequently, Makins ensured that the momentum was kept up in the negotiations with the Americans. The importance of this was demonstrated on 4 December when, following the announcement the day before of the withdrawal of British troops from Egypt, Macmillan was able to balance the news that the reserves had fallen to just below the desired $2000 million threshold with the announcement that, with US backing, the British government would seek a drawing on its IMF quota and a waiver on the US Loan.

Within two days, US oil supplies were on their way to Europe and by 22 December Britain received almost $2 billion in US-backed loans and aid from the IMF and the EXIM Bank. Britain and the United States later agreed to abolish the waiver. In future the British would have the right to defer interest and principal payments a total of seven times. Sterling had been narrowly saved but confidence in the currency had been weakened. It was clear that it would take years of cautious management, building up the reserves, and the avoidance of any more setbacks, to restore domestic and international confidence in sterling. The Suez Crisis had effectively set the agenda for Makins's term at the Treasury.[52]

In addition to his duties at the Treasury, Makins sought through his speaking engagements to rebuild public confidence in the Anglo-American relationship. He did not underestimate the difficulty of accomplishing this for, as he told the Current Affairs Unit of the English Speaking Union (ESU) on 12 November, Britain's special position in Washington had been impaired. He urged the ESU to follow Eisenhower's lead and to work to restore hope to the Anglo-American relationship.[53] In speeches to the American Chamber of Commerce in London on 27 November and to the Fishmongers' Company Dinner on 12 December, Makins reaffirmed his profound belief in the Anglo-American partnership.[54] He had never thought that a solid relationship could be built simply on sentiment or on common traditions and a language. It had to depend on shared interests and, at the government level, on the joint defence of those interests on the world stage. Moreover, public opinion in both Britain and the United States had to have a clear understanding of how those interests and objectives coincided. One of the impediments to this was the shift in the economic and strategic balance of power within the Anglo-American relationship in favour of the United States, which was resented by the British. This, and other latent trends, had been brought to the surface as a result of the shock of the impact which the Suez Crisis had had on Anglo-American relations.

Makins detected a rise in anti-Americanism in Britain at a time when anti-British feeling in the United States was on the decline. He saw this as part of a general exchange of characteristics across the Atlantic. As Britain's power declined and it came under increasing pressure, it tended to act more impulsively, which had been an American characteristic in the past. In contrast the burgeoning power of the United States allowed it more time for sober deliberation in international affairs, which had long been seen as a British trait. This complicated the Anglo-American relationship, especially for Britain. He thought that a much greater effort would be needed than before, first to repair the damage done to the relationship by the Suez Crisis, and then to maintain it properly.

Makins was correct in predicting, in a speech to the Winchester branch of the ESU on 16 March 1957, that the imminent meeting in Bermuda between the new prime minister, Harold Macmillan, and President Eisenhower would 'set the seal on the resumption of the now traditional relationship and confidence between our two Governments'.[55]

The Bermuda Conference confirmed also the irrevocable shift in the balance of power within the Anglo-American relationship in favour of the United States. Britain was now 'officially' the dependent junior partner in the 'alliance'. Following the withdrawal of Israeli forces from Egypt, as a result of heavy American pressure, and the reopening of the Suez Canal on 24 April (under an agreement based on the original 'Six Principles'), the Suez Crisis ended. It had been responsible for, in Makins's view, 'an abnormally violent fluctuation in Anglo-American relations'.[56]

Sir Roger Makins's involvement in the Suez Crisis, first as British Ambassador in Washington, then as Joint Permanent Secretary at the Treasury, clearly demonstrated his belief in the vital importance for Britain of the 'alliance' with the United States. He thought that this should be overridden only *in extremis* when there was 'an issue of profound substance dividing us'.[57] The Suez Crisis was not, in his opinion, such an occasion. As ambassador he had helped, through his correct reading of the American position and his transatlantic connections, to delay the use of force long enough to allow other factors to come into play and nearly resolve the Suez Crisis. He had also sought to ease the tension in the Anglo-American relationship through his talks to influential American audiences. When, after his return to London, force was used without American approval and the transatlantic rift occurred, he had played an influential role at the Treasury and in his speeches to British audiences, in conjunction with Macmillan, in the restoration of cordiality to the Anglo-American relationship. In achieving this, his extensive knowledge of the US political scene and his personal friendships with the key players on both sides of the Atlantic proved to be invaluable assets. He had served as the transatlantic diplomat during the Suez Crisis.

NOTES

1. I am indebted to Virginia and Christopher Makins for according me unrestricted access to all relevant material in the Sherfield Papers, which have recently been deposited with the Bodleian Library; MS Memoirs, chapters on North Africa and Washington Embassy.
2. A. Danchev, *Oliver Franks – Founding Father* (Oxford: Clarendon Press, 1993), pp.109–35; P.Boyle 'The "Special Relationship" with Washington' in J.W. Young (ed.), *The Foreign Policy of Churchill's Peacetime Administration 1951–1955* (Leicester: Leicester University Press, 1988), p.32.

3. Sherfield Papers, MS Memoirs, Washington Embassy, p.22.
4. Ibid., p.23.
5. D. Cameron Watt, 'Re-evaluating the Eisenhower Administration' in W.R. Louis and H. Bull (eds.), *The Special Relationship* (Oxford: Clarendon Press, 1986), pp.75–76.
6. Sherfield Papers, MS Memoirs, Suez Crisis, p.2; Sherfield Papers, A. Gorst & W.S. Lucas, 'Interview with Lord Sherfield', undated.
7. Sherfield Papers, MS Memoirs, chapters on Geneva and Foreign Office 1934–39, and Suez Crisis, p.31; author's interview with Lord Sherfield, 17 Sept. 1996.
8. S. Kelly, 'The Washington Embassy of Sir Roger Makins, 1953–1956', unpublished paper delivered to the Anglo-American Seminar at the L.S.E., 26 Nov. 1996.
9. Sherfield Papers, MS Memoirs, Suez Crisis, p.1.
10. CAB 129/66, C(54)53, 15 Feb. 1954; *Foreign Relations of the United States, 1952–1954, Vol.IX, Part 1* (Washington DC: USGPO, 1986), pp.1683–4; W.S. Lucas, *Divided We Stand* (London: Hodder & Stoughton, 1991), pp.32–4.
11. Lucas, *Divided We Stand,* pp.40–57; R. Lamb, *The Failure of the Eden Government* (London: Sidgwick & Jackson, 1987), pp.166, 169, 180; Sherfield Papers, MS Memoirs, Suez Crisis, pp.3, 16–17.
12. Sherfield Papers, MS Memoirs, Suez Crisis, p.10.
13. Ibid., pp.7–11.
14. Ibid., pp.11–16; Kelly, 'Washington Embassy', p.10.
15. Lucas, *Divided We Stand*, pp.89–90.
16. Sherfield Papers, MS Memoirs, Suez Crisis, pp.16–21.
17. *Foreign Relations of the United States, 1955–1957, Vol. XV* (Washington DC, USGPO, 1990), pp.726–7; Lucas, *Divided We Stand*, pp.128–9; Sherfield papers, Lord Sherfield, MS 'Sidelights on Suez', Part 1, p.2.
18. *FRUS, 1955–1957, Vol. XV*, pp.830–2; Lucas, *Divided We Stand,* pp.129–30.
19. Sherfield Papers, Personal Correspondence (hereafter PC), Black Box (hereafter BB) II, C/PER/IV/IV, Roger Makins to Ernest Makins, 18 July 1956.
20. D. Kunz, *The Economic Diplomacy of the Suez Crisis* (Chapel Hill: University of North Carolina Press, 1991), pp.68–72; K. Kyle, *Suez* (London: Weidenfeld & Nicolson, 1991), pp.128–9; Lucas, *Divided We Stand*, pp.135–7, R. Rhodes-James, *Anthony Eden* (London: Weidenfeld & Nicolson, 1986), pp.448–50; Sir Anthony Eden, *Full Circle* (London: Cassell, 1960), p.422; S. Lloyd, *Suez* (London: Jonathan Cape, 1978), p.71.
21. Sherfield Papers, MS Memoirs, Suez Crisis, p.23.
22. Ibid., p.24.
23. FO 800/728, Millard memo, 21 Oct. 1957, p.6.
24. Sherfield Papers, MS Memoirs, Suez Crisis, pp.24–5.
25. FO 371/119080/JE14211/87, Makins to FO, tel. 1613, 30 July 1956.
26. Ibid.
27. PREM 11/1101, Makins to FO, tels. 1845–1847, 9 Sept. 1956.
28. Sherfield Papers, MS Memoirs, Suez Crisis, pp.30–31.
29. Sherfield Papers, PC, BB II, C/PER/IV/IV, Roger Makins to Ernest Makins, 11 Sept. 1956.
30. Sherfield Papers, MS Memoirs, Suez Crisis, pp.30–31.
31. Ibid., p.31.
32. Ibid., p.31.
33. Ibid., p.33.

34. Ibid., p.32.
35. Ibid., p.33.
36. PREM 11/1102, Makins to Eden, 5 Oct. 1956.
37. Sherfield Papers, Green Box (hereafter GB) 41, speeches of 8, 9, 11 Oct. 1956.
38. Ibid.
39. Sherfield Papers, MS Memoirs, Suez Crisis, pp.35–7.
40. Ibid., p.51.
41. Ibid., p.39; information from Clarissa Pryce-Jones (daughter of Sir Harold Caccia).
42. Ibid., p.40; L. Johnman, 'Defending the Pound: The Economics of the Suez Crisis, 1956' in A. Gorst, L. Johnman, W.S. Lucas (eds), *Post-War Britain: Themes and Perspectives, 1945–64* (London: Pinter Press, 1989), pp.172–3.
43. Harold Macmillan, *Riding the Storm* (London: Macmillan, 1971), pp.2–3; author's interview with Lord Sherfield, 17 Sept. 1996.
44. Kunz, *Economic Diplomacy*, pp.131–3.
45. Sherfield Papers, MS Memoirs, Suez Crisis, p.42.
46. Ibid., pp.43–5.
47. Sherfield Papers, A. Gorst and W.S. Lucas interview, p.8.
48. Sherfield Papers, MS Memoirs, Suez Crisis, p.38; Lucas, *Divided We Stand*, pp.299–301.
49. Sherfield Papers, MS Memoirs, pp.46–47; T236/4189, Makins to Macmillan, 16 Nov. 1956; T236/4190, Makins to Macmillan, 22 Nov. 1956; Lucas, *Divided We Stand*, pp.309–13.
50. Sherfield Papers, MS Memoirs, Suez Crisis, pp.48–9; T236/4190, Makins minute, 4 Dec. 1956.
51. Sherfield Papers, GB 41, notes for speech to Monday Luncheon Club, 10 Dec. 1956.
52. Sherfield Papers, MS Memoirs, Suez Crisis, pp.48–50.
53. Sherfield Papers, GB 41, speech of 12 Nov. 1956.
54. Sherfield Papers, GB 41, speeches of 27 Nov. and 12 Dec. 1956.
55. Sherfield Papers, GB 41, speech of 16 March 1957.
56. Sherfield Papers, GB 41, speech of 10 April 1957.
57. PREM 11/1101, Makins to FO, tels.1845–47, 9 Sept. 1956.

The Diplomats' Diplomat:
Sir Pierson Dixon,
Ambassador to the United Nations

EDWARD JOHNSON

Sir Pierson Dixon, Britain's Ambassador to the United Nations at the time of Suez, had one of the most onerous tasks of all British officials during the crisis.[1] He was called on to defend Britain's use of force against Egypt, in the public forum of the UN, where Britain had few supporters, when he was often in complete ignorance of events in London and the Middle East. This contribution examines Dixon's defence of Eden's policy during the week of military action which began with the Israeli invasion of Egypt on 29 October and ended with the cease-fire on 6 November. It was then that Dixon's role was most prominent, and a full understanding of it and and his attitude to Eden's policy can only be achieved by some detailed examination of his actions during the fast-moving events of that week.

'Bob' Dixon was a highly accomplished and experienced diplomat who had been private secretary to Eden 1943–45 and to Ernest Bevin 1945–48, a role which took him to the wartime conferences at Yalta and Potsdam and to the post-war Council of Foreign Ministers meetings. He had then been appointed British Ambassador to Czechoslovakia, a post he held for two years until returning to the Foreign Office in 1950 where he remained until succeeding Gladwyn Jebb at the United Nations in 1954. Dixon was a diplomat's diplomat, a firm believer in the values and virtues of diplomacy to solve international disputes. He had been vigorous in his opposition to Nasser's nationalization of the Suez Canal Company, but he did not countenance the use of force to solve the Canal question especially when it was used as part of a secret, contrived and underhanded plan. He clearly thought Britain was in the wrong and had grave reservations about the action which he was called on to defend in the

UN. It was a defence which subjected Dixon to great moral and physical strain.[2] The physical strain came from the sheer pressure of work during the crisis. The effort involved in attending meetings at the UN and putting Britain's case, of overseeing the despatch of telegrams, receiving incoming ones from London and responding by telephone to the Foreign Office at all hours of the night and day must have subjected Dixon to alarming pressures. The stress was clearly too much for Dixon's French colleague, Bernard Cornut-Gentille whose nerves collapsed under the pressure of work as early as 31 October. Yet the moral strain on Dixon, which was the more damaging and longer lasting, arose from his opposition to Eden's use of force against Nasser.

The defence of force was never going to be an easy task for the representative of one of the founding members of the UN especially when the aggrieved state was the leader of the Arab world, and when both superpowers, but particularly the US government, were resolutely opposed to British policy. The defence was made more difficult by Dixon's exclusion from the circle of policy makers and officials who knew of the Sèvres agreement. Eden did not consult his former private secretary about the arrangements with the French and the Israelis, presumably because he knew Dixon well enough to know that he would be opposed.

Dixon had given indications of his views while on leave in London during August and also from despatches sent from New York during September.[3] In these he had made clear that once the Suez issue was taken to the United Nations it would be difficult to resist moves towards negotiation and compromise, and most importantly that the UN would not, in his opinion, underwrite any Anglo-French use of force against Nasser. Dixon also had received clear indications from Henry Cabot Lodge, the head of the American delegation to the UN, that the US would be opposed to the use of force.[4] Thus when the British took the Suez issue to the UN on 23 September a process of defusing the tension began, as Dixon had indicated. The British and French proposed the 'Six Principles' to govern the management and operation of the Canal and much of Dixon's time was spent negotiating with the UN Secretary-General, Dag Hammarskjold and the French and Egyptians on the details of the agreement, which he did with the support of the British Foreign Secretary, Selwyn Lloyd who was in New York from 2 October to 15 October. Dixon had therefore no indication of the background to events which were to break with the Israeli invasion of Egypt. This put him at a great disadvantage. It meant that for part of the week from 29 October to the cease-fire on 6 November he was operating very much in the dark in New York, unsure about what would be coming through next from London. It compromised his position on a number of occasions and put him on the back foot from the start of the crisis. Even so, both Eden, who did more than anyone to place Dixon in the straitened diplomatic role that he found himself, and the British Foreign Secretary Selwyn Lloyd were full of praise for his performance and defence of British policy at the UN.[5]

It was a defence in two parts. In the first period Dixon sought to delay the UN in order to allow the Anglo-French forces to gain a military foothold in the Canal Zone which might pay political dividends with Nasser later. Once it became clear however that the US government was driving the UN hard, was not prepared to sanction any delay and wanted a cease-fire and the invading troops out of Egypt, Dixon, with London's backing, then attempted to link the cease-fire to the successful creation of a UN force and to make some connection between it and the Anglo-French forces. This was a policy doomed to failure because of the unrelenting US opposition to British action but Dixon did his part in arguing the British case. However his defence of Eden's policy was, understandably, not always consistent. While he gave what advice that he could to Eden and Selwyn Lloyd about the best way of managing the British case in the UN, his fundamental opposition to the use of force also shone through on at least two occasions when he warned them of the grave consequences for Britain in the UN and the wider international community if it continued with its policy of force in Egypt. In fact Dixon's final warning, sent on 5 November, may well have played some part in convincing Eden that the military operation had to be called off.

Dixon's exclusion from the circle of collusion meant that he was caught out by the Israeli attack on Egypt, news of which reached him on the afternoon of 29 October. His first reaction, in line with Lodge and Cornut-Gentille, was to support a convening of the Security Council to 'call on Israel to withdraw her forces to the Israel side of the armistice demarcation line'. He cabled the Foreign Office accordingly[6] unaware that his own government was about to issue ultimata which would allow the Israelis to advance to within ten miles of the Suez Canal. While Dixon was certain the Israelis should withdraw, he did not wish to drive them into the dock at the UN and let Nasser off the hook. He therefore awaited instructions from London which were due the following day. The Americans however were not so patient and sought to rush the Security Council into session. This led to the first of a number of rows between Dixon and Lodge. Both were at the New York Metropolitan Opera House on the night of 29 October where Dixon's secretary, Douglas Hurd, ferried notes between them. Lodge informed Dixon of the US intention to request a meeting of the Security Council for the following morning and handed him Eisenhower's recent press statement, which made references to obligations under the Tripartite Declaration. Lodge claimed he saw a different side of the British Ambassador that night. Dixon was a fairly unemotional, reserved man and rather oblique in his manner; he 'had always been amiable but at this conference the mask fell off and he was virtually snarling'. He rejected the US reference to the Tripartite Declaration as 'silly and moralistic', asserting 'that the British would never go along with any move against Israel in the Security Council'.[7]

Shortly after this heated exchange, Dixon requested instructions from Lloyd on how far he could go, 'in associating myself with what appears to be a determined attempt on the part of the United States to bring the Israelis to heel'.[8] While he expected the Israelis to be censured for their action, he opposed US policy which he thought would send a reprieve to the Egyptians.[9] By the early morning of 30 October, Lloyd let in some light and gave Dixon some indication of Anglo-French intentions to halt hostilities. This was a vague reference to the ultimata that were to be addressed to the Israeli and Egyptian governments later on that day. Dixon was told to play for time and ensure if possible that no resolution, American or otherwise, was submitted to the UN.[10] Any resolution would almost certainly have delayed the imminent Anglo-French ultimatum and called on the Israelis to withdraw to their side of the armistice lines, something that was not part of the Sèvres accord.[11]

From this point Dixon sought to nullify American actions against Israel, so aggravating relations with Lodge. When the Security Council met on the morning of 30 October, Lodge recorded that Dixon and Cornut-Gentille were both 'white-faced and hostile to any conciliatory suggestions' and seemed merely intent on delaying tactics.[12] Dixon now refused to support the US call for the Security Council to meet as it would stop the Israeli advance.[13] The American delegation observed that Dixon had realised his position now conflicted with his views of the previous day, but he did not want to be quoted on this.[14]

Dixon's exclusion from the Sèvres circle further compromised him when the Anglo-French ultimata were delivered to the Egyptian and Israeli governments later the same day. Dixon had not been given any detailed notice of these. Lloyd had merely intimated to him some Anglo-French action without specifying what it might be. However, the full Security Council was given unofficial notice of the ultimata when, in its morning session [it began at 11am EST; 4pm GMT, 30 October] Sobolev, the Soviet representative, read out an early press report of Eden's statement to the House of Commons which included the terms. Dixon was 'much taken aback' and claimed lamely 'that he was waiting for the text of an important statement by Eden to the House of Commons'.[15] This was received in time for the afternoon session, where Dixon, 'obviously shaken',[16] read it out. Then, on the basis of the Anglo-French ultimata, he appealed publicly,[17] and then privately,[18] to Lodge not to press on with the US draft resolution in the Security Council. Lodge was not to be delayed however and Dixon thought he was under instructions 'to oppose us at every point'. Lodge even added a paragraph to the US resolution calling for an immediate cease-fire so undermining the Anglo-French ultimata.

Under instructions by telephone from London, Dixon, with his French colleague, then vetoed the US resolution, the first ever British use of the veto in the UN. The Soviet Union then re-introduced the original US resolution without Lodge's added cease-fire paragraph, on which Lloyd appeared to be willing to abstain and pressed Dixon to lobby the French delegation to do likewise. However the French had been instructed by Pineau, the French Foreign Minister, to use the veto again and the British followed in the name of unity. On this Dixon had his reservations. He was sure a British abstention on the Soviet resolution would have defused some of the hostility in the Security Council and stayed its hand, possibly even deflecting it from its subsequent course of action which was to call the General Assembly into emergency session under the Uniting for Peace procedure. He did cast the second veto, but only after being fortified and encouraged by a telephone conversation with Selwyn Lloyd.[19] It ended 'a thoroughly unsatisfactory day's work' for Dixon, as UN delegates expressed their shock at Anglo-French action, the Norwegian representative going so far as to declare it 'an appalling blow to Western unity'.[20]

As the crisis developed, its management moved away from London and Paris to Washington and New York as the US government sought to frustrate the military objectives of its allies. With this movement Dixon began to play a more prominent role, and his exclusion from those in the know over the Sèvres agreement began to matter less. In London Archibald Ross, the Superintending Under-Secretary for the Levant Department in the Foreign Office, confirmed that Dixon would have considerable latitude in the defence of Britain's case in the UN.[21] This defence was becoming increasingly important as the chorus of diplomatic opposition swelled in New York. As the UN, driven hard by the US delegation, put unrelenting diplomatic pressure on Britain and France to agree to a cease-fire, Dixon was to find himself pulled in two directions. He continued to defend Britain's case as best he could, warning the Americans against precipitate action and advising London on how it might hold the UN at bay thereby giving the Anglo-French forces time to get ashore in Egypt. At the same time, he was to become increasingly despondent about Britain's use of force in Egypt and the effect it would have on Britain's international standing and her place in the UN.

In trying to slow down the UN, Dixon realised the key lay with the US delegation whose 'tantrums'[22] he privately condemned. He saw Lodge on the morning of 31 October and warned him of the dangers of arraigning the British and French as aggressors in the Security Council, or hauling them before the General Assembly. Either action would drive both powers from the UN which would then collapse. In the circumstances, Dixon requested 'a cool review of the position as between friends' and felt he convinced Lodge of the need to slow the pace of events and also provided him with a better understanding of Britain's position.[23] If Lodge was convinced, Dulles was not and he put his weight behind the Yugoslav government's proposal, in the light of the vetoes, to refer the issue to an emergency session of the General Assembly under the Uniting for Peace procedure.[24] Dixon was sure that the Americans were 'desperately anxious to avoid a condemnatory resolution against us and France which they might find themselves obliged to support'.[25] In fact the US did press the Soviet Union to withdraw its condemnation of Britain in return for US support to take the matter to the General Assembly. Dixon showed some gratitude to Lodge for this, but this normally reserved man was still emotional on the matter, informing Lodge that he would attack the US in the

Security Council if a resolution condemning Britain was tabled.[26]

The strength of opposition to Britain was brought home forcibly when the Security Council met at 3pm [EST] on 31 October and Hammarskjold rebuked the British and French and even threatened to resign, so incensed was he at the Anglo-French action and vetoes.[27] According to Brian Urquhart, Dixon privately reacted angrily and accused the Secretary-General of unfairness in that the Soviet Union had not been so pilloried on the innumerable occasions when it had used the veto. Yet Hammarskjold simply expected better from the British and the French, particularly the British.[28] Hammarskjold's expectations were further eroded when news emerged later that day that Anglo-French airforces were bombing targets in Egypt, to which Dixon, not informed and yet again unable to reply with unassailable authority, could merely claim that they were military ones.[29]

By the afternoon of 31 October, it was clear that the UN was out to stop the British and French in Egypt and was not to be delayed by the British veto. The issue was transferred to the General Assembly under the Uniting for Peace procedure, the first time it had been used. It then fell to Dixon both to impress on his government the strength of opposition to its policy in Egypt and also to limit the resentment felt in the UN towards the British. Accordingly he wished to 'bring home the strength of our case at least to the more responsible delegations'. It could not be done solely by speeches but required the British to put forward concrete proposals which in the long term could assist a Middle East settlement but which in the short term would separate the Israelis and the Egyptians and protect the Canal.[30] The Anglo-French forces, once arrived in the Canal Zone, could do this; then if the Israelis withdrew, the Anglo-French forces would follow. Dixon requested instructions from London to underwrite this plan if it was to work and noted that the French delegation were working along the same lines.[31] Selwyn Lloyd was encouraged and allowed Dixon to promote it in the UN,[32] an indication that the British were now seeking some diplomatic lifeline to cling to, had misread the level of likely opposition and needed a face-saver to justify their action, even before Anglo-French forces had landed in Egypt.

Having proposed a way of handling the opposition in the UN, Dixon then had to advise his government on whether to attend the meeting of the General Assembly called for Thursday, 1 November. He doubted the legality of the move to the General Assembly but felt he should attend to avoid Britain's case going by default. Yet Dixon realised London would wish to keep in step with the French, and their delegation at the UN expected Paris to stay away.[33] In the event Pineau decided to represent France, a position which Dixon advised against. Dulles was to attend for the Americans and Dixon, looking to the future of Anglo-French-US relations, thought it better for the American Secretary of State to be confronted by officials and not Ministers.[34] The British agreed that Dulles should be met by someone and gave Dixon special credentials to represent Britain.[35]

Dixon went into the General Assembly having received a telegram from Kirkpatrick in the Foreign Office indicating that in the Commons that afternoon, 1 November, Eden was to refer to the UN assuming Britain's responsibilities in the Canal Zone.[36] Eden of course did precisely that by inviting the UN, 'to take over the physical task of maintaining peace in that area'.[37] The time differences involved allowed Dixon to have the text of Eden's speech with him in the General Assembly. His opening address was followed by that of Dulles, by then fully acquainted with the collusion of the three powers in Egypt,[38] and the tabling of yet another American resolution which again the British could not support. This called for an immediate cease-fire, a withdrawal of all military forces from the area and for the Suez Canal to be reopened. Dixon considered it anti-British.[39] It was inconsistent with his government's policy and, in the absence of instructions from London, he had to vote against it.[40] However before he did so, he sent the first of his warnings to his government in a personal telegram to Selwyn Lloyd, in which he severely cautioned him on the dangers of a vote against the Americans. The US resolution had broad support, and was an expression of UN opinion against Britain and France. In language which could not be misinterpreted, Dixon noted that Britain's closest friends were becoming 'intensely worried at the possible consequences which might follow if we and the French remained for long in open defiance of the United Nations'. There was talk of moving onto collective measures against the two powers. Britain's friends were concerned that 'our open defiance of the United Nations may be compounded to the point where we have no option but to leave the organization'. It seemed to Dixon and to other delegates in New York that either Britain would leave the UN or would have to climb down. Even the Yugoslav delegation, who with the US had led the hunt against the British, were petitioning Dixon to find some formula which would avoid a prolonged challenge to the United Nations. It was in this light that Dixon was intrigued by Eden's statement inviting the UN to assume some responsibility in Egypt and reported that he expected some proposal to be tabled in the UN fairly soon.[41]

It came sooner than Dixon expected, at the end of the marathon General Assembly session which finished at 4.20am EST on 2 November. Lester Pearson, the Canadian Minister for External Affairs, in explaining his abstention on the US resolution, felt that any cease-fire needed an international force to police it. Here was a lifeline thrown by the Canadians to the British which Dixon and those in London grasped. Dixon endorsed Pearson's position and repeated Eden's offer to the Assembly.[42] In London, Selwyn Lloyd and Kirkpatrick had concluded by 1 November that a UN role in the Suez crisis might provide the British some means of shelter from the diplomatic storm that was breaking in New York and Washington. They suggested the same to Eden who completed his Commons' speech that day with the vague invite.[43] Kirkpatrick had also talked to Norman Robertson, the Canadian High-Commissioner in London and learnt from him that Pearson was likely to propose the creation of a UN military force to police a cease-fire in the Middle East and the convening of a special conference to resolve the problems of Arab–Israeli relations. Consequently the British government knew if it publicly advanced the idea of a UN force, there was some underlying momentum for it.[44] Dixon therefore encouraged Pearson, something of which both Kirkpatrick and Lloyd were aware.[45] But whereas Pearson wished to ease the British off a hook of their own making and bring them closer to the US government, Eden wished to link the UN force to British goals: if not the removal of Nasser then at least a settlement of the Canal question and a broad peace in the Middle East. Thus Eden did not see a UN force as restraining British occupation of the Canal – rather, the opposite.[46] The British indicated that they were prepared to cease fire on condition that Egypt and Israel would accept a UN force to keep the peace and the force was to remain until agreement had been reached on both an Arab–Israeli peace settlement and the management of the Canal. Until such time that the UN force was constituted both Egypt and Israel must accept limited detachments of Anglo-French forces. Thus did Eden seek to link the creation of a UN force to the allied forces that were at the time on their way to the Canal zone and put a gloss of respectability on British policy.

Dixon received word of these British conditions late on the night of 2 November. Lloyd wished him to 'see how our minds are working' and hoped the statement would be useful: Eden was to make the same points in the House of Commons debate at noon GMT on the following day, Saturday 3 November and Dixon was requested to present it to Hammarskjold by 9am EST, [2pm GMT].[47] Dixon signalled his approval of the general line as 'very statesmanlike' indicating that some delegations would see it as 'a constructive attempt on our part to give the United Nations an opportunity to solve the outstanding questions in the Middle East'. But again he warned that there were still some member states, the 'rats' who would aim to put the British and French 'on the mat at another Assembly meeting'. Dixon thought it useful to get the Americans and Canadians on side and suggested that London inform all member states of British intentions with an appeal for support: if this could be done it might undercut some of the hysteria of the UN delegations.[48]

However, Dixon found it was the British position which was soon undercut when Hammarskjold telephoned him with United Nations Truce Supervision Organization reports from Egypt that the British were to attack non-military targets in the Cairo area. In view of the severity of the situation, Hammarskjold circulated this report as a UN document, putting it formally in the public domain. This report caused Dixon real distress: having seen some way out of the political mire, it seemed that Britain's footing had slipped again through its own failings. At this point he took a stand on the use of force and did not pull his punches when he telegraphed London that any action on non-military targets 'would make a mockery of our repeated assertions that our intervention was an emergency police action confined to the occupation of a few key points along the Canal' and he sought Lloyd's authority to deny these reports. If he was not allowed to do so, Britain's position in the UN would become untenable. Britain could not bomb open cities and expect any sympathy; it would undermine Britain's position in the UN and 'in these circumstances the only honest course for Her Majesty's Government and the French Government would be to withdraw their representatives and leave the United Nations'.[49] Dixon now saw that he must push hard for a cease-fire. Britain's word would count for nothing in the UN unless he could announce that Anglo-

French forces were 'suspending all further military activities until we know whether the United Nations are prepared to deal with the whole situation effectively'. There was no other way of securing Britain's objective in the Middle East, 'without alienating the whole world'.[50]

Seldom can a post-war British Ambassador have spoken with such candour to his government. In the circumstances it struck home. Selwyn Lloyd telephoned Dixon to authorize him to state that no attacks were to be made on areas where civilian casualties were inevitable. Lloyd would give Hammarskjold his word on this.[51] But Eden was not prepared to endorse Dixon's appeal for a cease-fire. The Anglo-French paratroopers had yet to go in and the sea-borne invasion force was still at sea. Eden needed a foothold in Egypt to bargain with and a cease-fire denied his government this: Dixon would have to wait.

In the mean time, Pearson had produced a draft resolution, which called on the Secretary-General to submit a plan for a UN force to the General Assembly within 48 hours to secure and supervise the cessation of hostilities as provided for in the earlier American resolution [No.997]. Dixon was told to welcome this provided British amendments were added. These proposed for a committee of UN members, not Hammarskjold, to plan the force which should utilize those military forces immediately available: the British and French Musketeer forces.[52] Again the British were seeking to link Anglo-French units with the deployment of a later UN force, thereby gaining a measure of international legitimacy for their invasion. In addition, Lloyd stressed to Dixon that the UN force had to be linked to a Middle East solution and a settlement of the Suez Canal dispute. Thus the allied landings could not be delayed but Lloyd guaranteed the minimum use of force in overcoming opposition.[53] Unfortunately for the British, the political momentum for the UN force was developing so quickly as to become unstoppable, and significantly the US idea of the UN force was different from the British view. With the weight of the US delegation behind it,[54] the unamended Canadian resolution [998] was adopted early on the morning of 4 November. Without the British amendments, Lloyd directed Dixon to abstain. He told the General Assembly that urgent police action was still required and it seemed to him 'that in some respects the resolution goes too far and in others not far enough. It was for that reason that I was not able to vote for the resolution, but, equally, I was able to abstain.'[55] In the same session he voted against an Afro-Asian resolution as it broadly repeated the earlier US Resolution 997.[56] However, it did authorize Hammarskjold to arrange a cease-fire and to report on its compliance within 12 hours.

The pace was now building to get the UN force established before the Anglo-French troops could land in Egypt. Hammarskjold, buoyed by three cease-fire resolutions in the General Assembly requested all parties to halt military operations by 8pm GMT on 4 November.[57] This was subsequently extended by Hammarskjold to 5am GMT, 5 November [midnight EST]. Hammarskjold had already done the preparatory work on the plan requested under the Canadian Resolution 998 and was due to give an interim report to the General Assembly. Dixon now needed guidance from London as to what to do. Could he announce a cease-fire as Hammarskjold had requested by midnight and would he be able to vote for the interim report on the UN force that Hammarskjold had prepared?

On the first question of the cease-fire, Kirkpatrick despatched guidance to Dixon at 12.56am GMT, on 5 November [7.56pm EST on 4 November]. Kirkpatrick was acutely aware of Dixon's position. He feared, 'our reply will NOT make your task easy.'[58] Ministers had decided that Anglo-French landings due for 5am GMT on 5 November had to be made. The British would cease all military action, if Israel and Egypt and the UN accepted the Canadian plan – the one Dixon had not been allowed to support. In the meantime the British had to get ashore to use the presence of Anglo-French troops as later leverage on Nasser. The Foreign Office, in consultation with Dixon, constructed a formal reply to Hammarskjold around these points, retaining the British conditions for a cease-fire.[59] Dixon himself amended the British response, as the original draft implied the UN force would have only limited functions not attached to a broader Canal agreement.[60] He was able to deliver it at 2.30am EST [7.30am GMT] on 5 November to the Secretary-General, by which time the allied forces were ashore in Egypt.[61]

On the second question of the vote on Hammarskjold's plan for a UN force [GA Resolution 1000], Dixon abstained. He informed the General Assembly that the resolution was submitted in the middle of the night for London and he did not have instructions.[62] However it seems Dixon had consulted Kirkpatrick on the resolution, but may not have had written guidance on it.[63] So, although the British welcomed the idea of a UN force in their reply to Hammarskjold, they could not vote in support of its creation. In part the reason lay in Hammarskjold's exclusion of permanent members of the Security Council from the UN force, something which Dixon noted was designed to keep the Russians out of the Middle East as well as avoiding discrimination against the British and the French.[64] It did however cut across British expectations that they would be the vanguard of a UN force, something which again Dixon had to warn London was no longer realistic.[65]

Dixon had to issue further warnings to his government when, on the morning of the 5 November, Hammarskjold phoned him with information of the RAF's bombing of Cairo and Heliopolis. This forced Dixon to warn Eden's government yet again of the likely repercussions of bombing cities. He had warned his government before; he now repeated these warnings 'with renewed emphasis'. The General Assembly would 'be in a very ugly mood and out for our blood.' It would want to know why Britain had not complied with the calls for a cease-fire and why it had contravened its declared policy by bombing civilian areas. Britain could expect the Soviet Union to press for collective measures to be taken in the Security Council. Dixon requested information on Britain's bombing policy and on Egyptian casualties and 'information as to when our limited operation with its limited objectives is going to stop'. He recognised that in the light of General Keightley's precautions to avoid civilian casualties, these charges against Britain might appear unjust but:

> We are inevitably being placed in the same low category as the Russians in their bombing of Budapest. I do not see how we can carry much conviction in our protests against the Russian bombing of Budapest, if we are ourselves bombing Cairo.[66]

Once again the Eden government was stung into a rebuttal of the charges made against it. Dixon was given authorization to declare that bombing had been conducted with the utmost consideration for civilians and that photographic evidence proved it. He could announce a cease-fire had been ordered for the area of Port Said for that day, 5 November and that all bombing in Egypt would cease forthwith.[67]

When the General Assembly re-convened on 5 November, to Dixon's surprise the British were not put on the carpet. Member states now had Hungary and Soviet action in Budapest on their minds and Dixon noted an improvement in the atmosphere in the UN. He then sent London an *aide-memoire* from Hammarskjold which indicated that as both Egypt and Israel had accepted a cease-fire and the General Assembly had authorised the UN force command, the British conditions for halting military operations appeared to have been met and the Secretary-General repeated his plea to Eden's government for a cease-fire.[68]

Having spoken in the most forthright tones to Eden on the need for a cease-fire, Dixon now in an apparently contradictory fashion, tried to delay the UN to allow the British to achieve their military objectives. He felt if British forces could achieve these by Wednesday evening [7 November] and could broadly agree with the Canadian plans for the UN force, the UN might settle down. He had detected in Pearson and Hammarskjold a more sympathetic appreciation of Britain's position and a willingness to delay a further General Assembly meeting. It was at this point that Dixon made his plea to Hammarskjold that 'quite serious proposals were projected at us without notice late at night when Europe was asleep and we were then forced to take up a position in public immediately.' If progress was to be made, proper consideration of plans had to be given by both the British and French governments. Therefore the tempo of the UN would need to be slowed down, sentiments with which both Hammarskjold and Pearson agreed.[69]

After talking to Pearson and Hammarskjold, Dixon heard disturbing reports that the cease-fire called for the Port Said area had been countermanded but he was re-assured by a personal phone call from Eden in the middle of the night in New York to assure him that no air bombing had taken place since the earlier British assurance nor would any take place in future.[70] During this conversation, Eden informed his former private secretary that Britain would soon have secured its military goals. In reply Dixon judged that if the US could be induced to 'slow down the hunt' against Britain he would be able to stall the UN until the end of the week, roughly 9 or 10 November.[71] This would have been ample time for Eden.

But US pressure on the Eden government and in particular on the pound sterling was intensifying. The Cabinet met on the morning of 6 November, only just over one hour after Eden's talk with Dixon, with evidence from Macmillan, the Chancellor of the Exchequer, but not necessarily from the Treasury, that Britain's reserves were plummeting and economic ruin stared the country in the face. US assistance was not forthcoming and thus pressure to halt the operation in Egypt strengthened. This, combined with Soviet moves in the UN which might, as Dixon thought, presage some independent Soviet action in the Middle East was a powerful factor in the move to cease fire. But as Keith Kyle has succinctly noted, the Eden government was caught by the fulfillment of its own demands. By the morning of 6 November, the British conditions which it had laid down in the reply to Hammarskjold only three days before had been met; there was no justification to continue fighting.[72] Consequently Dixon received a spate of telegrams in the late morning of 6 November informing him that British forces were to cease fire at midnight GMT.[73] Having been prepared to slow down the pace of the UN to allow the British to get a greater foot-hold in Egypt, Dixon must have been bewildered to find less than seven hours later that fighting was to stop.

With the cease-fire agreed, UN attention shifted to forcing the withdrawal of the invading forces from Egypt. Selwyn Lloyd flew out to New York on 12 November to take charge of the negotiations linking the withdrawal of British troops and the arrival of the UN contingents. This was not intended by Lloyd as a veiled criticism of Dixon, on the contrary, he wished to take some of the heat from him:

> First and foremost I had to come to the relief of Bob Dixon and his delegation. They had done a magnificent job in a trying situation. Dixon himself had not faltered or put a foot wrong. I felt that now I, as their political chief, must also face the music.[74]

Until the end of November Lloyd took on the responsibility of trying to squeeze as much as he could from Hammarskjold over British withdrawal and the functions of the UN force. The British policy did not change: the UN force should be linked to wider Middle East goals, not merely the disengagement of the Anglo-French-Israeli forces, and the British should not withdraw until it was clear the UN force was to tackle these issues. If the British attitude did not move, nor did the American. Under persistent pressure from the US government and the United Nations, Selwyn Lloyd read the political runes. By the end of November he returned to London convinced that Britain would have to withdraw without being able to use the presence of British troops as a lever on Nasser. Lloyd signalled on 3 December the Cabinet's decision to withdraw according to a time-table agreed by Burns, the UN force commander and General Keightley, the

Commander-in-Chief of the Allied Forces. By Christmas 1956, all allied forces, except some remaining salvage crews, had departed Egypt.

What assessment can therefore be made of Dixon's role in the Suez crisis in the period which covered the fighting ? There is no doubt that he acted as a loyal official and defended Britain in what were extremely difficult circumstances. These were aggravated by his exclusion from those who knew of the collusion, an exclusion which led to him being compromised over his initial reaction to the Israeli invasion and his public ignorance of the Anglo-French ultimata. Eden chose not to tell Dixon because he knew him well enough to realise that he would have been opposed. However, soon after the release of the ultimata, Dixon, the man with the most subtle mind in Whitehall according to Macmillan,[75] must have been able to draw some fairly clear conclusions about collusion which the US and Soviet delegations had already deduced and in the US case were to have confirmed to them almost immediately by the French.

Dixon felt a great sense of isolation defending Eden's government in the UN in which there was no hiding place once the British had issued their ultimata: he was in the front line as head of Britain's UN delegation. He was also the most senior British official in the US as Sir Harold Caccia, the British Ambassador to Washington designate, had not yet taken up his post following the departure of Sir Roger Makins. Dixon's isolation was heightened by the fact that two of the members of the British delegation, Douglas Hurd and Mary Galbraith, were new to the posts and although he had a good professional relationship with Crosthwaite, his deputy, he would not have shared any private feelings on the crisis with him.[76] But then Dixon was by nature an unemotional, indirect, oblique man who did not share his feelings with others.[77] We should also remember that once Cornut-Gentille collapsed through stress, Dixon became the senior official on both the British and French delegations: his sense of being alone in the front line defending the British case must have been stark.

It was a defence which had to deal with expected attacks from the Soviet bloc but most annoyingly from the American delegation and Lodge. Dixon did not like Lodge. Lodge was a politician and Dixon a diplomat and he found the American too forthright and to the point.[78] But the American policy of ostracising Britain in the UN forced Dixon to come to the point and to warn Lodge of the calamitous consequences for Anglo-US relations and for Britain's future in the

UN if the British were labelled aggressors, something which in fact the British and Anglo-US relations were spared.

Dixon's relationship with Eden and Selwyn Lloyd was also not without its element of tension. He had to warn them that Britain might have to leave the UN. This seems, on first glance, to have been a fairly dramatic declaration from an unemotional man, but Dixon may have considered that it would be Britain's only course of action if the use of force and particularly the bombing of civilian areas continued. It was the latter which caused him the most distress and on which he decided to take his stand of 3 November when he cabled Selwyn Lloyd registering his opposition in the strongest terms to the bombing of Egyptian towns, indicating that Britain could not remain a member of the UN while it persisted with such a policy. Was he right to take such a stand? The problem for him was that because he did not know the full details of the military plan, he was unsure whether the situation was going to improve or worsen. If he was to take a stand and warn his government it was difficult to know when was the appropriate time. He chose 3 November, although his private secretary feels that this was inopportune because it was never going to be possible to avoid civilian casualties, but clearly Dixon felt he had to register some protest.[79] He had to do so again on 5 November and on both occasions he was appeased by promises from Lloyd and Eden: one can only wonder if those promises had not materialized whether he would have resigned.

Finally we may question why, having warned the British of the dire consequences of continuing with the military operation, Dixon should have been prepared to delay the proceedings of the UN for Eden? Dixon wished for a slackening of the pace in the UN after the hectic activities of the previous week. It would have allowed him time to study the constructive ideas of Pearson and Hammarskjold on the UN force and time also for him to come off the defensive. He had during the previous week been facing a barrage of diplomatic bouncers. How he must have wished for a few friendly long hops! He saw the opportunity to delay the UN which meshed with Eden's need to occupy the Canal Zone and Eden had given his word that there would be no more bombing: the issue which incited the General Assembly and caused Dixon the most difficulty. He had no qualms about seeing Nasser defeated although he would rather have preferred a diplomatic victory. But he seems to have considered that Eden, having started to use force, had compounded his error by stopping. Did his warning of

5 November lead to Eden stopping? It may have been a factor but it was probably less powerful than the economic alarms being rung by Macmillan. Overall his effect on policy was probably limited. Archibald Ross confirmed that Dixon was to be given a wide degree of latitude in presenting Britain's case in the UN, but in effect he had little room for manouevre. He was given instructions on the way to vote, such as the vetoes cast on the US and Soviet Security Council resolutions and the votes in the General Assembly. His loyal defence of Eden's government over Suez was recognised by Evelyn Shuckburgh, his biographer, in *The Dictionary of National Biography* after his death:

> He sustained his ordeal with great dignity and self-control and his conduct during this crisis helped Britain to regain respect and influence in the United Nations in subsequent years.[80]

Dixon's outward self-control clearly masked inner turmoil and his diary entry written one year after the events, provides a salutary summary of his views on Suez. It had been, he felt, 'a miscalculation and a mistake', an action which had reduced Britain to 'a 3rd class power'and he recalled

> the sick-at-the stomach feeling with which I defended our case here. It came of the conviction that the operation was misconceived and probably would fail. The effort of concealing these feelings and putting a plausible and confident face on the case was the severest moral and physical strain I have ever experienced.[81]

NOTES

1. The author would like to thank Piers Dixon for allowing him to consult his father's diaries and for providing him with extremely useful background material in the preparation of this chapter, and Lord Hurd of Westwell who very kindly gave of his time to talk about Sir Pierson Dixon and his role in the crisis.
2. P. Dixon, *Double Diploma: The Life of Sir Pierson Dixon, Don and Diplomat* (London: Hutchinson, 1968), p.278.
3. See FO 371/119174/JE14214/20, JE14214/21, JE14214/64, JE14214/87G.
4. FO 371/119177/JE14214/94, Dixon's letter to Lloyd, 11 Sept. 1956.
5. Sir Anthony Eden, *Full Circle* (London: Cassell, 1960), p.531 and S. Lloyd, *Suez 1956: A Personal Account* (London: Jonathan Cape, 1978), pp.198–9.
6. FO 371/121746/VR1074/433, Dixon to FO, tel.967, 29 Oct. 1956.
7. *Foreign Relations of the United States [FRUS], 1955–1957, Vol.XVI, Suez Crisis July 26–December 31, 1956* (Washington, DC: USGPO, 1990), doc.413.

8. FO 371/121746/VR1074/431, Dixon to FO, tel.973, 29 Oct. 1956.
9. FO 371/121746/VR1074/434/G, Dixon to FO, tel.974, 29 Oct. 1956.
10. The British did not like the US draft resolution which was due to be placed before the Security Council. It had been handed by Dulles to John Coulson, the Minister at the British Embassy, Washington, at a meeting in the State Department in the early evening of 29 Oct., *FRUS, 1955–1957, Vol.XVI*, doc.409. Dixon may have received a copy from Coulson or from Lodge. It is more likely that he received it from Coulson as Lodge recorded that at the Opera House Dixon said, 'He had heard that the Department of State intended to introduce a "fantastic" resolution calling for economic sanctions if the Israeli forces were not withdrawn.' Ibid., doc.413.
11. FO 371/121746/VR1074/432, FO to Dixon, tel.1381, 30 Oct. 1956. Note that Lloyd sent telegram 500G to Washington on the same day, informing Coulson not to let the State Department know what had been sent to Dixon. Coulson was not to say anything which might imply British support for the US line or their resolution, see FO 371/121746/VR1074/429.
12. *FRUS, 1955–1957, Vol.XVI*, doc.423.
13. PREM 11/1105, Dixon to FO, tel.975, 30 Oct. 1956.
14. *FRUS, 1955–1957, Vol. XVI*, doc.423 .
15. B. Urquhart, *Hammarskjold* (London: The Bodley Head, 1972), p.173.
16. Ibid.
17. PREM 11/1105, Dixon to FO, tel.981, 30 Oct. 1956.
18. FO 371/121746/VR1074/447, Dixon to FO, tel.989, 30 Oct. 1956.
19. Ibid.
20. Ibid.
21. FO 371/118903/JE1094/29, Ross memo, 31 Oct. 1956.
22. FO 371/121746/VR1074/443, Dixon to FO, tel.986, 30 Oct. 1956.
23. FO 371/121746/VR1074/451, Dixon to FO, tel.993, 31 Oct. 1956.
24. *FRUS, 1955–1957, Vol.XVI*, doc.444.
25. FO 371/121746/VR1074/457, Dixon to FO, tel.997, 31 Oct. 1956.
26. *FRUS, 1955–1957, Vol.XVI*, doc.450.
27. Urquhart, *Hammarskjold*, p.174, although note that Urquhart claims Hammarskjold never intended to resign and even showed his speech to Dixon and Cornut-Gentille before he made it. However, the Americans took his speech as a petition of confidence in his post and Hammarskjold had even requested this from Lodge before the meeting, see *FRUS, 1955–1957, Vol.XVI*, doc.445.
28. Urquhart, *Hammarskjold*, p.175.
29. *United Nations Security Council Official Records* [SCOR], 11th year, 751st mtg, 31 Oct. 1956.
30. FO 371/121746/VR1074/450, Dixon to FO, tel.992, 31 Oct. 1956.
31. Ibid.
32. FO 371/121746/VR1074/452, FO to Dixon, tel.1449, 1 Nov. 1956.
33. FO 371/121746/VR1074/452, Dixon to FO, tel.998, 31 Oct. 1956.
34. FO 371/121746/VR1074/461, Dixon to FO, tel.1001, 1 Nov. 1956.
35. FO 371/121746/VR1074/452, FO to Dixon, tel.1449, 1 Nov. 1956, and Dixon, *Double Diploma*, p.267.
36. FO 371/121748/VR1074/524, Kirkpatrick to Dixon, tel.1444, 1 Nov. 1956.
37. *Hansard, Vol.558*, col.1649, 1 Nov. 1956.
38. At noon in Paris [6am EST] Douglas Dillon had sent a despatch relaying a

conversation with Pineau that morning in which the French Foreign Minister confirmed collusion, see *FRUS, 1955–1957, Vol.XVI*, doc.453.

39. Dixon, *Double Diploma*, p.267.
40. *United Nations General Assembly Official Records [GAOR]*, 1st emerg. spec. session, 562nd mtg, 1–2 Nov. 1956.
41. FO 371/121747/VR1074/473, Dixon to Lloyd, tel.1009, 2 Nov. 1956.
42. *UN [GAOR]*, 1st emerg. spec.session, 562nd mtg, 2 Nov. 1956.
43. Lloyd, *Suez 1956*, p.200.
44. L.B. Pearson, *The International Years: The Memoirs of the Rt. Hon. Lester B.Pearson, Vol.2, 1948–1957*, J.A. Munro and A.I. Inglis (eds) (London: Victor Gollancz, 1974), p.246. See also DO 35/6334, Ottawa to CRO, tel.1041, repeated to UK delegation UN, 1 Nov. 1956.
45. See the minute by Pink, 2 Nov. 1956, relaying a telephone conversation with Dixon in FO 371/121752/VR1074/646, and FO 371/121747/VR1074/488, Dixon to FO, tel.1020, 2 Nov. 1956.
46. PREM 11/1105, *aide-memoire* by Bishop, 2 Nov. 1956.
47. PREM 11/1105, Lloyd to Dixon, tel.1494, 2 Nov. 1956.
48. FO 371/121747/VR1074/489, Dixon to FO, tel.1026, 2 Nov. 1956.
49. FO 371/121747/VR1074/490, Dixon to FO, tel.1033, 3 Nov. 1956.
50. FO 371/121747/VR1074/491, Dixon to FO, tel.1035, 3 Nov. 1956.
51. FO 371/121747/VR1074/490, FO to Political Office with the Middle East Forces (Nicosia), tel.3514, repeated to UK delegation UN, 3 Nov. 1956.
52. FO 371/121747/VR1074/496, FO to Dixon, tel.1236, 4 Nov. 1956. Both this telegram and no.1235 [below] were to confirm what Lloyd had said by telephone to the delegation in New York.
53. FO 371/121747/VR1074/495, FO to Dixon, tel.1235, 4 Nov. 1956.
54. *FRUS, 1955–1957, Vol.XVI*, doc.481, footnote 2.
55. *UN [GAOR]*, 1st emerg. spec. session, 563rd mtg, 3–4 Nov. 1956.
56. Ibid.
57. UN doc.*A/3287*, annex 4, 4 Nov. 1956.
58. FO 371/121747/VR1074/503, Kirkpatrick to Dixon, tel.1563, 5 Nov. 1956, emphasis in the original.
59. UN doc.*A/3293*, letter to the Secretary-General, 5 Nov. 1956.
60. See the minute by R.F.Stretton on the history of the reply sent to Hammarskjold, 5 Nov. 1956, in FO 371/121751/VR1074/627 and PREM 11/1105, Dixon to FO, tel.1062, 4 Nov. 1956.
61. FO 371/121748/VR1074/515, Dixon to FO, tel.1069, 5 Nov. 1956.
62. *UN [GAOR]*, 1st emerg. spec. session, 565th mtg, 4 Nov. 1956.
63. See Stretton's minute in FO 371/121751/VR1074/627.
64. FO 371/121748/VR1074/516, Dixon to FO, tel.1070, 5 Nov. 1956.
65. FO 371/121748/VR1074/515, Dixon to FO, tel.1069, 5 Nov. 1956.
66. FO 371/121748/VR1074/517, Dixon to FO, tel.1071, 5 Nov. 1956. On 4 Nov. the Soviet Union had launched a major offensive to crush the Hungarian uprising in Budapest.
67. FO 371/121746/VR1074/443, FO to Dixon, tel.1597, 5 Nov. 1956.
68. PREM 11/1105, Dixon to FO, tels.1078 and 1079, 5 Nov. 1956.
69. FO 371/121748/VR1074/534, Dixon to FO, tel.1085, 6 Nov. 1956.
70. Dixon, *Double Diploma*, p.272, see also confirmation of this exchange in PREM

11/1105, Dixon to FO, tel.1080, 5 Nov. 1956 and Eden to Dixon, tel.1601, 6 Nov. 1956.
71. Dixon, *Double Diploma*, pp.272–3.
72. K. Kyle, *Suez* (London: Weidenfeld & Nicolson, 1991), p.465.
73. PREM 11/1105, FO to Dixon, tels.1614, 1615 and 1624, 6 Nov. 1956.
74. Lloyd, *Suez 1956*, p.213.
75. A. Horne, *Macmillan 1957–1986* (London: Macmillan, 1989), p.326.
76. Piers Dixon to the author, 20 Nov. 1997.
77. Lord Hurd to the author, 16 Dec. 1996.
78. Lord Hurd to the author, 16 Dec. 1996.
79. Lord Hurd to the author, 16 Dec. 1996.
80. E.T. Williams and C.S. Nicholls (eds), *The Dictionary of National Biography 1961–1970* (Oxford: OUP, 1981), pp.298–9.
81. Dixon, *Double Diploma*, pp.277–8.

The Past as Matrix:
Sir Ivone Kirkpatrick, Permanent
Under-Secretary for Foreign Affairs

ANN LANE

> Self-delusion…is a fault to which we as a nation are especially prone.
>
> Sir Ivone Kirkpatrick, *The Inner Circle*

One generalisation frequently made about the British foreign policy process is that it cannot be explained without close reference to the impact of the past, not only by the experiences through which decision makers have lived, but also as a consequence of the latter's conceptions of history.[1] 'Foreign policy is…rarely the result of calm reflection on current problems' but rather the outcome of decisions made under pressure when instinct or traditions 'grounded in group experience' generally prevail.[2] The Suez Crisis of course is an excellent example of the way in which such factors can affect decision making, and the case of Sir Ivone Kirkpatrick, who as one of the principal invokers of the Munich analogy in support of the use of force, seems to demonstrate how historical legacy and personal experience can combine to cloud an adviser's judgement.

Kirkpatrick, as Permanent Under-Secretary at the Foreign Office, was the chief civil service adviser on Foreign Affairs to the Foreign Secretary, Selwyn Lloyd and the Prime Minister, Anthony Eden. In this capacity he has been the recipient of much of the blame for the course on which Britain embarked in October 1956. Although he left little record for the historian to effect a detailed reconstruction of the development of his thinking at the time, his contemporaries at the Foreign Office and several of the ministers whom he served have given clear indications of his views at critical stages as the crisis unfolded. Kirkpatrick emerges as an early and unequivocal supporter of

Anthony Eden's inclinations, a position which was also accepted by and large by Selwyn Lloyd. It is primarily on such records, and on the surviving official documentation which lends additional support to these accounts, that his reputation resides. The evidence shows that Kirkpatrick supported and elaborated the arguments used by Eden at various stages of policy making right up to 15 October, and thereafter remained fervently – perhaps obsessively – loyal to the Prime Minister. Although he facilitated the secrecy surrounding the collusion episode, he disagreed unequivocally with the Challe Plan itself and counselled against its acceptance. Kirkpatrick's input into policy making was determined by his identification with Eden's style and outlook, which emerged during the last Churchill administration, if not earlier; by personal experience and by a predisposition towards authoritarianism which not only informed his judgement on the substantive questions raised by the Suez Crisis, but also determined the manner in which he discharged the duties of his office.

Kirkpatrick's contribution to the decision-making process in the British government during the Suez Crisis cannot be understood without reference to his earlier experiences and personality. Permanent Under-Secretary since November 1953, he possessed characteristics which under different circumstances would have been assets, but which proved to be weaknesses which the Suez Crisis magnified. This 'Irishman who never minded a fight' was known in Whitehall for his caustic wit, incisive mind and predisposition towards cynicism – qualities which probably made him the kind of sharp-edged commentator whose company is so often enjoyed among those of a more restrained disposition. Macmillan, Foreign Secretary in 1955, in particular, found him congenial: 'Very unconventional, quite a character,' he observed, 'Very strong will…he was always right, awfully bright.'[3] These same attributes would have given him formidable powers of intimidation in a working environment predisposed to deference and subordination. Roderick Barclay, Chief Clerk of the Foreign Office between 1953 and early 1956, certainly regarded Kirkpatrick as a negative force. 'Instead of trying to stand up for members of the Service against public or political criticism,' he complained, 'he tended to assume without investigation that such criticism was justified.' Kirkpatrick's responsiveness to those in power, a fault for which he was criticised after the Suez Crisis, was reflected in his inclination to side with the Treasury during budgetary negotiations on the Foreign Office's behalf. 'One was liable to find,' Barclay wrote, 'that one's own Permanent Under Secretary had joined forces with the opposition.'[4] Indeed, few of his contemporaries speak of him with real warmth and Barclay is not alone in being openly critical. It may even be that Kirkpatrick found the job just a little too onerous. Macmillan possibly thought so for he observed that 'this enormous department rather worried him...great memoranda and jaw, jaw, jaw...'[5] If this were so, and the evidence is little more than circumstantial, it might perhaps explain why he failed during a moment of real crisis when judgement and objectivity were of paramount importance.

Despite a noted independence of mind, and the self-confidence to challenge the views of those in seniority over him, Kirkpatrick knew how to follow orders and in turn, liked giving them. Gladwyn Jebb, who regarded Kirkpatrick as a personal friend, described him as 'an intelligent, combative, sardonic, courageous, but in some ways rather limited Irishman' who would have made 'an excellent General'.[6] His experiences in the British Control Commission in Germany had accustomed him to expect his orders to be obeyed even when there was disagreement. 'I have never favoured pandering to agitation,' he subsequently wrote. This trait, reinforced by a predisposition towards rigidity, enabled him to press on, impervious to the considerable discontent among his colleagues.[7] A quick thinker himself, he was 'intolerant and sometimes lacking in judgement in his handling of staff'.[8] In day to day business within the Foreign Office this manifested itself in a kind of officiousness, an excessive fussiness about the manner in which things were done. Over seven pages of his memoirs were dedicated to reprinting a memorandum distributed throughout the Foreign Office in 1947 which set out the way in which officials should conduct themselves in order to match the standards set by their predecessors.

Kirkpatrick was the product of a traditional upper-class background and education. Born in 1897 into a family of strong military traditions he had taken a commission on the outbreak of war in 1914 in the Royal Inniskilling Fusiliers. His association with the Foreign Service – or rather the covert activities associated with the conduct of foreign policy – began in 1917 in British propaganda and intelligence activities.[9] This experience, combined with a later spell as foreign adviser to the BBC and controller of the European Service during the 1939–45 war placed him in a sphere of activity which he seems to have relished. Perhaps his inherent elitism and disregard for objectivity temperamentally suited him to propaganda work. Certainly it impressed upon him the importance of publicity in foreign policy; as early as October 1946 he was recommending with regard to Britain's post-war problems in the Middle East that while these were not being created by Russia, 'our difficulties are being deliberately aggravated by a savage Soviet campaign of anti-British propaganda...a reply must be made with all the means at our disposal.'[10] He does not seem to have devoted much in-depth attention to Middle Eastern affairs, but this view informed his judgement on these matters until the end of his career. His memoirs, published in 1959, indicate his belief that the British failure to get their message across, particularly in the United States, was an explanation of the disaster of 1956.[11]

Kirkpatrick's disregard for 'research or analysis or prolonged discussion', which was so notable a feature of his minutes at the time of Suez, has been ascribed, with more than a touch of schadenfreude to his lack of a university education. Joining the Foreign Service after the First World War, he spent much of the formative part of his career in dealing at first hand with various European dictatorships, an experience which impressed upon him – in company with so many of his generation – the simple lesson that appeasement of dictators leads to still greater demands and eventually to war.[12] However, to single out Kirkpatrick for special condemnation for adopting the appeasement analogy in 1956 is to misconstrue the climate of the times. Appeasement had been a yardstick by which foreign policy choices were evaluated (and denigrated) since the late 1930s.[13] This tendency was reinforced by the preoccupations of commentators and historians with the origins of the Second World War; anyone involved with policy towards Nazi Germany during that period could not be anything but sensitive to the charge of accommodating the demands of would-be dictators.

Post-war considerations of alternative responses to the Soviet Union had established appeasement as a measure of policy choices in British policy-making circles. The debates about Soviet intentions found Kirkpatrick firmly on the conservative side. Ten years later the argument that the Soviet Union was seeking to undermine and replace British influence in the world was still informing his judgement: 'I do not believe,' he wrote to Eden on 3 October 1956, 'that it pays with the

Russians to acquiesce meekly when they distort the facts.'[14] Like Eden, Kirkpatrick was convinced that the Russian hand was behind Nasser, and he was uncompromising in his views about Soviet intentions in the Middle East when Khrushchev and Bulganin visited Britain in April 1956. The Russians, he observed, arrived in Britain 'in a mood full of blatant confidence' and 'told us very frankly that whilst in every other part of the world there would be no conflict they would make as much trouble for us in the Middle East as they possibly could.' This opinion, which did much to magnify the nationalisation crisis in his mind, did not moderate with the passage of time; recounting these events in his memoirs he added, darkly, 'They were as good as their word.'[15] Paradoxically, he seems to have favoured a conciliatory policy towards Egypt during the early 1950s and recommended early withdrawal from the Canal Base. This judgement was informed primarily by pragmatic strategic considerations consequent upon the arrival of the hydrogen bomb in the American and Soviet armouries which diminished in his mind the importance of conventional warfare. Indeed, when viewed within such a framework, the Canal Base could no longer be regarded as so very important given its vulnerability to the single strike. Recommending acceptance of the terms of the Anglo-Egyptian Treaty in 1954, Kirkpatrick observed that 'the power and numbers of these frightful weapons will be so great that the chance of our wanting to conduct a campaign in the Middle East will be less than it is to-day'.[16] This statement seems indicative of realist perceptions but Suez revealed that his judgement was informed to a considerable degree by historical precedents pertaining to Britain's role in the world. This combined dangerously with an overestimation of Soviet capabilities and an outdated conception of the nation's survival as dependent upon the exercise of great power responsibilities.

The impact Kirkpatrick was able to have on the Suez episode is derived in part from the deterioration in relations between Eden and his Foreign Office officials during the last Churchill administration. Eden had lost faith in the Office, especially in its handling of the Middle East. The Diplomatic Corps, he thought, were too biased towards the Arabs and once at Number Ten, Eden blamed the Foreign Office's '"casual and inactive" attitude, bred of prejudicial complacency, for Britain's notable lack of success in the region'.[17] In Kirkpatrick, Eden had found the ideal instrument for an interface between himself and the officials at King Charles Street, and his willingness to promote Kirkpatrick's career is evident in his highly unpopular advancement of the latter's name in February 1952 as the Secretary-General of NATO. This suggestion was pushed 'just long enough to irritate his colleagues and exacerbate the difficulties of selection' until, to the relief of all concerned, an alternative was proferred.[18] However, it is significant that Kirkpatrick shared some of Eden's outlook, including a suspicion of European entanglements and an inclination towards isolationism on the matter of trade.[19] Moreover, Kirkpatrick's attitude towards appeasement of Germany may, like Eden's, have been less clear cut than he later wished to suggest: in 1961, Eden noted 'the Embassy in Berlin (including Ivone Kirkpatrick)' had been 'appeasement inclined'.[20] Both may have been haunted by their association with past misjudgements.

The immediate origins of the Suez Crisis resided in the dismissal of General Glubb by King Hussein of Jordan in March 1956, an event which Kirkpatrick instantly attributed primarily to Soviet machinations. On 5 March, he informed the American Ambassador, Winthrop Aldrich, that in general the British were of the opinion that 'the Russians are out to liquidate the Baghdad Pact, that Nasser for his own reasons was helping them in this task, that events in Jordan were part of this pattern and that our policy should be directed toward strengthening the Baghdad Pact and showing that it was profitable to be our friend'. Despite protestations from Amman, where King Hussein was at pains to emphasise the importance he attached to continued British friendship, and from Cairo from whence Nasser asserted his innocence, Eden's vindictiveness towards Nasser found a ready supporter in Kirkpatrick who was convinced that while the Egyptian dictator was the moving force, the Jordanians should be punished for the dismissal of Glubb by withdrawal of the British subsidy.[21]

Kirkpatrick had come out in favour of the denunciation of the Anglo-Jordanian Treaty at a crisis meeting convened by Eden at Chequers the previous day. According to Evelyn Shuckburgh, then superintending Middle Eastern affairs within the Foreign Office, he was not alone in this: everyone present, which included Anthony Nutting, General Sir Gerald Templer, Lord Salisbury, Sir Walter Monckton and Sir Norman Brook, 'wanted to be rather tough'.[22] A letter to President Eisenhower the following day, drawing on the conclusions of this meeting, conveyed Eden's suspicions that Nasser's relations with the Russians were a good deal closer than he was admitting and that 'Recent events in Jordan are part of this pattern...a policy of appeasement will bring us nothing in Egypt'.[23]

Undoubtedly, Eden's predisposition to intensity and hyper-tension exacerbated an already stressful working environment, and his refusal to listen to reason on this question is well documented in surviving accounts. This episode is important for establishing the manner in which the subsequent crisis unfolded and for the early demonstration it afforded of Kirkpatrick's identity with Eden's outlook. Eden, Shuckburgh noted, 'seems to want to march troops in and arrest the [reformist] "High Executive Committee"...We have now got to a state where each telegram that comes in causes Ministers to meet, telephone one another, draft replies, and curse everybody'. Clearly suffering from over-work in a job he admitted loathing, Shuckburgh's diary nonetheless records that he was not the sole victim of the Prime Minister's arbitrary manner. Kirkpatrick (and Nutting also), felt themselves to be alternately 'rejected by the Prime Minister as no good, not on the job, unhelpful'. Shuckburgh concluded that 'No one is trusted to the extent that his advice is regarded when unwelcome'.[24] If this is so, then Kirkpatrick's early identification with Eden on the general lines of policy would have established him as an ally, to be brought in when necessary to reinforce an opinion or to counter opposing viewpoints as these arose. While such an atmosphere was hardly conducive to sound decision making, it is unclear to what extent an attempt was made to press alternative courses of action upon him. This is surely the crucial point; Kirkpatrick had emerged at the outset as one whose views in this regard were not altogether dissimilar and it is likely that the two men reinforced each other's prejudices, thereby entrenching more deeply Eden's inclination to seek retribution. In his memoirs, Eden recorded how in 1956 'I.K. [Ivone Kirkpatrick] certainly in favour...in every conversation or meeting we had, and we had many'.[25]

1956 was the twentieth anniversary of Hitler's occupation of the Rhineland and given the fevered atmosphere of frustration and impotence already pervading British Middle Eastern policy, it must be borne in mind that the parallels were readily perceived across a wide spectrum of opinion. Macmillan's diary entry for 27 July, cited in Horne's narrative, described Nasser's nationalisation speech as 'very truculent – an Asiatic Mussolini'. Horne adds a context to this noting that a similar theme was running through the press; for example, the *Socialist Daily Herald* declared 'No more Hitlers'. Hugh Gaitskell, leader of the Opposition, in the House of Commons on 2 August, observed: 'It is all very familiar. It is exactly the same that we encountered from Mussolini and Hitler.'[26] Moreover, Eden's disposition to evoke Hitler when discussing Nasser was nothing new. Churchill was heard to remark following discussions with Eden regarding Egypt in 1954 that 'he never knew before that Munich was situated on the Nile'.[27] Kirkpatrick, who had accompanied Neville Chamberlain on his ultimately fruitless trip to Munich, was readily persuaded of the validity of the 1930s analogy and eagerly stressed the tragic consequences of Franco-British inaction then, thereby fanning an already considerable blaze. The point is, however, that this was not a minority opinion at the time. Indeed it touched a nerve in the British political fabric which immediately polarised debate and charged supposedly rational argument with emotion in which the search for deeper insight was impeded, with tragic consequences.[28]

Kirkpatrick's ability to command Prime Ministerial attention was empowered further by the technical arrangements set in hand to handle the crisis. Formally, Kirkpatrick's input was channelled through the Defence (Transition) Committee under the chairmanship of the Cabinet Secretary, Sir Norman Brook. This 'rather ominous Committee,' as it was described by William Clark, then Eden's Press Secretary, was composed of Permanent Under-Secretaries and represented a 'formidable group of grey heads...the effective Civil Service Cabinet of this country'.[29] In addition to whatever informal and ad hoc contacts he had with the Prime Minister, Kirkpatrick was also in formal control of the Permanent Under-Secretary's Department (PUSD) which provided a critical link between the overt and covert side of Foreign Office business. Kirkpatrick's ability to cut the Foreign Office out of the policy-making loop was contingent upon the existence of this alternative communications network. This factor proved critical to the whole operation.[30] Roger Louis writes that 'Kirkpatrick effectively sealed off the usual channels of Foreign Office telegram traffic at all levels, to conduct an ultra-secret operation'.[31] The ruthlessness with which this was accomplished, and the absence of subsequent explanation, encouraged the bitterest criticism from within the Office. This in turn has coloured the way in which historians have written Kirkpatrick into their accounts. In sum, the identification of the Foreign Office's chief official with Prime Ministerial dogmatism, combined with the system of *ad hoc* committees, had the effect of marginalising the Foreign Office.

One of the chief advocates of the use of force, Kirkpatrick became closely involved during August in the process of finding a pretext for taking military action to recover the Canal. There is no evidence that he challenged the assumption that force be used or that he felt any private qualms in this sense. Others were not so sanguine and during the first London Conference in August, Harold Beeley (then Assistant Under-Secretary), in agreement with Archibald Ross (who had replaced Shuckburgh in June as Under-Secretary responsible for Middle Eastern affairs), attempted to intervene with Kirkpatrick to inject some caution into the search for a pretext: 'Military action against Egypt would,' he argued, 'have very serious repercussions in neighbouring countries...we must clearly aim at defeating Colonel Nasser without resort to force.' Indeed, he added that 'the gravest consequences would follow from a failure [of the use of force] to deprive Colonel Nasser of control over the Canal'.[32] There followed an exchange of correspondence which revealed the degree to which Kirkpatrick had become incapable of registering the existence of choice: 'It seems to me,' he replied rather patronisingly, 'easy to communicate these views – which are sound and, I think, generally accepted here, but it is more difficult to draw up a programme which will achieve this end... Defeating Nasser without resort to force...I shall be grateful for ideas.'[33] Beeley's solution of mustering international consensus to impose a form of sanctions was evidently considered by the Permanent Under-Secretary as too inferior a suggestion to be worthy of exploration. He was similarly oblivious to the protestations of the Foreign Office's chief legal adviser, Sir Gerald Fitzmaurice, who on seeing Beeley's minuting had weighed in on Beeley's side. Kirkpatrick initialled the papers to show that they had been seen but there is no indication that the issues raised by either of these men were formally discussed, far less that they were pressed on Selwyn Lloyd or Anthony Eden.[34] Kirkpatrick did not confine his dogmatism to his Foreign Office colleagues. At the end of August the external service of the BBC, the publicity outlet which Kirkpatrick believed critical to the success or failure of foreign policy making, was effectively reminded that the quality of its support for the government over Suez could have implications for future funding rounds. On 28

August he threatened the BBC's Director General, Ian Jacob, with the prospect of curtailing the Corporation's grant in aid, warning him that 'Ministers were becoming increasingly dissatisfied with the BBC in general'; his true purpose was belied by the statement that the subject was unlikely to be raised 'in acute form until after we had finished with the Suez crisis'.[35]

The clearest statements of Kirkpatrick's attitude towards Nasser appeared during the exchange of correspondence between Eden and Eisenhower during the first ten days of September when Kirkpatrick, unsurprisingly given his official position, assumed the role of Eden's draftsman. Following Eisenhower's 'devastating' communication on 3 September, Kirkpatrick set out for Lloyd the main factors of the problem for consideration as he then saw them. This minute is extraordinary for revealing the didacticism of his thinking. Beginning by listing in brutal fashion the forces which would muster against Britain should the military option be employed, he observed that 'the Americans would not support us' and worse would be 'openly critical'. Support from other quarters, he continued, would not be forthcoming, the effect in the Arab states would be bad; the economic consequences would be 'at the very least, an intolerable burden on our economy'. There is little room for arguing that he misunderstood the position in practical terms. What makes this the more extraordinary is that despite – or perhaps in spite of all this – he felt able to sustain an argument in favour of the use of force, an argument which, he was convinced, was 'overwhelming': 'We cannot possibly risk allowing Nasser to get away with it,' he advised. Accordingly, Kirkpatrick repeated his argument that the 'best tactics', assuming that Menzies failed in his mission to seek Nasser's agreement to Foster Dulles' plan for internationalisation, 'will be to begin by economic and psychological means of pressure'. American fear of the British threat to use force, he argued, might enable Britain to 'bulldoze them into suitable economic and psychological measures simply by threatening that if they do not agree we shall have no alternative but to have recourse to force.'[36] Kirkpatrick concluded that such a policy would mean postponing 'certain military measures' but that it 'would be safer than to charge blindly ahead'. The minute was signed off by Eden's Private Secretary, but there is no evidence of a formal reply.

Using the metaphor clearly preferred by the Prime Minister which had been current since July and before, Kirkpatrick drafted a reply to Eisenhower which Eden amended and sent to the President on 6

September. The draft, which William Clark described in his diary entry that evening as 'a very noble bit of prose', drew at length on the Rhineland analogies which were clearly 'in the forefront of the PM's mind'.[37] It was read in Washington at the time, as it reads to-day, as a justification of the use of force to maintain British influence in the Middle East.[38] Although Eisenhower's reply stressed his agreement with the British estimate of Nasser's intentions and purposes, he tried to inject some much needed perspective. The statement that the British had to contest Nasser's nationalisation of the Canal out of honour for the British standing in the world was a monstrous distortion which Eisenhower tried to illuminate by suggesting that Eden was 'making Nasser a much more important figure than he is'.[39] With the conviction of the ideologically driven, neither Eden nor Kirkpatrick were capable of registering the significance of this point. Seizing instead on Eisenhower's statements regarding the overall menace of current difficulties in the Middle East, and the need to concert their efforts to meet the challenge, they replied that they were 'encouraged' by this message and felt 'there is large measure of agreement'.[40] In Washington, meanwhile, Foster Dulles cut to the heart of the matter when he told the President that the Eden–Kirkpatrick note was not very well thought out and that he did not think 'you could go to war to preserve influence'.[41] Nonetheless, the point about making of Nasser more than he was had struck a nerve. Kirkpatrick addressed the issue in a letter to his friend Roger Makins, then Ambassador in Washington, dated 10 September. Allowing no room for doubt, Kirkpatrick lamented the President's wrong-headedness. Admitting that Nasser in himself was unimportant and that Egypt by herself was not powerful enough to mortally damage British prestige, he continued:

> if we sit back whilst Nasser consolidates his position and gradually acquires control of the oil-bearing countries, he can and is, according to our information, resolved to wreck us. If Middle East oil is denied us for a year or two, our gold reserves will disappear. If our gold reserves disappear, the sterling area disintegrates. If the sterling area disintegrates and we have no reserves, we shall not be able to maintain force in Germany, or, indeed, anywhere else. I doubt whether we shall be able to pay for the bare minimum necessary for our defence. And a country which cannot provide for its defence is finished.[42]

Selwyn Lloyd reproduces this at even greater length in his memoirs, attributing it to Kirkpatrick, 'his principal adviser', in response to charges that 'ministers acted with complete disregard for the Foreign Office advice given to them'.[43] The more interesting point for the historian, however, is why the central contradiction this paper contained was not sternly challenged. The answer may lie in the contents of SIS reports emanating from Cairo (and elsewhere) from where station chief, Freddie Stockwell, confirmed that Nasser was an agent of communist revolution throughout the region.[44] Certainly, SIS who had separate plans afoot for settling the Nasser question, was providing evidence for those wishing to believe it, of Russian penetration of the region. The latter was of course regarded as the trump card in any hand being played to win American endorsement of intervention in Middle Eastern politics. Kirkpatrick's minuting, with its references to 'our informant' and 'our sources' is littered with hints that he was relying on secret sources which of course were available to only a very restricted circle. Such hints may have discouraged potential dissenters from representing alternative interpretations. Of course any argument constructed on the basis of highly restricted information is nearly impossible to counter, except among those similarly informed. Within the Foreign Office, only Kirkpatrick, Patrick Dean and Geoffrey McDermott knew of British intelligence plans against Egypt and although Kirkpatrick is thought to have expressed concern at Eden's wish to kill Nasser there is no evidence that he tried to modify MI6's plans.[45]

Some historians have argued that Kirkpatrick's influence with the Prime Minister began, from this point onwards, to diminish. 'From September,' Scott Lucas writes, 'Eden increasingly circumvented Kirkpatrick as Dean, promoted from Assistant Under-Secretary to Deputy Under-Secretary in August, became the PM's channel for ad hoc action.' This is a contention for which there is evidence from the middle of October onwards, but up till then it is more a conjecture. The source is Lucas's interview with Archibald Ross who said that 'as things began to hot up [Eden] did take Dean over as his FO man...it was not so much the Foreign Office submitting advice as Eden using a member of the Foreign Office to do what he thought had to be done'.[46] Geoffrey McDermott, Chairman of the Joint Intelligence Sub-Committee offers corroboration.[47] Furthermore, during Lloyd's trip to New York, the proponents of the use of force found themselves temporarily outpaced by the peacemakers.[48] Nevertheless, as an unwavering supporter of the Eden camp which was becoming increasingly embattled by the logic of its self-serving arguments, Kirkpatrick surely remained central to the policy process, even though the import of his political contribution was being diminished by imminence of military operations and their attendant considerations.

The extent to which Kirkpatrick felt himself to be embattled, a reflection perhaps of his intellectual isolation, is recorded by Shuckburgh who called in on him during an informal visit to the Foreign Office on 24 September; 'never' he wrote, had he heard 'such black pessimism'. In response to mild criticism of Eden, Kirkpatrick exploded that 'the PM was the only man in England who wanted the nation to survive; that all the rest of us have lost the will to live'. To Shuckburgh's embarrassment, the tirade continued as Kirkpatrick lambasted the press for being 'concerned only to criticise the Government' and for tormenting him by coming to the Foreign Office and putting 'awkward questions to the News Department designed to weaken the British hand in the dispute'.[49]

If Kirkpatrick's importance was being circumvented by increasing Prime Ministerial attention to the secret services, it was the moment of decision which occurred between 14 and 16 October which resulted in Kirkpatrick's marginalisation from the inner circle. Knowledge of the Challe plan was to be kept to a very restricted group, one which included Kirkpatrick with whom Nutting was instructed to discuss the idea.[50] The best account of what followed is contained in Anthony Nutting's memoir. Nutting, unlike Lloyd, observes traditional discretion, declining to name his officials, but it is fairly clear that it was with Kirkpatrick and Ross that he conferred, on Eden's instruction and in Lloyd's absence on Monday 15 October. Alistair Horne, who cites the 'unexpurgated' version of Nutting's manuscript, says that 'even he [Kirkpatrick] "felt that it was a crazy idea. Never one to trust the French, he said that they would be certain to let us down…"'[51] The more they discussed it, Nutting writes, the 'less we could see a single argument in favour of going along with this sordid manoeuvre.' Lloyd appeared to have got from Fawzi in New York 'effectively all that we needed to safeguard our interests as users of the Canal'. The French proposals meant that aside from the moral issue, the Americans and the United Nations would be opposed and the Commonwealth divided. Nutting informed Lloyd of the plan on the latter's arrival at

Downing Street from the airport the following morning. Despite Lloyd's agreement, Nutting found 'the issue had already been decided, whatever the Foreign Secretary might say or feel'.[52] Foreign Office influence on the course of events was now effectively at an end.

Kirkpatrick was placed thenceforth in the role of facilitator. To him fell the job of excluding the entire Foreign Office, with the exception of Dean, Ross and MacDermott, from knowledge of collusion. Eden utilised SIS's radio links and ciphers to communicate with David Ben-Gurion and Israeli military intelligence as well as with the French co-conspirators, thereby by-passing the Foreign Office communications network. Dick White, head of MI6, was drawn into the conspiracy accordingly.[53] Kirkpatrick's task was to act as liaison with Pierson Dixon at the United Nations and to concoct, by whatever slight of drafting his long experience afforded, deft explanations of the position at critical moments for Britain's diplomats in the Middle East. The delicacy of his position was demonstrated when Dixon, oblivious of what was afoot in London, spoke up in support of Jordan at the time of the renewed Israeli assault on the Hashemite Kingdom. Eden was furious. On 27 October, Kirkpatrick prepared some notes and a draft minute for Lloyd to send to the Prime Minister arguing in Dixon's defence that he could hardly have said less in the context of the Jordanian complaint. Lloyd's telegram to Dixon on 30 October, following news of the Israeli invasion, conveyed the sense of this and hinted at Anglo-French plans to take action independently of their allies. The following day, a letter was sent to Dixon under Ross's signature but bears evidence of Kirkpatrick's hand. It had been prepared in draft on 27 October and held presumably so that Lloyd could convey his instructions first. Repeating Lloyd's request to 'lie low for a bit', Kirkpatrick continued, 'This does not mean that we think there was anything wrong with your support of Jordan in the initial stages of the debate', and reiterated the point made to the Prime Minister: 'I entirely agree that nothing less than your expression of sympathy and conciliation would have satisfied the requirements of the alliance.'[54] This act of providing simultaneously support and obfuscation was to continue throughout the ensuing crisis. Kirkpatrick appears to have actively enjoyed this duplicity in so far as it gave him license to evade, if not actually mislead the press corps. At a lecture to the Imperial Defence College at the end of October he mischievously observed that 'if you want to play a trick in the diplomatic game you do not always want to have to tell the press in advance.[55] Even more disquieting, perhaps, was his unconcern in having to mislead the American Ambassador, Winthrop Aldrich. Having issued the British ultimatum to the Egyptian Ambassador in mid-afternoon on 30 October, Kirkpatrick, with evident delight, received Aldrich at King Charles Street a little over an hour later. Aldrich, who had been fobbed off earlier in the day, had requested an interview with Lloyd but got Kirkpatrick instead, at a time deliberately chosen so that the American could not alert his President to intervene.[56] Despite Aldrich's view that there would be 'hell to pay', Kirkpatrick felt able to report 'a quite pleasant interview'.[57] This, and the deception which had earlier preceded the meeting contributed significantly to Eisenhower's subsequent fury.[58]

While the British and French delegations in New York vetoed American and Soviet resolutions calling for a cease-fire, Kirkpatrick, in an artfully composed telegram, presented the government's position on the Israeli action to all British missions as background guidance: The Israeli attack on Egypt, he explained, seemed 'undoubtedly to be an act of aggression'. How could it have been otherwise? On the other hand, Egypt had brought this on herself, first by insisting that the state of war with Israel was continuing, second by defying the Security Council, and third by openly threatening to encompass the destruction of Israel. 'British policy was to take the most decisive steps to bring hostility to an early end.' Preparing the way for Anglo-French military action he added that the British government was advised 'on the highest legal authority that they are entitled under the Charter to take every measure open to them within and without the UN to stop the fighting and to protect their nationals and interests which are threatened by these hostilities'.[59] This did not fall short of an outright lie and Fitzmaurice, on seeing the telegram, took immediate steps to distance himself, recording that throughout the crisis the legal team had consistently opposed the use of force.[60] Meanwhile Kirkpatrick recommended to Baghdad that Prime Minister Nuri Said be advised that our immediate action in the Canal Zone 'is merely a temporary fire brigade operation'. Giving once more a cryptic indication of what was really afoot, he warned the Ambassador to be careful to avoid committing Britain to calling on the Israelis to withdraw to the armistice lines in the immediate future.[61] Within the Foreign Office the significance of the British ultimatum and veto of UN condemnation was quickly understood and an atmosphere of 'initial perplexity' turned into 'despondency and resentment'.[62] On 31 October Kirkpatrick found himself in receipt of a letter from Shuckburgh which formulated the question at the centre of everyone's concerns; was it not necessary, he enquired 'to adjust the impression which our "ultimatum" had given that the Israelis are to be allowed to remain on Egyptian territory?' Only by insisting on withdrawal, he argued, 'can we prove that the action we have taken really is on behalf of our own Suez Canal interests, and not on behalf of Israeli expansion'.[63]

Shuckburgh visited the Foreign Office in person on 1 November to lunch with Harold Beeley who told him that everyone except 'Kirk' was "equally depressed and astonished" by Anglo-French negotiations'.[64] This account does not entirely square with others; Selwyn Lloyd records that he had a talk with Kirkpatrick on the morning of 1 November and that they were 'both worried by the United States's reactions' and the speed with which it had allowed the matter to be taken to the United Nations. Indeed, Kirkpatrick had that morning expressed the view that Britain was bound to leave the UN or be expelled unless some other way could be found quickly.[65] As a palliative, Lloyd and Kirkpatrick agreed that offering to hand over the peace-keeping function to the United Nations might improve the Anglo-French position and persuaded a willing Eden to mention this in his speech in the House of Commons that afternoon so that Dixon could refer to it in the United Nations General Assembly debate.[66] To Pierson Dixon, Kirkpatrick sent a personal telegram carrying his own 'reflections' as a stop gap until something more concrete was forthcoming. Outlining three possible scenarios he argued that if the General Assembly disapproved of the Anglo-French action and were not prepared to authorise decisive UN action to separate the combatants and secure a treaty, then they should be 'manful enough to say that they stand for falling back into a regime of chaos followed by certain war'.[67] Within the Office, Kirkpatrick found himself obliged at last to address his senior staff. On Monday morning, 5 November, he called them together for a short meeting that had its origins in a note to Kirkpatrick from Paul Gore-Booth expressing the deep dismay of the staff following recent developments. Gore-Booth's account records that Kirkpatrick 'did his best to answer questions to which there was no answer'. Sticking to the Rhineland analogy, for how else could the present predicament be explained, he reminded his staff that Ministers were no more obliged to ask for the advice of officials than they were to take it, assuming it was sought in the first place. Gore-Booth neatly summed up his account of the occasion with a reminder to his readers that 'Just as Mr Chamberlain did not choose to have full advice from the Foreign Office in 1938, so did Sir Anthony Eden tragically avoid it in 1956'.[68]

The anti-American feeling which was generated in British official circles by the American stance during the Suez Crisis was reinforced on 24 November by American abstention in the General Assembly debate on the Afro-Asian motion calling for withdrawal 'forthwith'. Indeed, Kirkpatrick told Aldrich three days later that if the United Nations let Britain down, he would advise Ministers to abandon the Organisation altogether.[69] Denis Healey's account of this period suggests that Kirkpatrick was the among the principle instigators of the anti-Americanism which pervaded the British Establishment at this juncture, and claims that he 'broke off relations with the United States completely', forbidding the Foreign Office to have contact with its American counterparts.[70] This may well be true, but it was reciprocated with equal force in Washington; while Eisenhower and Dulles refused to deal with Eden, Aldrich by-passed the Foreign Office and liaised directly with other British Cabinet Ministers. The resort to force had finally broken American tolerance.[71]

Kirkpatrick was due to retire from the Foreign Office on his sixtieth birthday in February 1957 when he would be succeeded by Sir Frederick Hoyer Miller. Kirkpatrick's official reflections on the Suez Crisis and the future of Britain's Middle East policy are recorded in his correspondence with Gladwyn Jebb, then Ambassador to France, during November and December in connection with the Middle East Policy review conducted in the wake of the Suez debacle.[72] Kirkpatrick's observations are significant for their emphasis on the limitations placed on British policy making by their alliance with the United States. 'In particular,' Kirkparick wrote, 'it looks as though it will not be possible for us to hold on in the Arab states without some degree of American support for our position. And you know,' he added cryptically, 'how up and down American support can be.'[73] In fact Kirkpatrick was merely restating the position which Attlee and Bevin had understood in other contexts in the wake of the Potsdam Conference and which before them Churchill and even Eden himself had shown signs of grasping well before the Second World War's end.

Quite why this truth was so determinedly overlooked in the conflict with Nasser is difficult to explain outside the framework of lingering perceptions of great power responsibilities and the all-too-human desire to refight lost battles in the hope that a victory in one will somehow cancel out the misjudgement which led to downfall in the other.

Kirkpatrick's rationalisation of this situation, which is couched in conventional Cold War terms of the possible extension of Soviet influence into the region, is similarly interesting for the parallels which can be drawn with mid-1940s discussions about Europe and the Mediterranean. He concluded that 'we think there is just no prospect of the Russians agreeing to hold off the Middle East if we hold off ourselves. The whole direction of their policy latterly makes one suppose the precise contrary'.[74] One of the paradoxes of this episode is that Anglo-French humiliation at Suez led to more direct American involvement in the Middle East. The territory encompassed in the battleground of Soviet–American confrontation had been expanded by the demise of the colonial powers.

Kirkpatrick's contribution to policy making during the Suez Crisis, while channelled formally through the Defence (Transition) Committee, functioned more informally through his personal communications with the Prime Minister in which capacity he appears to have acted as a source of constant support. There is no documentary evidence to prove that it was Kirkpatrick who supplied the Munich analogy in support of using force against Nasser, but there is also no evidence to suggest that he ever discouraged, or even questioned its use. In restraining the inclination of others to challenge the thrust of Eden's policy, he was at best an accessory. This role took on more sinister and ultimately damaging connotations once Kirkpatrick found himself obliged to extend it to exclusion of the entire Foreign Office from the decision-making process, a task which was achievable in the short term by virtue of his control over the interface between the Foreign Office and the covert communications network operated by SIS.

The indictment of Kirkpatrick, while at times unduly harsh, is nonetheless difficult to refute. His predecessor, William Strang, in a contemporaneous publication, observed that the qualities required for the diplomatist are 'strict objectivity' and 'the ability to draw on knowledge and wisdom possessed by others, and to synthesise it fully for one's own use'.[75] This ability may have been something in which Kirkpatrick was deficient. Indeed, his combative nature and perfunctory style of decision making would have precluded the process of reflection and considered judgement predicated in Strang's dictum. It may be unfair to attack Kirkpatrick for his loyalty, as some historians have done on the grounds that he thereby made the debacle possible because Eden 'could not do it alone'.[76] Kirkpatrick was the product of an age when duty and obligation to higher authority were observed more rigorously than is the case in modern times. Where Kirkpatrick can be more justly criticised, however, is for his encouragement of Eden's self-evidently dangerous obsession with Nasser as a Middle Eastern Hitler. This was a view which, once it was permitted to act as a rationale for policy decisions, could only lead to miscalculation.

Kirkpatrick's terse account of his period as Permanent Under-Secretary is significant for omitting any direct comment on these events. However, between the lines lies a personal indictment of the post-war international system and in particular the United Nations as an instrument concerned 'not to secure and enforce justice' but 'only to prevent war'.[77] Britain's position in the world, he at last had realised, had changed fundamentally. Britain was no longer free to make foreign policy in accordance with her 'eternal interests' and independent of her allies. 'In the Western world,' he observed, 'no country can any longer pursue an independent foreign policy. The liberty of action of each is in varying degrees restricted by the need to obtain the concurrence of one or more members of the alliance.'[78] Acknowledging, in effect, the cognitive dissonance which seemed to grip him in 1956, he observed that of the dangers besetting policy makers, 'the greatest is self-delusion. It is a fault to which we as a nation are particularly prone'.[79] The conclusion of his one-time colleague and biographer, Con O'Neil, is inescapable: the flight from judgement implicit in self-delusion is not a luxury which the Permanent Under-Secretary at the Foreign Office is at liberty to indulge.[80]

ACKNOWLEDGEMENTS

The author would like to thank the Academic Council and the School of Politics at the Queen's University of Belfast for providing the funds which made this research possible.

NOTES

1. See, for example, C. Hill, 'Past and Present in British Foreign Policy', in M. Smith, S. Smith and B. White (eds) in *British Foreign Policy: tradition, change and transformation* (London: Unwin Hyman, 1988), pp.24–49. See also P. Kennedy, *The Realities Behind Diplomacy: background influences on British External Policy 1865–1980* (London: Fontana, 1981), especially pp.379–84.

2. D. Reynolds, *Britannia Overruled: British Policy and World Power in the 20th Century* (London: Longman, 1991), pp.60–3.

3. A. Horne, *Macmillan 1894–1956* (London: Macmillan, 1986), p.359.

4. R. Barclay, *Ernest Bevin and the Foreign Office 1932–69* (Bucks.: Latimer, 1975), pp.19–20.

5. Horne, *Macmillan 1894–1956*, p.359.

6. Lord Gladwyn, *The Memoirs of Lord Gladwyn* (London: Weidenfeld & Nicolson, 1972), p.269.

7. I. Kirkpatrick, *The Inner Circle* (London: Macmillan, 1959), p.221.

8. Barclay, *Ernest Bevin*, pp.19–20.

9. C. Andrew, *Secret Service: The Making of the British Intelligence Community* (London: Sceptre, 1986), pp.241–3.

10. FO 371/59664/N15609/5159/38, minutes of meeting of Committee of Policy Towards Russia, 17 Oct. 1946.

11. K. Hamilton *et al* (eds), *Documents on British Policy Overseas*, Series I, Vol.VII (London: HMSO, 1995), docs. Nos. 56.i and 74.i.

12. C. O'Neil, 'Ivone Kirkpatrick', E.T. Williams and C.S. Nicholl (eds), *Dictionary of National Biography 1961–70* (Oxford: Oxford University Press, 1981), p.617.

13. See P. Kennedy, 'Appeasement in British Foreign Policy, 1865–1939', in *Strategy and Diplomacy 1870–1945* (London: Fontana 1984), p.39.

14. FO 800/741/PM/IK/56/194, Kirkpatrick to Eden, 3 Oct. 1956.

15. Kirkpatrick, *The Inner Circle*, p.262.

16. W.R. Louis, 'American Anti-Colonialism and the Dissolution of the British Empire', in *The Special Relationship: Anglo-American Relations since 1945* (Oxford: Oxford University Press, 1986), p.275. See further W.R. Louis, 'The Tragedy of the Anglo-Egyptian Settlement of 1954', in W.R. Louis and R. Owen (eds), *Suez 1956: The Crisis and its Consequences* (Oxford: Clarendon Press, 1989), p.70.

17. V.H. Feske, 'Suez: The British Foreign Office and the Quai d'Orsay', in G.A. Craig and F.L. Loewenheim, *The Diplomats 1939–1979* (Princeton NJ: Princeton UP, 1994), p.170.

18. A. Danchev, *Oliver Franks: Founding Father* (Oxford: Clarendon Press, 1993), p.141.

19. R. Rhodes James, *Anthony Eden* (London: Weidenfeld & Nicolson, 1986), p.351.

20. A. Adamthwaite, 'Overstretched and Overstrung: Eden, the Foreign Office and the Making of Policy, 1951–55', *International Affairs*, Vol.64, No.2 (Spring 1988), p.254.

21. FO 371/121541/VJ1201/51, Kirkpatrick minute, 5 March 1956.

22. E. Shuckburgh, *Descent to Suez: Diaries 1951–1956* (London: Weidenfeld & Nicolson, 1986), p.342; FO 371/121541/VJ1201/41/file.

23. Eden letter to Eisenhower, 5 March 1956 in A. Gorst and L. Johnman, *The Suez Crisis* (London: Routledge, 1996), p.44.

24. Shuckburgh, *Descent to Suez*, p.346.

25. Rhodes James, *Anthony Eden*, pp.554–5.

26. Horne, *Macmillan 1894–1956*, p.395, *Hansard, House of Commons Debates*, 2 Aug. 1956.
27. Shuckburgh, *Descent to Suez*, p.25; Feske, 'Suez', p.171.
28. D. Carlton, *Britain and the Suez Crisis* (Oxford: Basil Blackwell, 1988), p.46.
29. W. Clark, *From Three Worlds* (London: Sidgwick & Jackson, 1986), diary entries for 1 and 24 Aug. 1956, p.168.
30. W.S. Lucas, *Divided We Stand: Britain, the United States and the Suez Crisis* (London: Hodder & Stoughton, 1996 ed.), pp.101–2.
31. Louis, 'American Anti-Colonialism', p.276.
32. FO 371/119128/JE14211/1390, Beeley minute, 18 Aug. 1956, on which Archibald Ross minuted, 'I agree', 20 Aug. 1956.
33. FO 371/119128/JE14211/1390, Kirkpatrick minute, 21 Aug. 1956.
34. FO 371/119128/JE14211/1390, minutes by Beeley and Fitzmaurice, 31 Aug. 1956.
35. FO 953/1643/PB1011/43, Kirkpatrick to Rennie, 28 Aug. 1956. See T. Shaw, *Eden, Suez and the Mass Media: propaganda and persuasion during the Suez Crisis* (London: IB Tauris, 1996), p.124.
36. FO 371/119154/JE14211/2127, Kirkpatrick to Lloyd, 4 Sept. 1956.
37. Clark, *From Three Worlds*, diary entry for 5 Sept. 1956, p.183.
38. PREM 11/1177, Eden to Eisenhower, 6 Sept. 1956; Sir Anthony Eden, *Full Circle* (London: Cassell, 1961), pp.464–6; Lucas, *Divided We Stand*, p.182.
39. PREM 11/1100, Eisenhower to Eden, 8 Sept. 1956.
40. *Foreign Relations of the United States, 1955–57* [FRUS], *Vol. xvi* (Washington DC, USGPO, 1990), 'Summary of Developments in the Suez situation, 11 Sept. 1956. Report prepared by the Executive Secretary at the Department of State'.
41. Lucas, *Divided We Stand*, p.183.
42. FO 800/735, Kirkpatrick to Makins, 10 Sept. 1956.
43. S. Lloyd, *Suez 1956: A Personal Account* (London: Jonathan Cape, 1986), pp.130–31.
44. T. Bower, *The Perfect English Spy: Sir Dick White and the Secret War 1935–90* (London: Mandarin, 1995), pp.188–9.
45. Lucas, *Divided We Stand*, p.196.
46. Ibid., pp.195–6.
47. G. MacDermott, *The Eden Legacy* (London: Leslie Frewin, 1969), p.137.
48. Lucas, *Divided We Stand*, p.222.
49. Shuckburgh, *Descent to Suez*, p.360
50. K. Kyle, *Suez* (London: Weidenfeld & Nicolson, 1991), p.297; D.R. Thorpe, *Selwyn Lloyd* (London: Jonathan Cape, 1989), p.231.
51. Horne, *Macmillan 1894–1956*, p.432; see further Feske, 'Suez', p.189, footnote 160.
52. A. Nutting, *No End of a Lesson: The Story of Suez* (London: Constable, 1967), pp.96–7; Lloyd, *Suez 1956*, p.166.
53. Bower, *The Perfect English Spy*, p.195.
54. FO 371/121746/VR1074/436, Lloyd to Eden, 27 Oct. 1956; VR1074/435 Kirkpatrick's draft letter to Dixon, 27 Oct. 1956 and Ross to Dixon, 31 Oct. 1956.
55. Shuckburgh, *Descent to Suez*, p.362.
56. H. Thomas, *The Suez Affair* (London: Weidenfeld & Nicolson, 1967), p.137.
57. FO 371/118902/JE1094/4, Kirkpatrick minute of interview with US Ambassador, 30 Oct. 1956.
58. Carlton, *Britain and the Suez Crisis*, pp.69–70.
59. FO 371/121784/VR1091/431, FO circular tel. to Middle East posts, 30 Oct. 1956.

60. FO 800/747, Fitzmaurice to Kirkpatrick, 31 Oct. 1956. See Kyle, *Suez*, p.391, note 42.
61. FO 371/121783, Kirkpatrick's draft tel. 2343 to Baghdad, despatched 31 Oct. 1956.
62. P. Gore-Booth, *With Great Truth and Respect* (London: Constable, 1974), p.229.
63. Shuckburgh, *Descent to Suez*, p.363, note 4.
64. Ibid., pp.362–4
65. Clark, *From Three Worlds*, entry for 1 Nov. 1956, pp.202–4.
66. Lloyd, *Suez 1956*, p.200.
67. FO 371/121748/VR1074/524, Kirkpatrick to Dixon, tel. 1444, 1 Nov. 1956.
68. Gore-Booth, *With Great Truth and Respect*, p.230.
69. PREM 11/1106, Kirkpatrick to Dixon, 27 Nov. 1956. See also Kyle, *Suez*, p.509.
70. D. Healey, *The Time of My Life* (London: Penguin, 1989), p.173.
71. W. Aldrich, 'The Suez Crisis: A Footnote to History', *Foreign Affairs*, Vol.45 (1967); D. Cameron Watt, *Succeeding John Bull: America in Britain's Place 1900–1975* (Cambridge: Cambridge University Press, 1984), p.133; Carlton, *Britain and the Suez Crisis*, pp.87–8.
72. Kirkpatrick's valedictory would presumably shed some light on his state of mind but this is still withheld from the public domain.
73. FO 371/121237/V1054/13/3, Kirkpatrick to Jebb, 11 Dec. 1956.
74. FO 371/121237/V1054/13/3, Kirkpatrick to Jebb, 11 Dec. 1956.
75. W. Strang, *The Foreign Office* (London: Allen & Unwin, 1955), pp.182–3.
76. Louis, 'American Anti-Colonialism', p 276.
77. Kirkpatrick, *The Inner Circle*, p.266.
78. Ibid., p.265.
79. Ibid., p.268.
80. O'Neil, *Dictionary of National Biography 1961–70*, p.617.

Conclusion

JOHN W. YOUNG

The debate about the influence of officials on foreign policy, as on government policy in general, has a long pedigree. At the start of the twentieth century, with politics becoming more genuinely democratic and Foreign Office officials throwing off their role as mere clerks, Liberal backbenchers and radical journalists 'claimed that far from being neutral advisers and executors of the elected government's wishes...officials had sought to influence and even direct policy contrary to the wishes of...the Cabinet...'[1] Hence the accusation that the Foreign Secretary, Sir Edward Grey, led Britain on the road to the First World War due to the pernicious influence of an anti-German clique in his department. The idea that civil servants, rather than giving objective advice on a range of policy alternatives, actually limit and frame those alternatives in a manipulative way according to a bureaucratic agenda, was best portrayed at a popular level in the 1980s television series, *Yes, Minister*. But it was also evident in such-widely read works by experienced ministers as Richard Crossman's Cabinet diaries, most notably in the opening pages of the first volume where, within days of becoming Minister of Housing, he felt his Permanent Under-Secretary was 'looking after me, grooming me', and confessed 'one has to be pretty strong-minded and curious not to be got down by this astonishing Whitehall hierarchy, by the way the establishment takes you into itself and folds you into its bosom.'[2]

Yet in contrast to this view, of civil servants dominating or manipulating their political masters, is the argument of Denis Healey, the former Defence Secretary and Chancellor of the Exchequer, that 'a minister who complains...his civil servants are too powerful is either a weak minister or an incompetent one'. This is a classic statement of the case that it is ministers – so long as they are firm and competent – who retain effective power. Rather less forthright, but pointing in a similar direction, is the statement by Michael Heseltine, another long-serving Cabinet minister, that the role of civil servants 'is to give…advice, the best they can' whereas 'the responsibility of a minister is to listen carefully…and make his own judgements…and to realise that if he's going to achieve the results that his political priorities demand, he is going to have to lead that machine.'[3] A study of the impact of Foreign Office officials under the post-1945 Labour government – now a well-trawled field for historians – has suggested that the truth may lie somewhere in between the *Yes, Minister* and Healey views, and that even a strong-minded and competent minister like Ernest Bevin allowed officials to develop certain policies without proper consultation among ministers. However, this was not necessarily a bad thing, because the agenda to which officials worked was one designed to safeguard British interests, maximise its influence, maintain friendship with key allies and identify pressing security threats. It was inevitable that civil servants had firm ideas about where British foreign policy should go after 1945 and inevitable too that they should try to have their preferred policies accepted by ministers. 'Rather than question the constitutional proprieties of such action, historians would best set their efforts to determining how far and when such a process took place.'[4]

This advice to historians to concentrate on what they do best – the reconstruction of events at a particular point in the past – is especially apt for those studying the role of officials during one of the seminal episodes of twentieth century British foreign policy, the Suez Crisis. For the experience of 1956 confirms that the balance of power between ministers and officials will differ between any two given points in time. It will also differ according to the issue being debated: certain foreign policy problems under the Eden government, which seemed of less importance than the Middle East, *were* dominated by civil servants.[5] The calibre, experience and determination of individual diplomats, military leaders, Prime Ministers and Foreign Secretaries is an ever-changing constellation and, due to time constraints, ministers always have to decide which questions to focus their attention upon. It may have been possible to accuse Edward Grey of being under the influence of a pervasive officialdom where German policy was concerned, but no one who studies the Suez would think of levelling that charge at Anthony Eden and the ministers, such as Harold Macmillan, Lord

Kilmuir and Alan Lennox-Boyd, who supported a tough line against Nasser and Egypt.

It is certainly the case that at first, following the nationalisation of the Suez Canal Company, most officials, whether diplomats or military men, favoured an active policy to confront Nasser and put the Canal under an international regime. But in the last weeks of the crisis the concern among officials about the course of British foreign policy was widespread. One senior Foreign Office figure, Paul Gore-Booth, who had seen many colleagues over the previous days, wrote to his chief Ivone Kirkpatrick on 2 November 1956, about 'the dismay caused throughout our ranks... People are doing their duty but with a heavy heart and a feeling that, whatever our motives, we have terribly damaged our reputation.'[6] Kirkpatrick, of course, was one of the few supporters of the invasion of Egypt in his department. Yet, in contrast to the situation among officials and almost to the end, *ministerial* doubters about the operation, notably the Defence Secretary, Walter Monckton, were a minority.

While the Suez Crisis was a unique event, and while it is impossible to draw too many lessons about the role of the British civil service from a single episode, nonetheless a number of points stand out from the essays in the current volume. The range of officials discussed is a wide one, from legal advisers to Treasury mandarins, from military chiefs to the Chairman of the BBC's Board of Governors. Not all were civil servants, but most were, and there are several ambassadors represented, allowing some general points to be made about their treatment by Eden and his inner circle. Other officials might have been chosen. Eden's private secretary in the overseas field, Guy Millard, perhaps, or the third of the trio of defence chiefs, the Chief of the Air Staff, Dermot Boyle. But there is no doubt that the most important officials, in London and abroad, are represented here: the three leading Whitehall mandarins (the Cabinet Secretary and the heads of the Foreign Office and Treasury), the two essential figures on the Chiefs of Staff Committee (Mountbatten and Templer), the liaison man between the Foreign Office and MI6 (Dean) and ambassadors to the key posts of Washington, Cairo, Paris and the UN, together with a number of others who illustrate the range of official involvement and shed light on less well-discussed facets of the crisis.

What then are the points which stand out from this collection about the role of officials in the Suez Crisis? The first is the argument just touched upon that officials fulfil a large number of roles, from defending Britain's case at the UN and negotiating with allies to planning military operations and providing legal advice. But the essays have also pointed out other areas of activity, such as the manipulation of the media, psychological operations and the use of covert action to undermine foreign governments. As well as the Foreign Office, Downing Street and the Treasury, the volume has also mentioned the work of MI6, the BBC and the Cabinet Office. The machinery of government is vast and, by concentrating attention on a number of individuals, the potential of the system to fragment has been highlighted. This danger of the fragmentation of officialdom is increased by the fact that, whatever the ideal of providing neutral advice, officials self-evidently *do* have their own beliefs, perceptions and interests, sometimes being quite manipulative and dishonest in pursuing these. Kirkpatrick and Cadogan in particular seem to have trusted Eden, to have distrusted the UN and the US, and to have opposed any 'appeasement' of Nasser, all because of their experience of facing Hitler in the 1930s. Their perception of the national interest made both men ready to exploit their positions in ways that could potentially damage the institutions over which they had charge. Thus Cadogan was ready to use the BBC as a propaganda tool for the Prime Minister, while Kirkpatrick used his links to MI6 in order to keep decisions being made through the final crisis while the bulk of the Foreign Office was left in ignorance about what was happening.

Kirkpatrick remained loyal even after the Prime Minister began to exclude him from decision making and, despite the civil service's liking for honesty, the Permanent Under-Secretary seems to have become quite duplicitous in trying to disguise the reality of collusion with Israel and to prevent US action. This was an extreme example of what might occur, of course. But to a lesser degree others followed particular agendas during the crisis which reflected their experience and positions. Thus Norman Brook, as Cabinet Secretary and (from October) head of the civil service, was determined to preserve the co-ordination and continuity of policy, while the various ambassadors were all influenced by the lessons and needs of their particular posts. In Paris, Jebb was keen to improve Franco-British relations and not at all happy to welcome Israel's involvement in this relationship. In Cairo, Trevelyan was deeply worried about any attempt to turn his Embassy, once more, into a decisive player in Egyptian domestic politics. In Washington, Makins was concerned to protect co-operation with the US and, in New York, Dixon's main wish was to keep the UN quiescent and uncritical of British policy.

Despite this diversity of posts, characters and opinions, the machinery of government had to operate as a whole and, behind all the individuals discussed in this volume, it is clear that a sophisticated structure of ministries and committees existed which tried to link the administration together. Indeed, however unusual the Suez Crisis was, the machine was structured, as Michael Thornhill points out, on traditional British lines. Some *ad hoc* committees were created, but those familiar with the workings of Whitehall know that such committees are springing up and being wound down all the time, because the challenges facing government are also ever-changing. For the most part Whitehall went on as always with the key ministries (the Foreign Office, Ministry of Defence and, in the last phase at least, the Treasury) being those one would expect to find most heavily involved in such matters and a number of permanent, 'named' committees, such as the Chiefs of Staff and Joint Intelligence Committee. The problem, as Scott Lucas argues, was that the machine ultimately *did* depend on personalities and that a few key interpersonal links, as between Eden and Kirkpatrick, or between Eden and Dean, could short-circuit the whole edifice, rendering much of it powerless and creating confusion.

Despite many personal differences over Suez, officials did evolve a consensus view on events. In July and August there was clearly a strong belief that 'something had to be done' about Nasser, not least for reasons of British prestige (an issue which reflected on the standing of officials themselves) but, after a confusing period in September and October, a new consensus emerged which saw the use of force as ill-advised and was aghast at the likely impact of collusion – not least because this particular piece of chicanery was seen as possibly more damaging to Britain's prestige than the nationalisation of the Canal had been. So, although it could not be claimed that all officials thought the same way, and while the views of particular officials may have varied from bellicose to pacific (as they did among ministers and, indeed, in society as a whole) there seems to have been a clear majority of officials in late October who disliked collusion, opposed the use of force and preferred a diplomatic solution to the Suez problem. The 'official mind' was not quite at one but it leant towards a particular way of resolving matters which was different from that chosen by the Prime Minister. But, again, the problem was that there were enough senior placed officials, like Dean, Templer and Kirkpatrick, who were ready to co-operate with Eden and ensure that the Prime Minister's wishes were carried through without serious questioning.

Also, whatever the growing doubts about Eden's line, one other point which stands out about officials' behaviour in 1956 is their loyalty to the government, their refusal to take private criticisms into the public domain and their ultimate readiness to carry on working at their posts. Only a very few officials resigned over Suez. This is an aspect of the crisis which has been commented upon before, and it clearly exercised the minds of some of those involved for years afterwards. One Treasury official, Leo Pliatzky, even confessed later that Suez 'was the only occasion…when I had to reflect how the work of the British Civil Service, with its commitment to work for the government of the day, irrespective of its policies, differed from officials in Hitler's Germany…'[7] The experience of 1956, when officials 'swallowed their doubts, carried out the politicians' instructions and kept tight-lipped', certainly bears out the view, given in a study of civil service ethics, that 'the professional discretion of civil servants and their duty to the Government of the day prevails even when it involves acute personal discomfort'.[8]

Why this should be the case is suggested in another study: 'The influence of the civil service on…policy-making is certainly very powerful, but what chiefly characterises its relations with the political…hierarchy is nevertheless its fundamental…docility. On the whole, its influence is brought to bear through the machinery itself…'[9] It is certainly not the case that officials were acquiescent for reasons of weak-mindedness or lack of character. Cagodan, Makins, Brook, Mountbatten and others were formidable, tough, experienced individuals. However, they operated to professional values which kept their differences within the bureaucracy. It was for politicians to operate in the public arena and (until at least the Clive Ponting case in the 1980s) civil servants frowned upon the idea of themselves expressing public disagreement with ministers, preferring instead to wield influence behind the scenes, honouring a code of secrecy, loyalty and discretion. In November 1956 those who did not resign over Suez could justify remaining in office as the best way to rebuild British power and influence. Fittingly, Brook was a model of calm acceptance of the Suez failure, determined to carry on his duties and keep criticisms of ministers to himself. But no doubt more mundane factors – a secure income, a satisfying career, an ambition for higher things – also influenced decisions to live with government policy. Dixon, Jebb and Trevelyan all had several years in top ambassadorial posts ahead of them; Makins had just become joint head of the Treasury. As for the military chiefs, Templer had fewer qualms about Operation MUSKETEER than had Mountbatten, but the latter was dissuaded from resignation, partly it seems because of a belief that the military were there to carry out the orders of a democratically-elected government (the key difference, surely, from officials of the Nazi regime) but also because he greatly enjoyed his role as First Sea Lord. It should also be noted that for all his complaints about Suez, Mountbatten was informed of collusion whereas the more bellicose Templer was not. Mountbatten's position in the Royal Family, his old friendship with Eden and the fact that he was acting Chairman of the Chiefs of Staff for much of 1956 no doubt contributed to this apparent anomaly.

But it was not just that officials remained at their posts when MUSKETEER was brought to a halt. Despite their qualms and questions, they also helped pave the way for the use of force. However badly he treated them, Eden needed his officials to handle the nuts and bolts of administration, to negotiate with the French and the Israelis, to draw up invasion plans, to defend Britain's case on the world stage and, through Norman Brook, to co-ordinate the machine at the centre. Political, military, economic and diplomatic activity all had to be kept operating. Officials were in fact involved in planning for a possible invasion as early as July and the legal advisers conducted a long debate about the use of force so that, even if most knew nothing about collusion, very many officials long knew that force was an option for dealing with Nasser. Brook, despite his growing doubts about Eden's fitness for the premiership and his preference for a diplomatic settlement, was a leading figure in plans for MUSKETEER.[10] Other cases tell a similar story. Thus, Humphrey Trevelyan may have believed that the only likely successor to Nasser was another extreme nationalist, but his Embassy was involved in both clandestine attempts to undermine the Egyptian leader and studies of political figures who might be drawn onto a British-created government in Cairo. And Mountbatten, for all his fears of substantial civilian casualties, decided it was his duty to plan for a successful operation including the bombardment of Port Said. Neither can officials, or at least some of them, escape the accusation that they fuelled Eden's obsession with Nasser as a kind of Middle Eastern Hitler, made doubly dangerous through the backing of the Soviets. Kirkpatrick did nothing to question the preposterous Hitler analogy and MI6 appear to have been particularly responsible for creating the image of Nasser as an agent of Moscow, but one who might be successfully replaced. This image fitted both the Intelligence Service's desire to pursue a determined anti-Communist policy and its belief in the efficacy of covert action.

If officialdom was ultimately quiescent in what ministers on the Egypt Committee decided, it still leaves the question of why Eden decided to keep so many officials ignorant of what was happening in the last fateful week of the crisis. It ought to have been clear that evidence of the Franco-British-Israeli collusion would become public; and it certainly did not help the execution of policy when even key officials were kept in the dark. With his vast experience of foreign affairs, Eden of all people should have recognised this. It seems to have been particularly difficult for Dixon to operate in a fog at the UN, a vital forum where world opinion was concerned, when the French Ambassador had suffered a nervous collapse and there was no British Ambassador in Washington. As a former private secretary to Eden, Dixon could have expected better. Yet the fact was that the Prime Minister *did* believe he could deny that collusion had occurred, and there were obvious reasons for keeping knowledge of actual military operations limited to a narrow group. Secrecy about bold operations can have its uses: it allows rapid action unencumbered by bureaucratic doubts; it minimises the danger of leaks; and it helps achieve the element of surprise against opponents. Henry Kissinger, another advocate of secret diplomacy, once argued that bureaucracies are designed 'to devise a standard operating procedure which can effectively cope with most problems', but that because of this they also create a rigidity in policy which a determined political leader must try to break. Kissinger also noted 'the curious phenomenon that decisions taken with enormous doubt...become practically sacrosanct once adopted. The whole administrative machinery swings behind their implementation as if activity could still all doubts'.[11] On a generous reading of Eden, then, perhaps he behaved as he did simply to overcome the reluctance of the Whitehall machine, confident that it would fall in behind the 'correct' policy, once adopted. But a less flattering argument would be that he simply wished to avoid hearing alternative policies, having decided to pursue the vendetta against Nasser at an early date, and that it was especially important to hide the fact of collusion because of the deviousness and duplicity this implied. As Clive Ponting has argued, on the basis of his own experience in Whitehall, 'Secrecy is used not to protect national security but to prevent political embarrassment; and papers that show the fallibility of government policy or the deviousness or duplicity of Ministers…are highly classified.'[12]

If nothing else the Suez experience illustrates that, if a group of ministers is determined enough, they can sometimes press on with a dangerous and questionable policy, overriding the doubts of their officials, confident that Whitehall will march, albeit reluctantly, behind. There will always be some officials who, through a sense of duty, personal loyalty or misguided beliefs, will back even controversial decisions. Most of the rest will still their doubts because of their deeply-held code of professional conduct. And opportunities for civil servants to slow down or re-direct policy can be closed off by ensuring that the vital decisions are confined to a few, willing hands: thus Eden, in 1956, refused to let Edward Bridges (the Permanent Secretary at the Treasury until Makins took over) see the minutes of the Egypt Committee even though military action would carry grave consequences and even after Bridges had been to Brook to complain about being sidelined in this way.[13] The only officials Eden was prepared to trust were those who backed his policy or who, like Brook, he *had* to rely on because of their special position in the hierarchy. Nonetheless it is also quite clear that such behaviour did not lead to efficient policy making, and those who complain about the iniquities of civil service influence over elected politicians need also to consider the dangers of those politicians by-passing established lines of Whitehall policy making and ignoring the advice of experienced, permanent, professional officials.

There was clearly a lot wrong with the detailed workings of British policy in 1956 – the intense rivalry between Mountbatten and Templer, for example, or the failure of MI6 to correctly analyse the Egyptian political situation – but these were probably no worse than at any other point in history. The more significant and widespread failure, and one which *was* specific to Suez, was the simple failure of ministers, and Eden in particular, to listen to sensible arguments against his policy and reconsider his options. Instead policy moved down one particular line and even then seemed hurried and confused. The list of arguments put by officials against force was a long one and included Makin's warning of likely US opposition to any invasion, Mountbatten's fear of Commonwealth opposition, Templer's complaints about the military deficiencies of MUSKETEER and the consistent advice from Sir Gerald Fitzmaurice that the use of force could not be justified. It is also true that the Treasury persistently warned of the likely economic impact of any attack on Egypt, Bridges having written in early September that it was a 'vital necessity from the point of view of our currency of ensuring…that we have maximum US support.'[14] But all such advice was ignored and only when MUSKETEER proceeded did the cold lesson of events bring home to Eden the multiple dangers of American opposition, Commonwealth division, world outrage and economic strain.

From what unfolded in the second half of 1956, it does not seem that any official, or group of officials, could have made a difference to the Suez fiasco. Even if Brook and Kirkpatrick had emerged as early, determined opponents of an invasion, and Templer had pressed his doubts about the military operation, Eden might just have ignored them, as he ignored so many others. No official seems to have had a consistent, close and real influence over the Prime Minister so far as planning for collusion and the invasion of Egypt were concerned, even Kirkpatrick being pushed aside in favour of the rapidly-promoted Dean. It is still not possible to get a complete picture of how Whitehall operated during the crisis. The full role of the Joint Intelligence Committee and MI6 are particular gaps in current knowledge. But it is clear that the policy-making machine, topped by the ministerial Egypt Committee, did not study a wide range of arguments, or look at alternative policies, or bring expertise properly to bear. This is not to say that official advice could have saved Britain from continued decline or misguided decisions in its overseas policy: many of the same officials who criticised Eden's decisions in late 1956 went on, in early 1957, to concentrate their energies on rebuilding the American alliance, when arguably they would have been wiser to look across the Channel, where the European Economic Community was about to be created. But a proper consideration of alternatives would undoubtedly have avoided the precipitate disaster that MUSKETEER became, if only because of the inbred caution and compromise among civil servants.

Conclusion

With a cursory analysis, it might be said that the system of British government *did* work during 1956, in that officials advised and ministers decided. But a close look at several of the leading officials involved has shown that the Whitehall machine functioned imperfectly, that official advice was too frequently brushed aside and that ministers made decisions based on prejudice and fear, in particular a fear that the failure to tackle Nasser would be a disaster for national prestige. Ironically, in trying to escape such a fate they only brought it about.

NOTES

1. P. Kennedy, *The Realities behind Diplomacy* (London: Fontana, 1981), p.61.
2. R. Crossman, *The Diaries of a Cabinet Minister, Volume 1, Minister of Housing, 1964–70* (London: Hamish Hamilton, 1975), pp.25–6.
3. H. Young and A. Sloman, *No, Minister: An Inquiry into the Civil Service* (London: BBC, 1992), pp.25–6.
4. R. Smith, 'Introduction' to J. Zametica, *British Officials, and British Foreign Policy, 1945–50* (Leicester: Leicester University Press, 1990), p.5.
5. This was true, for example, of Britain's reaction to the 1955 Messina conference, which proved of enormous long-term significance because it led to the founding of the European Economic Community. The then Foreign Secretary, Harold Macmillan, gave only intermittent and confusing advice to his officials and Eden took no interest in the issue at all, presumably because it seemed technical and unpressing. See J.W. Young, 'Britain, the Messina Conference and the Spaak Committee', in M. Dockrill and J.W. Young (eds), *British Foreign Policy, 1945–56* (London: Macmillan, 1989), pp.197–224.
6. Quoted in P. Hennessy and M. Laity, 'Suez – What the Papers Say', *Contemporary Record*, Vol.1, No.1 (Spring 1987), p.5.
7. Quoted in P. Hennessy, *Whitehall* (London: Secker & Warburg, 1989), p.165 and see pp.164–8 on the impact of Suez on the civil service.
8. K. Theakston, *The Civil Service since 1945* (Oxford: Blackwell, 1995), p.5; R.A. Chapman, *Ethics in the British Civil Service* (London: Routledge, 1988), p.303.
9. D. Vital, *The Making of British Foreign Policy* (London: Allen & Unwin, 1968), p.46.
10. It has however been argued that Brook, abetted by others, informed the US in advance about collusion and MUSKETEER: A. Verrier, *Through the Looking Glass* (London: Cape, 1983), pp.151–2.
11. H. Kissinger, *American Foreign Policy* (New York: W.W. Norton, 1974), pp.18 and 20.
12. C. Ponting, *Whitehall: Tragedy and Farce* (London: Hamilton, 1986), p.137.
13. P. Hennessy, *Cabinet* (Oxford: Blackwell, 1986), p.58.
14. Quoted in H. Dooley, 'Notes on Cabinet Planning during the Suez Crisis of 1956', *International History Review*, Vol.9, No.3 (Aug., 1989), p.497.

Bibliographic Essay

SAUL KELLY

The literary inquest into the Suez Crisis started as soon as it was over, with various offerings by journalists anxious to condemn or justify the actions of the Eden government e.g. Paul Johnson, *The Suez War* (1957) and T.E. Utley, *Not Guilty: The Conservative Reply* (1957). The most notable was by two Frenchmen, Merry and Serge Bromberger, which was swiftly translated into English by James Cameron as *The Secrets of Suez* (1957). Based on interviews with unnamed French politicians and military figures, this book claimed that Eden had arranged secret meetings with French and Israeli leaders at which it was agreed that they should collude in an attack upon Egypt in order to seize the Suez Canal and to topple Nasser. It also revealed the depth of bitterness felt by the French at Eden's 'betrayal' of them by his decision to accept a ceasefire before the Suez Canal had been captured.

The politicians soon entered the literary arena. Following allegations of collusion and 'betrayal' in the Brombergers' book, and Randolph Churchill's swingeing attack on him in *The Rise and Fall of Sir Anthony Eden* (1959), the fallen Prime Minister responded in *Full Circle* (1960). He denied collusion (and continued to do so until his death in 1977) and maintained that he had only tried to keep the peace in the Middle East. He blamed other British politicians, the French and particularly the Americans for undermining his position. This led the former US President Dwight D. Eisenhower, in his memoirs *The White House Years: Mandate for Change, 1953–1956* (1963) and *The White House Years: Waging Peace, 1956–1961* (1965) to defend the record of his administration over Suez, and particularly that of his former Secretary of State, John Foster Dulles (who had died in 1959 and had left no account of Suez). In contrast, one of Eisenhower's

232

speechwriters, Emmet Hughes in *The Ordeal of Power: The Inside Story of the Eisenhower Adminstration* (1963), portrayed the ex-President as a well-meaning but ill-prepared leader and Dulles as an incoherent ideologue, and claimed that they had been at loggerheads. While the Deputy Under-Secretary of State at the time of Suez, Robert Murphy in *Diplomat Among Warriors* (1964) was bitter about British actions during the crisis, Herman Finer in *Dulles Over Suez* (1964) supported Eden's argument with a lengthy assault on Dulles. This fuelled the debate over the Secretary of State's competence and whether he or Eisenhower had controlled US foreign policy during Suez.

Back in Britain, Erskine Childers, *The Road to Suez* (1962), A.J. Barker, Suez: *The Seven-Day War* (1964) and Leon D. Epstein, *British Politics in the Suez Crisis* (1964) gave straightforward accounts, respectively, of the diplomatic, military and domestic aspects of the crisis; but none could explore the 'hidden' aspects, like collusion. The former Conservative politician and Lord Chancellor in Eden's Government, the Earl of Kilmuir, *Political Adventure* (1964) continued to gloss over collusion in order to paint British actions in the best possible light. The Canadian author, Terence Robertson, *Crisis: The Inside Story of the Suez Conspiracy* (1964) gave a partial account of collusion, as did the Israeli Chief of Staff, Moshe Dayan, *Diary of the Sinai Campaign 1956* (Hebrew version 1965, English ed. 1967) and Michael Bar-Zohar, *Suez Ultra-Secret* (1967) and *The Armed Prophet: A Biography of Ben Gurion* (1967).

It was not until the tenth anniversary of the crisis that the first British accounts began to appear. Relying heavily on interviews with unnamed high level British and French sources (including the former British Foreign Secretary, Selwyn Lloyd, and the French Foreign Minister, Christian Pineau) Hugh Thomas, *The Suez Affair* (1966), revealed how Lloyd had travelled to Paris to negotiate the agreement for collusion known as the Sèvres Protocol. The BBC television series *Ten Years After* (published in 1967 as a BBC book by Peter Calvocoressi and Anthony Moncrieff) identified some of those sources, particularly Pineau and also interviewed Nasser. Sir Anthony Nutting, who resigned as Minister of State at the Foreign Office over Suez, confirmed this collusion in his provocative memoir, *No End of a Lesson* (1967), which Whitehall (in the form of the Secretary of the Cabinet, Sir Burke Trend, and the Permanent Secretary at the Foreign Office, Sir Paul Gore-Booth) tried unsuccessfully to prevent being published (see Peter Hennessy, 'No End of an Argument', *Contemporary Record*, Vol.1, No.1, Spring 1987).

Foreign Office discontent was revealed in Piers Dixon (ed.), *Double Diploma. The Life of Sir Pierson Dixon. Don and Diplomat* (1968), which contains useful material on the negotiations in the United Nations, as well revealing 'Bob' Dixon's strong misgivings about the use of force against Egypt. Geoffrey MacDermott, the operational liaison between the Foreign Office and MI6 in 1956, in *The Eden Legacy and the Decline of British Diplomacy* (1969), gave an intriguing account of British intelligence activities against Egypt. Its American counterpart was written by Miles Copeland, *The Game of Nations* (1969).

The New York Times correspondent in London during Suez, Kennet Love, in *Suez:The Twice-Fought War* (1969) interviewed participants in his shrewd assessment of British and US policies in the Middle East. Although the contributions from French military figures such as General Maurice Challe, *Notre Revolte* (1968), General Andre Beaufre, *The Suez Expedition* (1969) and General Paul Ely, *Memoires, Tome II Suez...le 13 mai* (1969) continued to harp on the theme of France's 'betrayal' by everyone except Israel, they contained useful information on the collusion process.

The 1970s saw the continued flow of self-justifying memoirs from Suez survivors, but few general studies of the crisis. Humphrey Trevelyan gave a fatalistic account of his time as British Ambassador to Egypt in 1956 in *The Middle East in Revolution* (1970). Harold Macmillan, who succeeded Eden as Prime Minister, gave a full but understated survey of Suez in *Riding the Storm, 1956–9* (1971). The recollections of the Lord Privy Seal at the the the time of Suez, R.A. (RAB) Butler, *The Art of the Possible* (1971) shows a troubled conscience which has not been confirmed by later evidence. The British Ambassador to France in 1956, Gladwyn Jebb, in *The Memoirs of Lord Gladwyn* (1972) vented his spleen at being excluded from a critical meeting in Paris in October 1956. Thus, he added weight to the fragmentary evidence that the Foreign Office seemed to have been by-passed by Eden during the crisis. Lord Gore-Booth's *With Great Truth and Respect* (1974) confirmed the unhappiness of certain Foreign Office officials over collusion and the attack on Egypt but denied that they had staged a 'revolt', only a protest.

There were also further revelations from American, Israeli and French sources. Townsend Hoopes in his entertaining, well-researched and complex portrait of *The Devil and John Foster Dulles* (1974) continued to make the case that the former Secretary of State, rather than Eisenhower, was the driving force behind US policy during Suez. The CIA liasion in London in 1956, Chester L. Cooper, *The Lion's Last Roar* (1978), revealed how US officials were divided over supporting their British ally. Moshe Dayan gave more detail on collusion in *The Story of My Life* (1976) and the Israeli Ambassador to the United States, Abba Eban, *An Autobiography*, added an interesting perspective of events from Washington. The recollections of Christian Pineau, *Suez 1956* (1978), in which he admits the secret French relationship with Israel and freely castigates Nasser and Eden, should be contrasted with the less emotional and careful account by the French Minister of Defence in 1956, Abel Thomas, *Comment Israel fut sauvé* (1978). Perhaps the most balanced memoir of those written by participants is that of the former British Foreign Secretary, Selwyn Lloyd, *Suez 1956* (1978). although it is somewhat spoilt by his extraordinarily legalistic attempt to explain how the British meetings with the French and the Israelis at Sevres did not constitute collusion. The best overview of the military dimensions of Suez is still Roy Fullick and Geoffrey Powell, *Suez: The Double War* (1970).

In the United States the debate on the nature of President Eisnhower's leadership brought a reconsideration of Suez, based on the declassification of American documents e.g. Donald Neff, *Warriors at Suez* (1981) and Stephen Ambrose, *Eisenhower the President* (1982) should be compared with Blanche Cooke, *The Declassified Eisenhower* (1981). David Carlton, *Anthony Eden* (1981) was the first historian to use the newly-available material in the Eisenhower Library to cast some new light on Suez, particularly over the succession struggle in the British Cabinet. Carlton's critical appraisal of Eden was also based on the diaries of Evelyn Shuckburgh, who as Private Secretary to Eden 1951–54 and the Under-Secretary of State at the Foreign Office dealing with Middle Eastern affairs 1954–56 was in a good position too serve the public and private Eden. Shuckburgh's abridged diaries were published as *Descent to Suez* (1986) to coincide with the thirtieth anniversary of the crisis. The same year saw the release of the edited diaries of Eden's Press Secretary, William Clark, *From Three Worlds* (1986), which are also informative on the actions and attitude of the Prime Minister and his problems with his Cabinet and the United States. They also reveal how No.10 Downing Street sought to manipulate the domestic mass media. Although the Parliamentary Under-Secretary of State at the Foreign Office in 1956, Douglas Dodds-

Parker, was reticent in *Political Eunuch* (1986) about his own role in the Eden Government's propaganda policy, he did indicate the importance he attached to the presentation of policy. The 'authorised' biography by the Conservative MP Robert Rhodes James of *Anthony Eden* (1986) was a sympathetic, but inadequate (given its over-reliance on the Avon Papers) attempt to counter Carlton's highly critical portrayal of Eden. It is rumoured that another 'authorised' life of Eden is to be written. Philip Williams (ed.), *The Diary of Hugh Gaitskell, 1945–56* (1983) and Philip Ziegler, *Mountbatten* (1985) shed light on the respective thinking and actions of the leader of the Labour Party and the First Sea Lord during the crisis.

Richard Lamb, *The Failure of the Eden Government* (1987) was the first writer to make use of the Suez documents released by the British government at the Public Record Office in 1987. His book contained much new detail but it was flawed by factual and analytical errors and by being too hastily written. The strategic, diplomatic and intelligence aspects of the crisis were addressed, respectively, by Anthony Gorst and W.S. Lucas, 'Suez 1956: Strategy and the Diplomatic Process', *Journal of Strategic Studies* (1988) and by Raymond Cohen, 'Israeli Military Intelligence before the 1956 Sinai Campaign', *Intelligence and National Security* (Jan.1988). David Carlton, *Britain and the Suez Crisis* (1988) provided us with best succinct account to date of the affair and of Macmillan's role in it. It contrasts favourably with the seriously flawed first volume of the official biography of *Macmillan* (1988) by Alistair Horne. The latter's dependence on the Macmillan Papers, and ignoring of the wealth of material in the PRO, meant that he simply repeated Macmillan's own account in his memoirs of his role in the crisis and his apparently minor role in the decision to attack Egypt. It should be compared with Lewis Johnman, 'Defending the Pound: The Economics of the Suez Crisis, 1956' in Anthony Gorst, Lewis Johnman and W.S. Lucas, *Post-War Britain: Themes and Perspectives, 1945–64* (1989). D.R. Thorpe, *Selwyn Lloyd* (1989) produced a more balanced account of his subject.

The Anglo-American background to the crisis has been analysed by H.W. Brands, 'The Cairo–Tehran Connection in Anglo-American Rivalry in the Middle East,' *International History Review* (August 1989), Ayesha Jalal, 'Towards the Baghdad Pact: South Asia and Middle Eastern Defence in the Cold War, 1945–55', *International History Review* (August 1989), and William Roger Louis, 'Dulles, Suez and the British'

236

in Richard Immerman (ed.), *John Foster Dulles and the Diplomacy of the Cold War* (1989). Mohammed Abd el Wahab Sayed-Ahmed, *Nasser and American Foreign Policy, 1952–1956* (1989) has written the only significant historical study from an Egyptian perspective. This was supplemented by Yigal Sheffy, 'Unconcern at Dawn, Surprise at Sunset: Egyptian Intelligence Appreciations before the Sinai Campaign, 1956', *Intelligence and National Security* (July 1990).

The first wide-ranging studies were by W.R. Louis and Roger Owen (eds), *Suez 1956: The Crisis and its Consequences* (1989) and Selwyn Ilan Troen and Moshe Shemesh (eds), *The Suez–Sinai Crisis of 1956: Retrospective and Reappraisal* (1990), which contributed in particular to our knowledge of Israel's relations with both Arab and Western states. David Devereux, *The Formulation of British Defence Policy towards the Middle East* (1990) placed Suez in the context of British strategic planning. Britain's deteriorating position in the Middle East was addressed by Scott Lucas in 'The Path to Suez: Britain and the Struggle for the Middle East, 1953–6', in Anne Deighton (ed.), *Britain and the First Cold War* (1990). Peter L. Hahn, *The U.S., Great Britain and Egypt, 1945–1956* (1991) portrays the complexity of the background to Suez and, in particular, the emerging importance of Egypt in American foreign policy in the 1950s. Diane Kunz, *The Economic Diplomacy of the Suez Crisis* (1991) stressed the economic aspect at the expense of the diplomatic, strategic and political angles. The only comprehensive studies are by Keith Kyle, *Suez* (1991) and Scott Lucas, *Divided We Stand: Britain, the U.S. and the Suez Crisis* (1991, rev. ed. 1996). Steven Freiberger's *Dawn over Suez* (1992) simply reduces the crisis to another case of the United States usurping the British position in the Middle East.

The Waldegrave 'Open Government' Initiative of the early 1990s has led to the further release of British government documents on Suez, which has enabled historians to investigate particular aspects of the crisis in greater detail. Richard Aldrich, 'Intelligence, Anglo–American Relations, and the Suez Crisis', *Intelligence and National Security* (July 1994) provides a useful review while the role of the information services has been addressed by Tony Shaw, *Eden, Suez and the Mass Media: Propaganda and Persuasion during the Suez Crisis* (1996). Anthony Gorst and Lewis Johnman, *The Suez Crisis* (1997) have provided a documentary survey, while Avi Shlaim has re-examined 'The Protocol of Sèvres, 1956: Anatomy of a War Plot', *International Affairs* 73, 3 (1997).

Abstracts

Alternatives to Nasser: Humphrey Trevelyan, Ambassador to Egypt

Michael T. Thornhill

One of the questions which remained unanswered after the opening of the files of the British government on the Suez Crisis in 1987 was what regime should replace that of Nasser if military action was successful. This article helps to answer this question by assessing the often divergent reports of Trevelyan and his Embassy officials on possible alternatives to the Nasser regime. The article also details the direct involvement of British 'diplomats' in subversive activities against Nasser's government. Humphrey Trevelyan emerges from the account as a wise man who understood the limits of military force and the pitfalls of political intervention. It demonstrates how the Cairo Embassy's attitudes on these issues shaped the advice being received in London during the diplomatic phase of the crisis.

'A Modern Major General': General Sir Gerald Templer, Chief of the Imperial General Staff

Anthony Gorst

Templer was an enthusiastic supporter of Eden's desire to use military force to solve the Suez Crisis. This enthusiasm resulted in Templer, who was the dominant figure on the Chiefs of Staff Committee, and to a lesser extent the other chiefs (the Chief of the Air Staff, Sir Dermot Boyle, and the First Sea Lord, Lord Louis Mountbatten) accepting a political war aim, the toppling of Nasser, which was militarily unachievable and which contributed to the constant changes in the military plan in August and September 1956. This article disentangles the role of Templer in policy making during the crisis and highlights the lesson that the CIGS drew from MUSKETEER, that future military interventions needed to be taken quickly and decisively in pursuit of a realistic war aim.

Abstracts

Playing the Role of a Cassandra: Sir Gerald Fitzmaurice, Senior Legal Advisor to the Foreign Office

Lewis Johnman

This examination of the role of Fitzmaurice and the general legal debate within the British government over the use of force reveals the determination of Eden to topple Nasser without declaring this as an aim of policy. Thus, the extreme narrowing of the advisory and policy channels threw much of Whitehall into confusion. The Suez 'insiders' (Eden, the Egypt Committee and a small number of senior officials) blocked or ignored any advice which did not suit their purposes and utilised entirely inappropriate means to justify their actions. This article shows that, as with so much of the advice being given during the Suez Crisis, 'what was ignored proved to be correct and what was accepted proved to be wrong'.

The Mandarins' Mandarin: Sir Norman Brook, Secretary of the Cabinet

Keith Kyle

For most of the Suez Crisis those, admittedly limited, number of civil servants who had clearance to receive documents (codenamed TERRAPIN) were kept fully informed by Ministers and controlled the plans for the use of force. This was especially true, as this article shows, of Brook, with his two committees – Defence (Transition), which met throughout the Crisis and co-ordinated the reports of the specialist groups, and the Egypt (Official) – and his role as Secretary of the Cabinet and of the Egypt (Ministerial) Committee. It was only during the last phase that most civil servants were excluded, with the exception of Brook. It fell to Brook, as Secretary to the Cabinet, to undertake the unpleasant task of destroying any incriminating documentary evidence of collusion. Following Eden's departure for Jamaica to convalesce, Brook's calm was a great boon as he worked to restore order to Whitehall and to keep the machine running.

Whitehall and the Suez Crisis

In the Know? Sir Gladwyn Jebb, Ambassador to France

Christopher Goldsmith

Most accounts of the Suez Crisis have tended to concentrate on the exclusion of Jebb from the Franco-British meeting on 16 October 1956, when Eden and Lloyd agreed to the Challe plan for collusion with Israel. But, as this article points out, it is also important to recognise that Jebb had earlier played a part in shaping the British response to the nationalisation of the Suez Canal Company, especially the development of a common Franco-British approach. As the Crisis developed, he became increasingly concerned about the implications of a continued commitment to a policy of force and the closeness of French relations with Israel – a worry which was reflected in his warning to Eden about the supply of French Mystere fighters to Israel. The Prime Minister chose to adopt another approach and took the first steps along the path to collusion and disaster.

The Limits of Opposition: Admiral Earl Mountbatten of Burma, First Sea Lord and Chief of the Naval Staff

Eric Grove and Sally Rohan

Mountbatten's consistent opposition to British policy over Suez was motivated by moral and political considerations as much as by Service and strategic interests. He took very seriously his position within the Royal Family, the governing class and the Navy and, therefore, pushed his opposition to MUSKETEER as far as he could without prejudicing these interlocking positions. The fact that Mountbatten did not resign over Suez was of considerable importance for the Navy when he successfully defended its interests during the Sandys Defence Review in 1957–58.

The Missing Link? Patrick Dean, Chairman of the Joint Intelligence Committee

W. Scott Lucas

Dean performed an important liaison role during the Crisis. He was not only Superintending Under-Secretary of State of the Permanent Under-Secretary of State's Department and Chairman of the Joint Intelligence Committee, which linked the Foreign Office, the military and MI6, but he also bypassed official channels and passed on messages to the secret services from the Prime Minister. Dean's story, as this article makes clear, was part of a much larger and more important catalogue of chaos and fragmentation within Whitehall which led to the pursuit of several foreign policies during Suez. Moreover, MI6's persistent and, some might argue, pernicious influence led to the disaster of November 1956.

Abstracts

Cadogan's Last Fling: Sir Alexander Cadogan, Chairman of the Board of Governors of the BBC

Tony Shaw

Coincidence, combined with the closed nature of the British governing elite, placed Cadogan, one of the most distinguished civil servants of his generation, in a uniquely wide-ranging position during the Suez Crisis. He operated in three apparently autonomous, but ultimately antagonistic, spheres: as Chairman of the English-Speaking Union's Commonwealth Current Affairs Unit, as a government director of the Suez Canal Company and as Chairman of the BBC's Board of Governors. Further complications arose from his close friendship with Eden dating from the inter-war appeasement years. This article demonstrates that Cadogan's overall impact on Suez lay more in the sphere of presentation of government policy than in its actual formulation.

In the Company of Policy Makers: Sir Donald Logan, Assistant Private Secretary to the Secretary of State for Foreign Affairs

Chris Brady

The policy-making role of Logan was negligible, but his place in the history of Suez is considerable. Logan was a man of genuine integrity who was present at an important moment in British history: the collusion meetings at Sèvres in late October 1956. He has told his story without embellishment and if only for this reason it is worth analysing. But he is also of interest because of his refusal to blow the whistle on Eden after the latter made his deceptive statement to Parliament on 20 December 1956. Logan epitomises the practical and realistic image of the British civil servant at this period.

Transatlantic Diplomat: Sir Roger Makins, Ambassador to Washington and Joint Permanent Secretary to the Treasury

Saul Kelly

Makins's role in the Suez Crisis is of particular interest to historians. His main duties as Ambassador in Washington during the early stages of the crisis were to keep on good terms with the Eisenhower Administration, conveying British policy to them and explaining US policy to London without losing the confidence of the Eden government. The main thrust of Makins's advice, after returning to London in mid-October 1956 to take up the post of Joint Permanent Secretary of the Treasury, was to stress the need to secure US support for an International Monetary Fund (IMF) loan for Britain and other financial and economic measures to avert the looming disaster for sterling and the economy. It was as a result of his transatlantic contacts that the British government eventually secured this vital financial and economic support, in return for withdrawing from Egypt.

The Diplomats' Diplomat: Sir Pierson Dixon, Ambassador to the United Nations

Edward Johnson

Dixon had the onerous task of defending Britain's use of force against Egypt in the UN – a forum in which Britain had few supporters – even though he was often 'kept in the dark' about the real aims of Eden's policy. Although Dixon later claimed that the Anglo-French action at Suez was 'a miscalculation and a mistake', at the time he did what he could to defend it publicly, while warning privately of the serious consequences for Britain of ignoring the UN. The personal effect of all this was 'the severest moral and physical strain he had ever experienced'.

The Past as Matrix: Sir Ivone Kirkpatrick, Permanent Under-Secretary for Foreign Affairs

Ann Lane

Kirkpatrick was a key player in the development of policy and one of the few who had an overview. He was a solid supporter of Eden's policy towards Egypt. His belief that Nasser was another Hitler, combined with his concern at the Soviet challenge to Britain's position in the Middle East, framed his approach to the Suez Crisis. In the end, however, Kirkpatrick was out-manoeuvred as the Suez operation became increasingly determined by military considerations. His defence of British actions to his senior officials, however, went beyond the call of loyalty to Ministers.

Notes on Contributors

Saul Kelly is Research Fellow in History at the University of Westminster. He is the author of articles on Anglo-American relations and *Britain, the United States and the Question of the Italian Colonies, 1945–1952* (forthcoming).

Anthony Gorst is Lecturer in History at the University of Westminster. He is the author of several articles on British defence policy and with W. Scott Lucas 'Suez 1956: Strategy and the Diplomatic Process' in *Journal of Strategic Studies* (1988).

Chris Brady is a lecturer in the Management Systems and Information Department of the City University Business School. He was previously an officer in the Royal Navy serving in Managerial and Intelligence capacities during the Falkland and Gulf wars. He is currently researching the role of game playing in the decision-making process.

Chris Goldsmith is a PhD student in the Department of Politics at the University of Leicester. He is working on a thesis on the Paris Embassy of Sir Gladwyn Jebb.

Eric Grove is a Senior Lecturer at the Centre for Security Studies, University of Hull and the author of *Vanguard to Trident; British Naval Policy Since 1945* (1987).

Lewis Johnman is Quintin Hogg Research Fellow in History at the University of Westminster. He is author of 'Defending the Pound: The Economics of the Suez Crisis, 1956' in A. Gorst, L. Johnman and W. Scott Lucas (eds) *Postwar Britain 1945–1964* (1989) and with A. Gorst *The Suez Crisis* (1997).

Edward Johnson is Principal Lecturer in Politics at the University of Central England in Birmingham. He has published on British views towards the UN and Dag Hammarskjold in the *Review of International Studies* and *Diplomacy and Statecraft*.

Keith Kyle is Visiting Professor of History at the University of Ulster. In 1956 he was the Washington correspondent of *The Economist*. He is the author of *Suez* (London, 1991) and a contributor to Wm. Roger Louis and Roger Owen (eds), *Suez 1956: The Crisis and its Consequences* (1989). His articles include 'Suez and the Waldegrave Initiative' in *Contemporary Record* (1995) and 'La Grande-Bretagne, la France et la crise de Suez' in *Histoire Economie et Societé* (1994).

Ann Lane is Lecturer in Politics at The Queen's University of Belfast and has written on post-war British foreign policy including *Britain, the Cold War and Yugoslav Unity, 1941–49* (1996).

W. Scott Lucas is Head of Department of American and Canadian Studies at the University of Birmingham and is the author of *Divided We Stand: Britain, the United States and the Suez Crisis* (1991).

Sally Rohan is a Senior Lecturer in the Defence Studies Department at the Joint Services Command and Staff College, Bracknell. Her research interests lie in the area of British defence policy and European defence organisation on which she has published several articles.

Tony Shaw is Lecturer in Modern History at the University of Hertfordshire. He has published several articles on international history and *Eden, Suez and the Mass Media: Propaganda and Persuasion during the Suez Crisis* (1996).

Michael Thornhill is Research Coordinator on the *New Dictionary of National Biography*, and is a member of the Modern History Faculty at Oxford University.

John Young is Professor of Politics at the University of Leicester and the author of *Britain and European Unity, 1945–1992* (1993) and *Winston Churchill's Last Campaign* (1996).

Index

Adenauer, Konrad 94
Aldrich, Winthrop 172, 204, 213, 215
Alexandria, plans to invade 36–9, 71
Algeria, British policy towards 84
ALPHA project 13, 161
Amery, Julian 120–1
Amory, Heathcoat 70
Anglo-Egyptian Defence Agreement (1954) 13, 203
Aswan High Dam project 16, 82, 133, 161–2

Baghdad Pact 13, 33–4, 81, 84–5, 93, 161, 162, 204
Barclay, Roderick 200–1
BBC
    Cadogan, Sir Alexander as Chairman 134–43, 224
    and Kirkpatrick, Sir Ivone 207–8
    political broadcasts 136–40, 145(n26)
Beaufre, General 40
Bedell Smith, Walter 158, 172
Beeley, Harold 48, 207, 214
Beith, John 81
Ben-Gurion, David 149, 150, 212
Bermuda Conference 174–5
Bevin, Ernest 80, 222
Birch, Nigel 74
bombing, British policy 190
Bottomley, Norman 139
Bourgès-Maunoury, Maurice 91, 149
Boyle, Dermot 4, 32, 223
Boyle, Sir Edward 2
Bridges, Sir Edward 2, 65–6, 75, 170, 229
British Embassy in Cairo
    destruction of records 11, 12, 25(n10)
    role in Egyptian politics 12, 13–14
Brockman, Ronald 103
Brook, Norman
    character of 64

collusion 74, 75–7
Defence (Transition) Committee 5, 66–8, 75, 206
    doubts of 3, 75
    and Eden, Anthony 65–6, 68–9, 76
    Egypt Committee 68–9, 72, 73–4
    Egypt Official Committee (EOC) 5, 18, 70–1
    loyalty of 5, 76–7, 224, 226–7
    and Makins, Sir Roger 75–6
    timetable of action 29
Bulganin, Georgi 118
Buraimi Oasis 160, 162
Butler, R.A. 49, 65, 69, 137, 152, 172

Caccia, Sir Harold 163, 170, 172, 193
Cadogan, Sir Alexander
    career of 126
    as Chairman of BBC Board of Governors 134–43, 224
    as Chairman Commonwealth-American Current Affairs Unit 128–30, 142
    as director of Suez Canal Company 130–4, 142
    and Eden, Anthony 7, 127
    influence of 7
Cairo
    bombing of 190
    British Embassy see British Embassy in Cairo
Canada, in United Nations 186
cease-fire agreement 43, 190–2
Challe, General 152
Challe Plan see Sèvres agreement
Chiefs of Staff Committee (COS)
    records of 44(n5)
    reorganisation 32–3
    role of 40–1
Churchill, Winston 64–5, 134

CIA
  attitude to Nasser 15
  and MI6 119, 121–2
Cilcennin, Viscount 101–2, 105–6
civil servants
  influence of 221–2
  loyalty of 3, 226
  role of 73
Clark, William 47, 65, 68, 75, 119, 138, 206, 209, 235–6
Cobbold, Kim 171
Coldstream, Sir George 53–4, 59
Collins, Elizabeth 103
collusion 2, 225–6, 233–5
  Israel's role 41, 73, 92
  memoirs of 233
  role of Brook, Norman 74, 75–7
  role of Eden, Anthony 150–1, 152–3, 153–4, 185–6, 228–9, 232
  role of Kirkpatrick, Sir Ivone 2, 120, 151, 200, 211–13, 224
  Sèvres meetings 6, 74–5, 92, 117, 146, 149–52
  see also Sèvres protocol
Commonwealth, impact on 102
Commonwealth-American Current Affairs Unit 128–30
Convention of Constantinople (1888) 47, 48, 52–3, 57
Cooper, Chester 122
Copeland, Miles 124(n8)
CORDAGE, Operation 41
Cornut-Gentille, Bernard 179, 180, 193
Coulson, John 196(nn10, 11)
Crabb, Buster 118
Crossman, Richard 221
Czech arms deal 13, 14

Dalton, Hugh 79, 80
Darracott file 70
Davis, Sir William 103
Dayan, Moshe 149, 152, 235
Dean, Patrick 6–7, 66, 117–24, 151–2, 210
Defence (Transition) Committee (D(T)C) 5, 66–8, 75, 77(n11), 206
Dibble, Tom 67
Dickson, William 32, 42, 100
Dilks, David 126
Dillon, Douglas 88, 197(n38)
Dixon, Sir Pierson
  career of 178
  defence of Britain's actions 8, 178–80, 195
  exclusion from Sèvres agreement 180–3, 193
  role of 193–5

as United Nations Ambassador 2, 50, 179–95, 212, 214, 225, 234
  and United States 181
Dodds-Parker, Douglas 130, 236
Dulles, John Foster
  and Cadogan, Sir Alexander 129
  and Eden, Anthony 159, 209
  and Makins, Sir Roger 158–9, 163, 165–8
  OMEGA plan 119
  opinions of 232–3, 235
  Suez Canal Users Association 50, 52–3, 87–8, 165–8
  and United Nations 185

Eban, Abba 235
Eccles, Sir David 173
Eden, Anthony
  anti-Americanism 76, 159, 161, 166–7
  and the BBC 136–8
  biographies of 236
  and Brook, Norman 65–6, 68–9
  and Cadogan, Sir Alexander 127, 136–7
  collusion 150–1, 152–3, 153–4, 185–6, 228–9, 232
  desire for military intervention 34, 47–8, 68–9, 166
  desire to remove Nasser 13, 36, 49, 95, 119, 124(n8), 228
  difficulty of working with 49, 65–6, 68
  and Dixon, Sir Pierson 194–5
  dual objectives of 49
  and Dulles, John Foster 159
  and Fitzmaurice, Sir Gerald 56
  and Jebb, Sir Gladwyn 80–1
  and Kirkpatrick, Sir Ivone 199–200, 203–4, 205, 210–11
  Middle East policy 65
  and Mountbatten, Lord Louis 98–9, 107–8, 111–12
  refusal to listen to advice 5, 47
  relations with France 88–9, 90–1
  and Trevelyan, Humphrey 16, 17
  and United Nations 186–7
Edgar, Donald 22–3
Egypt Committee 68–9, 72, 73–4, 102, 118
Egypt Official Committee (EOC) 5, 18, 25, 70–1
Eisenhower, Dwight 157–8, 167–8, 208–9, 232–3, 235
English-Speaking Union (ESU) 128–30, 142, 174
Europe, Britain's relations with 94
Evans, Trefor 14, 16, 19, 23–4

Index

Fawzi, Mohammed 89, 148–9
Fergusson, Bernard 38, 121
financial crisis, British 8, 170–3, 191–2
Fitzmaurice, Sir Gerald 2, 5, 47–62, 207, 213, 230
Flux, J.B. 23
France
    British relations with 6, 81–95, 120, 232
    Mystère aircraft supplied to Israelis 6, 90, 91
    Sèvres agreement 149–53, 181–2, 211–12
Franks, Oliver 123, 129

Gaitskell, Hugh 137, 138, 140, 154, 206
Galbraith, Mary 193
Garvey, Terence 23
Gazier, Albert 89–91
Georges-Picot, Jacques 130, 131, 133
Glubb, Sir John 13, 33, 65, 204
Goodhart, A.L. 49
Gore-Booth, Paul 2, 93, 214–15, 223
Gove, J.G. 23
Graham, John 148
Grantham, Sir Guy 110
Green, John 136
Grey, Sir Edward 221, 222
Grisewood, Harman 136, 138–9

Hailsham, Lord 74, 78(n35), 106, 108–9, 112–13, 115(n29)
HAMILCAR operation 36–7
Hamilton, John 16, 23–4
Hammarskjold, Dag 179, 184, 187, 189–91, 196(n27)
Hankey, Lord 66, 130
Harcourt, Lord 164, 172
Head, Anthony 38, 74, 107, 152
Healey, Denis 215, 221
Heath, Edward 70
Heikal, Mohamed 15–16
Heliopolis, bombing of 190
Hennessy, Peter 146
Heseltine, Michael 222
Hinchingbrooke, Viscount 154
Hitler, Adolf, Nasser analogy 9, 51, 52, 205–6, 208–9, 217, 228
Home, Lord 152
Hoover, Herbert Jr. 158, 161, 164, 171–2
Horne, Alistair 205–6, 211
Humphrey, George 161, 172
Hurd, Douglas 181, 193
Hussein, Ahmed 163
Hussein, King 13, 204
Hylton-Foster, Sir Harry 47

India, attitude to British policy 102
Information Co-ordination Executive 38
International Bank for Reconstruction and Development (IBRD), loan offer to Egypt 161, 164
International Monetary Fund (IMF), loan to Britain 8, 170, 171
invasion
    Anglo-French 42, 57–8
    Israeli 58, 180, 213–14
Iraq
    and Jordan 89
    power of 85
Israel
    arms supplies to 6, 84, 86
    British relations with 41, 73, 83–4, 122
    French relations with 9, 90
    invasion of Egypt 58, 180–1, 213–14
    and Jordan 41, 89
    role in collusion 41, 73, 92
    Sèvres agreement 92, 149–53

Jacob, Sir Ian 134, 137, 141, 208
Jebb, Sir Gladwyn
    career of 79–80
    character of 80
    and Eden, Anthony 80–1
    excluded from talks 6, 79, 90–3, 234
    and Kirkpatrick, Ivone 201
    response to Suez Canal nationalisation 82–3
    role in Franco-British co-operation 6, 83–95, 224
Joint Planning Staff (JPS), 'limited war paper' 35–6
Jordan
    Baghdad Pact 162, 204
    and Israel 41, 89
    'Templer Mission' 33–4
Joxe, Louis 86, 96(n21)

Keightley, General Charles 18, 30, 36, 39, 72, 107, 112, 190
Kellogg-Briand Pact (1928) 56
Kilmuir, Lord 2, 46, 49, 52–7, 59, 70, 222–3
Kirkpatrick, Sir Ivone
    anti-Americanism 167, 215
    and BBC 207–8
    and Cadogan, Sir Alexander 142–3
    career 201–2
    character 200–1
    collusion 2, 120, 151, 211–13, 224
    and Eden, Anthony 199–200, 203–4, 205, 210–11

and Fitzmaurice, Sir Gerald 51
and Foreign Office 206–7
and Jebb, Sir Gladwyn 91
marginalisation 121, 210–11
role during Crisis 216–17
support for invasion 121, 153, 199–200, 207, 223
United Nations role 186, 189
view of American policy 208–9
view of Soviet Union 9, 202–3
Kissinger, Henry 228
Krushchev, Nikita 118
Kunz, Diane 163, 171
Kyle, Keith 163, 192

Lampson, Sir Miles 13
Langridge, Dick 148
Laskey, Denis 148
legal advice
ignored by Eden 47, 56–62
to government 46–7, 49
Lennox-Boyd, Alan 223
Libya, as base for operations 48
Little, Tom 23
Lloyd, Selwyn
and Dixon, Sir Pierson 181, 194
and Jebb, Sir Gladwyn 91–2
and Pineau, Christian 86–7, 88–9
Sèvres meetings 117, 148–55
and United Nations 55, 188, 192, 214
Lodge, Henry Cabot 179, 180–1, 183, 193–4
Logan, Donald
career 146–7
character 146
loyalty of 3, 7–8, 153–5
role in Suez crisis 147–8, 154–5
Sèvres talks 3, 117, 122, 149–52
London Conference
First 49–50, 69
Second 88, 132
Louis, Roger 206
Lucas, Scott 163, 210, 225
LUCKY BREAK 119

McDermott, Geoffrey 92, 120, 125 (n12), 210
Macmillan, Harold
Anglo-American relations 161, 167–8, 170–2
biographies of 236
economic advice to 2, 170
Israeli position 85
and Kirkpatrick, Ivone 200–1
and Makins, Sir Roger 167–8, 170–1
MUSKETEER operation 36–7

Sèvres protocol 152
as successor to Eden 65
McNair, Lord 59–60
Maher, Ali 22
Makins, Sir Roger
as Ambassador in Washington 157–69, 225, 230
and Brook, Norman 75–6
as Joint Permanent Secretary to the Treasury 8, 66, 169–75
Manningham-Buller, Sir Reginald 47, 56
al-Maraghi, Ahmed Mortada 22, 28(n65)
Menon, Krishna 102
Menzies, Robert 136
Messina conference 231(n5)
MI6 4, 7, 12, 118–21
military operation
planning 34–40, 69–72
timing 29, 71–2
Millard, Guy 130, 223
Mollet, Guy 90, 94, 120, 149
Monckton, Sir Walter 69, 74, 101–2, 105–7, 204, 223
Moslem Brotherhood 23, 24, 28(n78)
Mountbatten, Edwina 103–4
Mountbatten, Lord Louis
on Chiefs of Staff Committee 32
and Eden, Anthony 98–9, 107–8, 111–12
MUSKETEER Operation 104–8, 227
opposition to armed intervention 6, 101–14
plan to seize Port Said 34, 35, 44(n26), 99–100
resignation threat 102, 106, 112–13, 227
and Templer, Sir Gerald 32, 33, 41, 104–5
view of Nasser 100–1
views on Suez Crisis 98–9
Murphy, Robert Jr. 164
Murray, Ralph 14, 17–19, 22, 24, 71, 122
Murville, Couve de 164
MUSKETEER, Operation 5, 30, 37–9, 75, 104–8, 227, 230
MUSKETEER (REVISE), Operation 39–43, 72, 108–11, 138

al-Nahas, Mustapha 21
Nasser, Gamal Abdel
Britain's desire for his removal 13, 22–4, 36–7, 70
comparison with Hitler 9, 205–6, 208–9, 217, 228
expansionism 127
possible successor to 4, 17–25, 26(n42)
and Soviet Union 119
and Trevelyan, Humphrey 11, 14–15, 16, 23

Neguib, Mohamed 20, 23
Nicolson, Harold 80
al-Nuqrashi, Mahmud 24
Nutting, Sir Anthony 56, 90, 119, 122, 204, 211–12

officials, role of 9, 223–31
OMEGA plan 13, 15–16, 118, 119, 162–3, 167
O'Neil, Con 217

'Partisans of the Right' 21
Pearson, Lester 80, 186, 188, 191
Peres, Shimon 149
Permanent Under-Secretary's Department (PUSD) 118–20, 206
PILEUP, Operation 132
Pineau, Christian
    collusion talks 149, 150, 235
    London talks 81–2, 86–8, 96(n21)
    New York talks 148–9
    at United Nations 182, 185
Pink, I.T.M. 50
Pliatzky, Leo 226
Ponting, Clive 1, 3, 229
Port Said
    Anglo-French landing 42, 44(n26)
    plans to invade 34, 35–6, 39–40, 71–2, 99–100, 110
Powell, Sir Richard 74
propaganda war 15–16, 22–3
psychological warfare 37–40, 121

Rhodes-James, Robert 163
Ridsdale, Sir William 128
Robertson, Norman 82, 186
Ross, Archibald 121, 183, 195, 207, 210

Said, Nuri 162, 213
Salah al-Din 21
Salem, Salah 137
Saudi Arabia, Buraimi Oasis dispute 160, 162
Sèvres protocol 12, 24, 56, 79, 152–3, 181
    see also collusion
Shuckburgh, Evelyn 195, 204–5, 211, 214, 235
SIS 210, 212
'Six Principles' 175, 179
Slade-Baker, John 23–4
Soviet Union
    blamed for Suez Crisis 168, 202–3, 204
    Budapest bombing 190–1
    Egyptian negotiations with 162–3
    supposed penetration of Middle East 119, 210, 216, 228
    United Nations 182, 183

Spaak, Paul-Henri 80
Stockwell, Freddie 210
Stockwell, General Hugh 30, 36, 40
Strang, William 216–17
Stuart, James 76
successor to Nasser, Britain's choice of 4, 17–25, 26(n42)
Suez Canal
    internationalism aims 49–53
    management of 67, 77–8(n18)
Suez Canal Company
    and Cadogan, Sir Alexander 130–4, 142
    nationalisation by Nasser 34, 46–7, 51, 57, 66, 82, 118, 130–1, 164
Suez Canal Users Association (SCUA) 40, 50–1, 52, 87–8, 165–7
Swinburn, James 23
Syria
    airfields 72–3
    plans to overthrow 122

TELESCOPE, Operation 42
Templer, Sir Gerald
    career of 31
    character of 29–30, 31–2
    as Chief of Imperial General Staff (CIGS) 4, 31–3, 67–8
    Jordan mission 33–4
    and Mountbatten, Lord Louis 32, 33, 41, 104–5
    Operation MUSKETEER 5, 30, 37–43, 107–8, 227
    view of military operations 4–5, 35
TERRAPIN 5, 73
Thomas, Abel 235
Thornhill, Michael 225
Three Power meetings 86
Trevelyan, Humphrey
    and Eden, Anthony 16, 17
    OMEGA plan 16
    opposition to invasion 11–12, 16–17, 224
    part in plans to overthrow Nasser 4, 22–3, 227
    previous career 12–13
    views of Nasser 14–15
Tull, John 22

United Nations
    General Assembly 42, 184–6, 214
    Pierson Dixon as Ambassador 178–95
    role of 59–60, 82–3, 87
    Security Council 50, 55, 182–4

United States
   Anglo-American relations 2, 121–2, 158–75,
     215, 236–7
   and Commonwealth-American Current
     Affairs Unit 129–30
   economic support for Britain 2, 8, 171–3,
     192
   involvement of 88–9
   opposition to intervention 15, 92, 94,
     116(n53), 165–7
   United Nations delegation 182–3, 215
Urquhart, Brian 184

Vallat, Francis 55, 61

Wafd 13, 20–1, 27(nn53, 57)
War Book 66–7, 77(n13)
Watson, Adam 17
Watt, Donald Cameron 159
West Africa, decolonisation 64–5
White, Dick 42, 212
Wisner, Frank 122
Wright, Quincy 54
Wylie, Sir Francis 130, 132

Young, George 122

Ziegler, Philip 103, 110